Clare Longrigg

MAFIA WOMEN

Chatto & Windus
LONDON

Published in 1997

1 3 5 7 9 10 8 6 4 2

Copyright © 1997 by Clare Longrigg

Clare Longrigg has asserted her right under
the Copyright, Designs and Patents Act, 1988
to be identified as the author of this work.

First published in Great Britain in 1997 by
Chatto & Windus Limited
Random House, 20 Vauxhall Bridge Road,
London, SW1V 2SA

Random House Australia (Pty) Limited
20 Alfred Street, Milsons Point, Sydney,
New South Wales 2061, Australia

Random House New Zealand Limited
18 Poland Road, Glenfield
Auckland 10, New Zealand

Random House South Africa (Pty) Limited
Endulini, 5A Jubilee Road,
Parktown 2193, South Africa

Random House UK Limited Reg. No. 954009

Papers used by Random House UK Limited are natural, recyclable
products made from wood grown in sustainable forests. The
manufacturing processes conform to the environmental
regulations of the country of origin.

A CIP catalogue record for this book is available from the British Library

ISBN 0 7011 6509 X

Typeset by Deltatype Ltd
Printed and bound in Great Britain by
Mackays of Chatham PLC

For my parents

Contents

Acknowledgements

This extensive list reveals how much I have depended on the expertise of others to put the book together. It would be even longer, but some of those who have helped me cannot unfortunately be named.

My thanks to the magistrates and specialists who were so generous with their time, especially Guido Lo Forte, Teresa Principato, Paolo Mancuso, Amato Lamberti, Liliana Ferraro, Salvatore Lupo, Antonio Laudati, Giuseppe Narducci, Maurizio Fumo, Maria Maniscalco, Frank Friel, Walter Coughlin, Saverio Senese and Antonio Manganelli. Particular thanks to the magistrates Salvatore Boemi, Alessandra Camassa, Nicola Gratteri, Giacomo Travaglino, Giuseppe Borrelli, Alberto Di Pisa and Maurizio Romanelli for their invaluable assistance.

Thanks to the journalists and photographers who generously helped me out, especially Enzo La Penna and Roberto Ormanni, Titti Beneduce and all at ANSA in Naples; Franco Castaldo, Enzo Mignosi, George Anastasia, Gigi Di Fiore, Antonio Nicaso and Diego Minuti, Shobha and Luciano Ferrara.

Thanks to Anna Puglisi and Umberto Santino at the Centro Siciliano di documentazione Giuseppe Impastato, for their help over the years, and for their tireless research and remarkable campaigning work.

Thanks to investigative journalists Andrea Cinquegrani and Rita Pennarola; thanks to Renate Siebert for her hospitality and encouragement. Thanks also to staff at the Istituto Gramsci in Palermo.

Thanks to the friends who made the book possible by their generous help, knowledge, ideas and encouragement, as well as hospitality over the years: Linda Pantano, Walter Rizzo, Valeria Abramo, Alessandra Dino, Monique El Faizy, Oliver Phillips,

Silvana Polizzi, Frances Kennedy, Enrico Fierro, Cettina Dono-frio, Anna Russo, Margherita Cacioppo, Sharon Krum, Simona Mafai, Giovanna Terranova and Michela Buscemi. Particular thanks to two Sicilian journalists and great friends whose knowledge I relied upon: Rino Cascio and Giorgio Petta.

Special thanks to Piera Fallucca, Aurelio Angelini and Valerio Angelini, who have always given me a place to stay in Palermo and offered me boundless hospitality and kindness.

I'm grateful to Professor Mario Serio for his expert legal advice. Thanks also to my agent Derek Johns and my editor Jenny Uglow. I'd also like to thank the *Guardian* for giving me time off to write the book. Thanks to Amanda Mitchison, who read the manuscript and made valuable suggestions. Thanks to Robin Hunt, to my sisters, Laura and Francesca, and to Sarah Johnstone, who has had to live with a lot of mafia women. Thanks finally to Adrian Buchanan.

Introduction

There are no women in the mafia.

It's probably the most durable stereotype of all, the image we see in films, in press photographs, and on the television news. In the foreground is a man's dead body, blood-spattered, half covered with a sheet; in the background a woman weeping into her palms. If she knows who killed him, she will be no more likely to speak than the punctured corpse.

The mafia is a great creator of myths. Since the last century, it has captured the popular imagination with a combination of mythology and terror – myths are cheaper than guns, and in some cases more effective. Mafia propaganda has always exalted the values held dear by ordinary people: according to the mafioso's code of honour, he defended the interests of the poor, stood by his friends, never harmed women and children – and *never* involved women in mafia business.

Until recently, information of a more specific nature was almost impossible to come by. Investigators did not expect people to disobey the law of silence, and before the emergence of mafia defectors, journalists were mostly writing in the dark, delving into folklore.

The Sicilian mafia's origins go back well into the nineteenth century, but even the origins of the name are obscure (at one stage the adjective *mafioso* meant fine, upstanding, handsome, or its equivalent in English dialect, 'tidy'). At the time of the unification of Italy in 1860, a class of middle-men emerged who managed estates in southern Italy for the absentee landlords and controlled the peasant farmers. These managers set themselves up as representatives of the disenfranchised poor, but ended up exploiting both peasants and landlords. By the twentieth century, the mafia exercised authority over peasant farmers and trades-people; it had become a secret society with a formal structure and central executive commission, and its members commanded fear and respect.

The expression Cosa Nostra was first used in North America, where Italian immigrants flooding into the US in the early 1900s organised protection rackets to extort money from newer arrivals. Masculinity and violence created their identity; their 'code of honour' linked them to the old country and lent respectability to their real purpose, which was to get rich. The mafia has always used state law to its best advantage: the big break came during prohibition, when the mafia made a fortune running illegal bars and casinos. As the authorities tried to crack down on organised crime, mafiosi were sporadically deported as undesirables – it couldn't have worked out better for the Italians, who returned home and set up illegal traffic with their contacts in the USA.

In 1943, the Americans employed mafia members to help them invade Sicily; in return, they were given positions of authority after the war. During the chaos of post-liberation Italy the black market flourished, run by the mafia. A historic meeting in Palermo in 1957 between Cosa Nostra bosses from New York and Sicily established the protocol of the heroin trade, and before long the sons of poor peasant families were getting seriously rich. During the 1970s they went into finance and property development to recycle the profits, and entered the world of legitimate business. The mafia's economic power, and its control over ordinary people, gave it leverage with politicians, who have relied on the mafia to deliver votes. In return, the mafia has been awarded contracts for public works including water, building and roads.

Although the word 'mafia' describes a single phenomenon, there are major differences between the organisations in different parts of Italy. All of them are defined by their use of violence, intimidation and imposition of silence, all of them exercise control over the local population by extorting protection money – which is effectively a sign of ownership. Each has its own male hierarchy and secret initiation rite. Where the organisation is more arcane, few women have been actively involved. But where the rules have become more relaxed, and the organisation more family-based, women have begun to take part.

In the west of Sicily, Cosa Nostra is based on a rigid hierarchical structure, with clans based on elected members rather than family ties; here, women's role is traditionally confined to propaganda. In eastern Sicily, one powerful Cosa Nostra family is surrounded by small criminal groups based on the mafia model but with informal affiliations. It is here that the *stidda* or 'splinter groups' were first identified: armed gangs who hire themselves out to mafia clans – some of which are led by women.

In Calabria, the 'Ndrangheta clans are based on family units, in which women play a central, authoritative role; these units have remained intact among the expatriate Calabrian communities in northern Italy and Canada. The Naples Camorra is a loose conglomeration of families with an informal structure, where women with sufficient courage and authority can make their own way.

In America, the organisation clung on to the old ways for years, but each successive generation has slipped away from its Sicilian roots as young Italian-Americans enter the mainstream American way of life. Women who get involved in the US mafia do it for the glamour, and the money, and don't tend to stick around once the going gets tough.

Italy still seems to nurse a great nostalgia for the hierarchical, rule-bound mafia, and the notion of a code of honour. Where the American press reports mafia crimes with barely concealed scorn, always giving the boss's nickname – the more ridiculous the better – Italian commentators seem strangely reluctant to condemn. When a letter from the wife of the boss of bosses, Ninetta Bagarella, was published in the press, in which she defended her family against unjust persecution, one magistrate replied: 'there are doubtless some very good things about the mafia . . .'[1]

These days, mafia defectors claim they no longer recognise the organisation they joined in their youth – the 'old mafia' which respected the rules – and that the honoured society has become debased and savage. But perhaps the organisation never really

bore any resemblance to the image cherished by American immigrants and by young men growing up poor in southern Italy, to
whom the mafia was their only chance of being someone.
Back in 1974, the mafioso turncoat Leonardo Vitale called the
organisation evil, with its false laws and false ideals: 'Helping the
poor and helping the weak by killing people? They must be
crazy!'[2]

The mafia 'law' of never harming women and children is often
quoted to differentiate between today's ruthless gangsters and the
honourable organisation of old, but it is a false comparison. A May
Day gathering of Communist Party faithful in 1947, at Portella
della Ginestra in the western Sicilian mountains, was targeted by
the mafia and their political masters. Unarmed men, women and
children were picnicking on the grassy plain when shots were
fired into the crowd; among the dead were a woman and four
children.

Respect for women is often vaunted on the mafioso's list of
qualities. But the mafia uses rape as a war weapon, to humiliate
the defeated. In 1973, Corleone boss Luciano Leggio had his
ambitious lieutenant Damiano Caruso eliminated. To finish the
job, Leggio also killed Caruso's mistress, and raped and murdered
her teenage daughter.[3]

The first 'penitent' mafiosi to confess explained many things,
but mystified others: their description of the mafia left women
out of the frame altogether. 'Never tell women anything about
Cosa Nostra: it's one of the rules,' said Sicilian supergrass
Tommaso Buscetta, who collaborated with magistrates in 1984.
'A mafioso could be punished with death if he breathed a word
about the organisation to his wife.'

When the first female witnesses began to collaborate in the
early 1990s, the outside world was amazed at how much they
knew.

The 1996 parliamentary report on organised crime included
for the first time a section on women, which brought their true
role sharply into focus. It revealed that in 1990 just one woman
had been indicted in Italy for mafia association; by 1995 this figure
had increased to 89.[4] Women reported for possessing and

trafficking in drugs increased from 37 in 1994 to 422 in 1995, while the number charged with recycling money increased from 15 to 106, and women arrested for loan sharking went up from 119 to 421.

These figures appeared to demonstrate a radical change in women's role. It looked as though women, previously excluded from mafia business, had suddenly started working for the various criminal organisations. Or was it that investigators, having always accepted the idea that women never get involved, had finally begun to study their movements a little more closely?

In fact, there are records of women involved in mafia crime throughout this century. Maria Grazia Genova, known as Maragé, from Delia, a small town in southern Sicily, was born in 1909 to a mafia family. She was arrested a total of twenty-two times; in 1949 she escaped from prison while awaiting trial for her part in a mafia war between rival families – a feud which cost the lives of more than forty people.

The picture of the silent, unseeing, incurious mafia wife was remarkably durable. The mistress, however, was different. In America, mafia molls like 'Diamond Lil' Reiss and Virginia Hill took hold of the public imagination. The mistresses of mafia bosses were glamorous figures, frequently seen on the mobsters' arms in casinos and speakeasies. The girlfriends were more independent than mob wives, who played a formal public role; mafiosi were more likely to confide in their girlfriends and use them in crimes, or to provide alibis. As a result, US police began to target mafia mistresses. In 1980, after she had been used and abandoned by a series of New York mobsters, Arlyne Brickman agreed to wear a wire and record a conversation with one of her ex-lovers.

Weighed down by ancient prejudice, Italian investigators lagged years behind the American police. It was not until 1992, when Giacomina Filippello took the stand to nail her dead lover's killers, that the Italian courts took note of the mafia mistress's privileged position. There was a lot of talk about mafia women becoming emancipated, but perhaps we were seeing not so much a change in women's status, as the emancipation of investigating magistrates.

When I started researching this subject in the late 1980s, I was motivated chiefly by irritation. There was evidence to suggest that women played an active role in the mafia, and yet the idea was usually dismissed as laughable. I was particularly irked by a 1983 court ruling in which a Palermo judge declared that women could not be guilty of money-laundering because they are not autonomous and are anyway too stupid to take part in 'the difficult world of business'. It seemed to me that this line of thinking deprived women of moral choice, in much the same way that pets cannot be held guilty of their masters' crimes. Some magistrates still maintain that a woman directing her husband's affairs is not committing a crime – that a mafia wife has no choice, and therefore no moral responsibility. In 1995 Naples magistrate Giuseppe Narducci told me: 'Women's role is in no way subordinate: they make decisions, they plan strategies and commit crimes. Some magistrates have a problem believing that women are equal, but they'll get over it.'

In the name of equality, I wanted women to be given a fair trial: in the dock with the men. Like many of the Sicilian women I spoke to, I found it hard to accept that women are not clever enough to commit crimes. I also found it difficult to believe that women are morally superior to men.

In Sicily there is a lot of confusion about the criminal capacity of women. The veneration of motherhood makes Italians unwilling to think of women as capable of destructive or dangerous behaviour, and this attitude has led to a number of questionable acquittals. In 1971 Ninetta Bagarella, fiancée of the Corleone mobster Totò Riina, persuaded a judge not to punish her for working for the Corleone clan, by telling a Palermo court: 'I am a woman in love. Is that a crime?'

Even though women are supposed to be excluded from the mafia, the Italian media love the image of a killer bimbo. Girls with guns have always held a sexual fascination – in southern Europe, not just in Hollywood – and the media tend to celebrate one single murderess more than hundreds of male killers. Any woman described by the Italian press in connection with the mafia is *bella*, 'beautiful', with black hair and black eyes, mysterious and proud – the reader can just join the dots.

More commonly, mafia women are perceived as saintly mothers. The traditional view of the mafia wife is of sacrifice, loyalty and silence: standing by her man through the tough times, and raising the children to be perfect gangsters. The mafia relies on this image to generate propaganda. Stories in the press about Ninetta Bagarella always emphasise what a beautiful woman she is, how loyal, selfless and resourceful, teaching the children herself because they couldn't go to school. (A furious moral debate is currently raging over whether these qualities make her a good mother, or whether she would have done her children a favour by taking them away from their mafioso father.)

Not only does the press defend such women, without whom none of their husbands' careers would have been possible, but women have been smart enough to manipulate the media. Some have given press conferences to denounce their turncoat husbands, showing a media awareness which hardly fits with the image of the ignorant mafia wife who never asks questions and never leaves the house.

Others had also long had their doubts about the mafia wife's traditional image as a silent victim. At the Giuseppe Impastato Centre in Palermo, researchers Umberto Santino and Anna Puglisi have always treated mafia myths with healthy scepticism. They began to assemble press cuttings on mafia women, and by the mid-1980s had published a thick volume.

On my visits to Palermo over the last eight years, I have met Sicilian women so dynamic, clever, feisty and independent that the image of the meek retiring mafia wife seems an unlikely fiction. It is usual for married women to keep their own names in Sicily, which to an outsider is a sign of autonomy (although unfortunately it adds to the already long list of names in the narrative). In 1993 the collaborator Piera Aiello challenged mafia wives to drop the pretence that they see and hear nothing, and to admit that they exercise considerable influence over their husbands: 'A wife always knows what is going on. A woman can lead her husband wherever she wants.'[5]

The first part of this book demonstrates the active part women play in the mafia. Although I had planned to recount the story of every convicted mafia woman, it quickly became clear that there were already far too many to include them all in one volume. The ever-expanding number led me to compile my own limited biographical list, which is included at the back of the book.

While there has been some kind of awakening amongst investigators, several other factors have contributed to the increase in the number of women arrested for mafia crimes.

The mafia is usually portrayed as a conservative, male-dominated hierarchy, but it is probably less backward and more adaptable than the rest of society would like to believe. Recent changes within the organisation have favoured women's promotion. When the growth of its stake in the international drug trade enabled the mafia to expand, the organisation was forced to absorb more workers – including women. Women took advantage of prejudice: they passed unsuspected across international borders, where there were seldom female customs officers on hand to search them. Women have been discovered at the centre of family businesses, importing and selling drugs. (In most cases the reaction of the press has been to belittle the female drug trafficker: the infamous Anna Russo became known in local folklore as 'Grandma Heroin'.) Subsequently, when the mafia went into investment banking to recycle drug money, women quickly got involved in white-collar crime, being equally skilled and much less visible than men.

Another catalyst for change has been the advent of the *pentiti* or 'penitent' mafiosi, who have revealed much of the mafia's hidden machinery. The so-called *legge dei pentiti* or 'penitents' law' passed in January 1991 offered protection to collaborators and their families. Defectors were given a monthly wage and a place to live; later the state provided new documents and a job. For the first time ever, the state offered mafiosi a real alternative. Five years on, there are 1,273 collaborators, 421 of whom are mafiosi. With so much unwelcome exposure, the organisation has had to tighten security, so the all-male initiation rite – the only formal barrier to women's participation – has been all but abandoned.

For a long time, Italian law favoured female criminals. Mafiosi used women's names to register companies, properties and bank accounts. The system worked perfectly because women – even wives of high-ranking mafiosi – were considered beyond suspicion. Since there was no legal definition of mafia, there was no way of connecting a bank account in a woman's name with a drug smuggling ring.

The United States was the first country to take serious measures to combat organised crime. In 1970 the Racketeering Influenced and Corrupt Organisations Act or RICO made it a criminal offence to contribute to the general aims and profits of the mafia. It took over ten years for Italy to catch up with its own version in 1982, the Rognoni–La Torre law (named after its authors), which defined the mafia as a criminal association which uses violence and intimidation to achieve its aims. Magistrates were able to pursue the mafia not as the perpetrator of individual crimes, but as a system to which whole sections of society contributed – including women. The first arrest warrants for women accused of money-laundering followed soon afterwards.

The mafia has evolved at the same rate as 'civilised' society: while Italian women were entering the world of employment, mafia women were infiltrating the institutions, buying into legitimate business – it was only a matter of time before they assumed executive positions. The La Torre law was the first step to discovering the real breadth of women's role in organised crime.

The second half of the book shows how changes in the law have exposed the role played by women, and have led to their arrest in increasing numbers for mafia-related crime. It also describes the emergence of a strong anti-mafia movement run by women who – for the first time ever – attempted to cross the social divide.

The Women's Anti-mafia Association was launched in 1982 by a group of women whose husbands – judges, policemen and politicians – had been assassinated. These 'illustrious' widows set about encouraging mafia women to come forward and testify against the mafia. At the 'maxi-trial' of 1986 in a landmark move, two women from mafia families sued the organisation for murder.

There are many heroines of the anti-mafia, courageous women who have broken the oppressive silence and denounced the mafia and the establishment that supports it – Mamma Carnevale, mother of a trade unionist murdered in the 1950s who demanded justice for her son; Rosaria Schifani (widow of one of the police bodyguards for Giovanni Falcone, the anti-mafia magistrate assassinated in 1992), who spoke out at Falcone's state funeral and criticised the corrupt institutions; Enza Panebianco, a young political activist who exposed the corruption of local government. Although their courage is exceptional, it is easier for us to understand their motivation. The aim of this book is to take a close look at the conflicts and contradictions at work inside the women who grow up *within* mafia environments. It is more difficult to understand what motivates such women to espouse the mafia's values, or to reject them, and what influences their choices.

The penitents' law of 1991 finally gave mafia women the option of removing their children from a culture of violence and starting again, in return for giving evidence. It was also the first time women were taken seriously as witnesses. Before 1991, women who dared to accuse mafia killers were openly mocked. After that, mafia wives who took the stand proved that far from being silent victims who asked no questions, women knew a great deal about mafia business: of the sixty-one female collaborators who have come forward since the Act was passed, roughly a third are mafia women.[6]

By 1992 there were several women collaborators in Sicily, Naples and Calabria being cross-examined on details of mafia clans. After years of being passed over by 'civilised society' as obedient chattels, it looked as though mafia women were going to be the key to breaking the organisation. It seemed only a matter of time before hundreds of mafia women would take the opportunity to cross the line that divided them from law-abiding society, leaving the oppressive values of the 'honoured society' behind.

In America the process has already begun: the mobster is no longer a role model among poor families (the son of a Philadelphia boss hanged himself after his classmates' taunts became unbearable). The US Cosa Nostra has served its purpose: to give its members the advantage of power and money in a hostile society. Many American mafia bosses have used their position and ill-gotten wealth to send their children to expensive schools and colleges, and set them up in respectable professions. These days, mafia codes of honour are something quaint that young mafiosi might memorise, but not believe in – it never takes long for a young hit man facing prison to confess and turn in his associates. The mafia women I met in America admitted that they had had a good time with their gangster boyfriends but had little respect for the organisation; for them the mafia had been something glamorous, fun and strictly temporary, that no one should have to die for.

When I arrived in Sicily in July 1992, to work on the story of how women were going to bring down the mafia, there was a lot of talk about how women could be a force for good: they wanted to raise their children in a decent society. Then, on 19 July, campaigning anti-mafia magistrate Paolo Borsellino was killed by a car bomb, just two months after the murder of his friend and colleague Giovanni Falcone. The assassinations seemed like a mortal blow to the anti-mafia movement. A week after Borsellino's death, Rita Atria, a young collaborator, killed herself.

But what one Palermo man had called the 'death of hope' turned into a furious backlash. For Cosa Nostra, the assassinations were a public relations disaster. Until then, many Sicilians had cherished a romantic vision of a mafia which defended the poor and disenfranchised against an autocratic state. But Falcone and Borsellino were working-class heroes, respected by people on both sides of the criminal divide. Cosa Nostra seemed to have lost any semblance of honour or purpose. Many of its members, encouraged by their wives or girlfriends, defected in horror at the unstoppable crime wave perpetrated by their leaders. Anyone who still believed that killing women was forbidden by the mafia's code of honour was disabused by the murder of Falcone's wife Francesca Morvillo and one of Borsellino's bodyguards, Emanuela Loi. The death of agent Loi was also a cruel blow to women who had struggled hard for a career in the military on equal terms with men.

Anger and grief fuelled a major onslaught against organised crime in Italy, with a new energy and determination on the part of police and magistrates (the Pizza Connection trial was finally concluded with guilty verdicts in early 1997 – over ten years after it began). Anti-mafia measures rushed through in July 1992 included maximum security prison for convicted mafiosi. But the mafia, versatile as ever, adapted itself to the new conditions – and women were key to the changes. The rigorous assault by law enforcement left many clans without a leader. The new security measures meant that the boss could not direct operations from inside prison as he used to. In many cases, the boss has had to entrust business to his wife, who has become the manager.

Instead of leading the tide of righteous citizens against crime, women turned out to be even more entrenched in mafia values than men. The number of male mafia defectors rose, but many of their wives refused to leave the underworld. Some have threatened to take the children away, trying to force their men to withdraw their testimony. Others have organised protests in court to disrupt the proceedings. Some have even plotted to murder the 'treacherous' defector – a father, a husband, or a son.

Women have proved more retrograde than their men: many have clung to the security they know, provided by the mafia, rather than take a risk and opt for change. The neat progression that I had mapped out, from female murderers to superwomen leading their families towards an honest future, did not reflect reality. Women were taking moral responsibility for their actions, and they were choosing the mafia.

The mafia bases itself on a version of family bonds – protecting its members, awarding them privileges, closing ranks against hostile elements – and the mother plays a central role. (Under Italian law, a family member cannot be accused of aiding and abetting.) It was not surprising that when it came under attack, the mafia fell back on family values. If the mafia no longer commanded respect, at least the mother, at the heart of the family, was unassailable.

'When the mafia is really in trouble, they call on their women,' says prosecutor Antonio Laudati. In the summer of 1996, when the Corleonesi were down, it was time for the big guns. The wife of the boss of bosses, Ninetta Bagarella, pulled off a propaganda coup with a letter to the press in defence of her family. She championed family bonds above any other considerations – including legality or social responsibility. A mother's love, she argued, exonerated her son of wrong-doing. And many, many Sicilians agreed.

1. Camorra Godmothers

'We had been married for eighty days when they shot my husband. And eighty days later I shot the man who killed him. I was only 18. And I was pregnant.'

Pupetta Maresca sits at her kitchen table, looking down at her fingertips. She speaks in a low voice, perfectly enunciated. 'I was with my husband all night while he lay dying. I made him tell me who had shot him. The police knew who it was, but they didn't arrest him. I had no choice.'

Maresca, now 57, lives in a spacious penthouse in Sorrento, a resort on the Amalfi coast, where painted fishing boats are moored in little coves and tropical gardens threaten to escape over their high walls. At the end of a long lane so narrow that cars only make it round the corners on the second attempt, Maresca, headlined in newspapers for over forty years as the first lady of the Camorra,★ the Naples mafia, lives in a flat with her husband's surname, Simonetti, on the door.

She is wearing a white shirt-dress and black and gold high-heeled mules; she is tiny and has filled out with the years, but her face is still beautiful. She has perfect skin, a neck that has been massaged with expensive unguents all its life, classical cheekbones and a pretty, pouting mouth painted pink. Her eyebrows, plucked to oblivion, are drawn on with slightly jagged pencil lines. As she shows me in, a small brown dog clamps its jaws around my foot, making vicious snarling noises.

'The dog bites,' she says.

We sit at the round kitchen table over a two-foot-square gift

---

★There are several explanations for the origin of the word, but the one currently favoured derives from a popular street game in Naples, la Morra, in which sums of money were gambled. Each district had a local organiser, who took charge of collecting bets and kept order. He was known as the Capo della Morra, hence Camorra.

box of little cakes iced in pink and green, while the television flickers silently in the corner.

Assunta Maresca grew up in Castellammare di Stabia, a small town south of Naples, the only girl in a family of four boys. Tiny, pretty and spoilt, she was nicknamed Pupetta, 'little doll'. Her family controlled Castellammare, and defended their territory fiercely: they were known as the Lampetielli, 'lightning flashes', because of their reputation for skilful use of flick knives. By 17 Pupetta was renowned for her beauty, and jealously guarded by her brothers, who beat her if she so much as caught a man's eye. But when she was courted by a powerful camorrista, Pasquale Simonetti, known as Pascalone 'e Nola, ten years her senior, a wealthy old-style *guappo* or boss, her brothers offered no resistance. The wedding in 1955 was a grand affair with 500 guests, and the whole town turned out to wish them well. Most people gave them the traditional envelopes stuffed with money, others brought jewels for the princess.

It took Pupetta a while to get used to her new status in her husband's manor. In the mornings there was a queue of people outside their house bringing the boss presents of wine or cheese and asking for his help. Someone's son had been arrested, could Pascalone speak to a lawyer? Someone else's daughter had been dumped by her boyfriend, who now refused to marry her – could Pascalone help them buy some furniture for a dowry to help things along? He was the arbiter, a Solomon, patron of the needy and the wronged. According to local folklore, he once summoned a lad who had seduced and abandoned a young girl, and gave him a wad of money. 'This is for your wedding – or your funeral,' he told the boy. 'You decide.'[1]

The Camorra has always enjoyed social consensus in Naples: the *guappo* was considered a law-giver, one who restored order; he interceded when people needed housing, or work, or a duel had to be fought, or a pregnant girl had to get to the altar. The camorrista made people respect the rules. He moved in a moral universe with which neither the police nor the clergy concerned themselves: the dramas of everyday life.

Pascalone – 'big Pasquale' – controlled the market prices of fruit and vegetables in Nola, and took his cut of sales. But there was another pretender to the exalted position of price-fixer, a gangster called Antonio Esposito who, like Pascalone, had amassed wealth and connections through trading in contraband cigarettes.

'They came to tell me my husband had been shot,' recalls Pupetta Maresca. 'It was eleven in the morning on 16 July. I went straight to the hospital. He had been hit in the stomach and was bleeding terribly. I stayed at his side and he hung on all night, comforting me, telling me it would be all right . . . He didn't want to die. I begged him to tell me what had happened, who had done this to him. That's how I knew who did it. He told me Esposito was behind it. Why else would I have thrown my life away in a prison cell, unless my husband had told me who killed him?'

After her husband's death, Maresca sat in her married home, alone, for long hours, contemplating her shattered dreams. 'I didn't see anyone apart from the few friends who came to visit me, but I was frightened in the house on my own and moved back to live with my parents. It was like a nightmare, after starting a new life with my handsome prince, to be back living with my mother again.'

She reported to the police that the camorrista Antonio Esposito had got a hit man to murder her husband, but the weeks went by and Esposito went about his daily business in public view. 'I told the police again and again, I told them *everyone* knew it was him, but oh no, they said, they had to have proof, they had to have proof. I wanted justice.'

Maresca could not risk her husband's murder going unpunished: it would have diminished his reputation, and robbed her of her status as the widow of an important boss. Pupetta Maresca, sister of the Lampetielli brothers, was not victim material. She knew she had to win her reputation as a woman of honour, publicly, with several witnesses. If the police would not bring the murderer to justice, she would have to do it herself.

She carried a gun at the time – her husband's gun, which she had taken from his bedside, she says, as a memento. Esposito started sending her threatening messages, indicating that he knew her every move. Almost exactly eighty days after Pascalone's death, her driver was taking her on her daily visit to the cemetery, accompanied by her 13-year-old brother, when she saw Esposito walking along the road, and stopped the car.

'He walked towards us and tried to open the car door. I thought, He's going to kill me. To tell you the truth, I fired the first shot.' Esposito fired back, hitting the car doors. Cowering in the back seat, she shot him again and again. When he fell, she and her brother threw themselves out of the car and ran for it.

She went into hiding, thinking she could hold out at least until she had the baby. But after two weeks, police found her staying with a friend of her mother's and arrested her.

During the trial, Maresca was interrogated at length about her reasons for shooting Esposito, and tried to explain her actions. Finally, she admitted that she had to take revenge for her husband's murder: *she had had no alternative.*[2] The young widow was found guilty and sentenced to fourteen years in prison.

Maresca lets her hair down; thick shoulder-length hair dyed mahogany, with half an inch of grey at the roots, and smooths it behind her ears with the languid gesture of someone accustomed to being told she is beautiful. 'Prison was a nightmare. It was run by nuns, wizened old hags who were consumed with envy. I was young, I had just got married, I had all my lovely silk underwear . . . they took it away and gave me a rough sack dress to wear, shapeless and several sizes too big. I threw it back at them. "You wear it!" I said.'

The new prisoner gave the nuns hell, making demands, making complaints, demanding to see the governor. No, she wouldn't let them cut her hair. No, these clogs were men's shoes, take them away. No, the saggy cotton knickers. Absolutely not. 'I was just 17, you can imagine me in the midst of all those old women rotting in jail. There were some young ones too, but they were from Calabria and Sicily: primitive girls.'

By killing the man who murdered her husband, Pupetta

Maresca had inherited her husband's authority: the other inmates waited on her, brought her hot coffee and clean bedclothes. The women would hang around trying to see her, or send her little notes asking her for help: could she ask her lawyer to talk to the magistrate? Could she do something for so-and-so's children who were in trouble? Could she talk to the prison governor on someone's behalf? Maresca became the boss of the women's prison. She had food brought in for the less fortunate, and stood up for their rights.

She gave birth in prison in the middle of winter, to a boy she called Pasqualino – 'little Pasquale' – and was allowed to keep him until he was three. 'They took him away to live with my mother. That was the most heartbreaking thing of all. It destroyed me. My son was afraid of everything, he had always lived inside, with me: he screamed if he saw a car, even a little donkey frightened him . . .'

There follows a long pause. She looks down at her fingers, delicately entwined, and sighs. 'What can I tell you about my son, signorina? It's too painful. Really too painful.'

On my second visit, Pupetta Maresca opens the door in the middle of buttoning her shirt over her bra, and kisses me airily on both cheeks. I am gratified to see that the brown dog has been shaved and she now looks somewhat abashed with her naked dugs scraping the floor. We sit at the kitchen table with a huge vase of wilting red roses between us.

When Pupetta Maresca got out of jail after fourteen years at the age of 31, her son Pasqualino was a stranger. He called his grandmother 'Mamma' and his mother 'Pupetta'. She went to visit her former cellmate, who introduced her to Umberto Ammaturo, a handsome camorrista with terrific sideburns who ran cocaine from South America via Nigeria to Italy,[3] and arms from Germany to Libya. They became lovers, and Pupetta moved in with him. She gave birth to twins, gorgeous blond children, the apples of her eyes. Her older son grew rebellious and loud-mouthed, hanging out with local hoodlums. Ammaturo couldn't stand the boy's arrogance: son and lover squared up to each other. By the time he was 18 Pasqualino was behaving like a junior *guappo*, but he lacked his father's style and his stepfather's cunning. Once, when he was leaving a nightclub with a group of lads, an argument flared up about who was going to pick up the tab. Pasqualino drew his gun and shoved one of them against the wall – who happened to be the nephew of a camorrista known as *'o malommo*, 'the bad man'.[4]

The boy, in a hurry to become a man, talked a lot about how he was going to avenge his father's death. For him it was a rite of passage – which was a problem, because his mother had already done the job. She had shot the man who ordered the murder, while the gunman, Gaetano Orlando, known as Tonino u' Bastimento, 'Tony the Scourge', a lesser figure in the scale of things, had spent several years in prison. But Pasqualino needed to prove himself. He told whoever would listen that he was looking for Tony the Scourge, that as soon as he was 18 he would find him and splatter his brains over the landscape. In January 1974, days after Pasqualino's eighteenth birthday, he was due to meet Ammaturo at the construction site of the Naples flyover about some work. He was never seen again.

'I need to know one thing . . .' Maresca's voice is scarcely louder than a whisper, but every word is clear and sharp as a blade. 'Just one thing . . . I need to know where they buried him. Is it possible that with all these mafiosi repenting and turning state's evidence, not one of them has said a word about my son?'

The prime suspect in the murder of her son was Pupetta Maresca's lover. And it was not just the investigators who thought so.

'I know he knows something about it,' she says. 'I've always thought so. Pasqualino was turning out just like his father, he wanted to be like him – wanted to have his father's authority. His presence was a threat. I asked Ammaturo again and again if he knew anything about my son's death, but he always told me he didn't know anything, he even hit me when I went on and on asking. I told him, "Yes you know, oh yes you do," ' she says in an icy whisper. 'But there's another thing I'm sure of. If he had told me, I would have killed a man for the second time in my life.' Her voice is glacial, pure hate. 'I am very sure of that.'

A Naples lawyer commented privately: 'Pupetta Maresca is carved out of stone. Umberto Ammaturo is not saying anything because he is afraid of her revenge. And he's right to be afraid.'

'Pupetta Maresca came to me a number of times, alleging that Ammaturo had killed her son,' says Judge Italo Ormanni, who was in charge of the investigation in Naples in the mid-seventies, and now presides at the criminal courts in Rome. 'She was always hysterical and weeping – I don't know how many handkerchiefs I got through on that particular case, because she always turned up without one. It became a standing joke with the carabinieri. But at the end of every session, after all the tears and the drama, she always refused to sign a statement.'[5]

The judge, convinced the boy was buried in one of the cement pillars supporting the city flyover, asked permission to knock it down and search for the body, but it was never granted.

So Pupetta Maresca, the woman who had taken the law into her own hands, who had shot her husband's killer because the police wouldn't arrest him, carried on sleeping with the man she believed had killed her son. Why? 'The thing is, Ammaturo was still the father of her children,' Ormanni explains. 'One of the twins had a bad heart and had to get treatment in Switzerland, and living with Ammaturo guaranteed her enough money for the cure . . . it also guaranteed her a certain lifestyle. They lived in a luxurious home, the top two floors of an apartment block. There was intense security, closed circuit TV, they had their own lift. Inside there was money wall to wall . . . marble everywhere, gold taps, a sunken bath so big they had a staircase to get into it. Pasqualino was the child of her first marriage, his father had died a long time ago . . . he had lived with her from time to time, but he came and went. She had a new life with Ammaturo.'

'The twins,' Maresca acknowledges, 'in a way, replaced Pasqualino.'

Although Pupetta and Umberto were portrayed in the press for a long time as the great love story of the underworld, she now says she loathes Ammaturo, who was violent and cruel to her. 'Have a look at my head,' she says, leaning forward, 'there are chunks of hair missing; he used to hit me on the head, where it doesn't show . . .' Ammaturo was a powerful camorrista in his own right, and he had other women, and yet – in a reversal of roles almost unique in the mafia – he is always referred to in the media as Pupetta Maresca's man.

Pupetta was useful to Ammaturo. Her beauty and her taste for drama made her the focus of press attention, leaving him to operate in her shadow. She shielded her brothers in the same way, to an extent that got her into serious trouble. According to Italo Ormanni, in the 1960s the Lampetielli became a powerful force in Castellammare through their trade in contraband cigarettes. In 1974, Raffaele Cutolo, self-styled boss of a new criminal organisation, the Nuova Camorra Organizzata, imposed a 'tax' on every case of cigarettes imported by the other Camorra families. Pupetta Maresca's family fought back. In 1978 Ciro, Pupetta's favourite brother, was shot several times. He survived, but while he was in prison four years later Cutolo's men threatened him again.

To draw fire from her brother, Pupetta Maresca created a spectacular diversion. On 13 February 1982 she called a press conference at the exclusive Press Club on the seafront in Naples. She turned up in a tight black leather suit with an 'extremely vulgar' fur collar, her shirt 'noticeably unbuttoned' and a leopardskin scarf round her neck. (These comments were made by Sergio De Gregorio, a Naples journalist, whose disparaging report of the event may or may not have had something to do with the fact that she was suing him for libel at the time.)

The first thing she did was send away a female journalist who had written something she didn't like. Then she launched her attack: 'If Cutolo touches one member of my family, I will have his gunmen killed, I will kill his lackeys, even the women and the babies in their cradles . . . This whole region is being strangled by an invisible power, creeping through every level of society. That insidious force is Raffaele Cutolo. He wants to rule, at any price – you're either with him or against him. Cutolo wants to become emperor of Naples, and this town is in chains because of him. All these deaths, the rivers of blood which are running through our city as people watch helplessly, all this is caused by one power-crazed madman.'[6]

The newspapers were wild for Pupetta's defiance and her *décolletage*. And they were thrilled by Cutolo's airy reply: 'La Pupetta should drop the histrionics . . . she really should have a little more dignity. She's made a complete fool of herself.'[7]

When she talks about Cutolo, Maresca's voice changes register, from her softly enunciated purr to a bark. Her loathing bursts through her perfectly cultured patina and she reverts to Neapolitan dialect. 'He had threatened to kill my brothers. What was I supposed to do? Oh, but I paid for it all right. That piece of shit started threatening me as soon as I made my little speech.'

Later the same year, Maresca was arrested, with her lover Umberto Ammaturo, for the murder of Aldo Semerari, a doctor who had been found with his severed head between his legs.[8] It is a charge she still denies, and which a former carabiniere (who cannot be named) also maintains was trumped up. She served four years for something she didn't do, she believes, because her mortal enemy Raffaele Cutolo used his contacts in the judiciary to put her there. Nothing burns in her mind more fiercely than that injustice. 'I was tortured by the judges who put me away, every day of those four years. The first fourteen years were different, because I had committed a crime, and it was right that I should pay. But those four years were terrible, because there is no peace for an innocent person in prison.'

Pupetta Maresca shows me the view from her terrace. It is vast, terracotta tiled, dotted with dog shit. It looks out over the palms and the roofs of old palazzi, over the church dome, tiled in yellow and green, towards the sea. 'My faith in God keeps me going,' she offers. 'If I didn't have that I don't know how I should survive. I am the spiritual daughter of Padre Pio. I often go and pray at his sanctuary.'

Throughout our conversations, in which we have talked about the murder of her husband and her son, Pupetta Maresca has not given me the impression of a person racked with grief. Even I – who am embarrassingly often moved to tears by tales of loved ones strangled and dissolved in acid – feel strangely unmoved by her account. She is completely cold. Beautiful and cold.

The notion of justice as an individual burden is diffused throughout the Italian mafia – in the Sicilian Cosa Nostra, the 'Ndrangheta in Calabria, and the Camorra in Naples. Each of the three distinct organisations has its own framework, but they are jointly characterised by disregard for the laws of the state. Such laws, and the personnel employed to enforce them, do not register on the men of honour's moral scale. The mafia has its own peculiar 'logic' which justifies any action in the interests of the organisation.

In the course of examining a Sicilian witness, a magistrate asked her whether it was usual, whether it was considered acceptable within a mafia clan, to settle scores and solve problems by shooting people. The magistrate's difficulty with the concept was such that it took him several attempts to articulate his question. The witness had no such problem. 'Of course,' she replied.[9]

A mafia hit man, who defected and turned state's evidence, described his moral outlook. 'A man going to do a hit does it out of solidarity, out of a sense of common duty. He does it because he believes it is the right thing to do. The first time I killed a man I was about 33, but I was still in primary school when I understood that the world is divided between those who kill and those who get killed . . . When people ask me how I could find it in me to kill another man, I tell them, in the neighbourhood where I grew up, that's just the way it is.'[10]

The organisation demands obedience of its soldiers, and mafia 'logic' dresses up murder in a mantle of duty and honour. But the mafia's code of honour is a fake. Judges in the trial of over 475 mafiosi in 1985–86 lost no time in tearing down the hypocritical construct. 'Murder is not something extraordinary, nor is it justified by the credo of Cosa Nostra, it is the means by which the organisation achieves its aims and affirms its power; the rest is mystification and lies.'[11]

What a mafioso describes as an honourable act is something more pragmatic: it serves the individual's rise, or survival, within the organisation. Pupetta Maresca killed her husband's murderer 'because she had to': she fulfilled her public obligation to her dead husband and protected her own status. Years later, when her son was murdered, she threatened to kill the man responsible, but it would have been against her interests to do it, so she let it go.

The mafia operates in a moral twilight created by people's needs, and exploits the very people it pretends to serve. In Naples, in the 1960s, unemployment was high, and a vast number of people lived at close quarters in conditions of abject poverty. The Camorra put people to work in its thriving illegal industry, selling food and medicines on the black market and smuggling drugs and cigarettes.

In 1963, Raffaele Cutolo, a young and clever boy from Ottaviano, a small town near Naples, was sentenced to life imprisonment, reduced to twenty-four years, for the murder of a young man who dared to touch his sister.[12] While he was in prison, surrounded by the poor and dispossessed, he started recruiting followers from the cells. The Camorra was in abeyance at the time. The old-style *guappo* like Pascalone 'e Nola, the traditional boss of the rural areas, was on the way out. Cutolo had no territory but the teeming cells, but with his new recruits, he set himself up as a charismatic leader of what he called the Nuova Camorra Organizzata, or NCO, and made a bid to rule the city. Cutolo, known as *'o professore*, 'the professor', conducted pseudo-religious initiation rites to give his followers a powerful sense of belonging, using people's desperation to fuel his ascent. In part he created the conditions from which he saved his followers: he incited violence and bullying inside the prison, and then offered the victims protection. Once outside, they had to work for him. He supported the prisoners' families; the money given them was part of a levy extracted with menaces from small businesses and other families.

Cutolo ruled by force of personality, but his operation also required clever financial management and sustained pressure on politicians and the local population. Since he couldn't do everything from inside prison, Cutolo put together a trusted group of directors, led by his sister Rosetta. Known as 'eyes of ice', Rosetta, five years his senior, became his manager. He gave her orders, and she ran the organisation.

Rosetta Cutolo was the power behind her notorious brother for over fifteen years. She became a legendary figure during the dozen years she was in hiding, and was further glamorised by Giuseppe Tornatore's film *Il Camorrista*, until she gave herself up to the police in 1993. She is currently serving a five-year sentence for mafia association.

When young, she was a dumpy, plain creature, with a big nose and long straight hair which she tied in a ponytail; the rare photographs of her taken in the 1970s show her dressed mannishly in a patterned shirt over a T-shirt, without make-up. It is said that she was once engaged, but gave up the love of her life to dedicate herself to her brother.[13] Giuseppe Marrazzo, the writer who helped create the Cutolo myth with his fictional-ised version of the camorrista's life, implied an incestuous relationship between brother and sister. 'Rosa Cutolo is the true, faithful right arm of the boss of Ottaviano . . . she has remained a spinster to dedicate her life to him.'[14]

She was pious as a young woman and, while she was in hiding, spent her time in the company of a priest (the unfortunate cleric was murdered by Cutolo's enemies in 1986).[15] But the moral universe was swallowed up by the cult of Raffaele Cutolo. Even as a small boy he had grand ideas: his father was a man of such piety he was known as *'o monaco*, 'the monk', but Raffaele said that when *he* grew up he was going to be pope. In his book *Poetry and Philosophy*, a collection of his pronouncements, he writes: 'I am a divinity, for me no laws exist, because I am greater than a judge.'[16] He has spent many years trying to convince prison psychiatrists he is mad in order to get a more lenient sentence – perhaps the effort of feigning psychosis has finally got to him, for he has become increasingly Messianic. 'Jesus said: if someone slaps you, turn the other cheek. I say: at that point you can kill them.'[17]

While Raffaele has created scandal, giving interviews and making speeches in the courtroom, his sister has kept a low profile. Rosetta ran her younger brother's organisation with a selfless dedication that added to his cult status. She collected money from local businesses with missionary zeal, and painted him as a kind of saint: 'We do good in my brother's name. Do you see these people here? They come to us for many reasons; if there are jobs to be allocated in the local town or elsewhere, we are given a quota to fill. We also help prisoners: every trader gives us a contribution, of his own accord, to support prisoners' families.'[18]

As Cutolo's pretensions grew more outrageous, the other Camorra families, including Pupetta Maresca's brothers, the Lampetielli, grouped together to fight the upstart. They called themselves collectively the Nuova Famiglia, and imitated his organisation by recruiting among the unemployed criminal fringe, inventing an initiation rite of their own. By the late 1970s, hundreds had died in a war for control of Naples and the outlying territory.

Rosetta passed on her brother's orders and cultivated his devoted following. One resident of Ottaviano told a reporter that without her, the organisation would have collapsed.[19] Shortly after Cutolo succeeded in getting himself transferred to a mental hospital, a bomb blew a hole in the perimeter wall and he escaped. Rosetta and her mother – the last people to see him before the escape – were arrested and charged with engineering Raffaele's escape, but were released after three days.

Some say that, in spite of his evident megalomania, 'the

professor' was always in awe of his older sister. According to Antonio Laudati, prosecutor at the National Anti-mafia Department, who has questioned Cutolo many times, Rosetta was the true force behind the organisation. 'Her brother has always been under the power of her forceful personality. He's been in prison for thirty years; during that time she became director of the Nuova Camorra Organizzata in her own right.'[20]

In spring 1980, a top-level meeting was held between representatives of the Sicilian Cosa Nostra and the Camorra clans, to try to put an end to the bloody war between the NCO and the rest, and find a peaceful way to carve up the territory between them. At the meeting, Raffaele Cutolo was represented by his lieutenant, Vincenzo Casillo, and his sister Rosetta.[21]

In October 1981, police raided her house in Orlando, and broke in on a meeting of fifteen of Cutolo's aides, including a local councillor and Cutolo's 19-year-old son, Robertino. Rosetta, who had been chairing the meeting, escaped with two of her men. She was not seen in public again for over ten years, during which time she directed operations from a series of safe houses in different cities.

By 1984 Cutolo had overshot himself. An ambitious attempt to bargain with the authorities backfired: when the Christian Democrat Ciro Cirillo was kidnapped by Red Brigade terrorists, the negotiations for his release were conducted between politicians, terrorists and the Camorra. Cutolo, having made a trade-off with government ministers, found himself in solitary confinement, in a maximum security prison. As he became power crazed and paranoid, his closest allies met increasingly violent and unpleasant ends, while Rosetta sat tight. If he still had any power, she was the only executor he trusted, but by the mid-eighties the NCO was finished. Although Rosetta was wanted by the police, according to her lawyer she lived at least some of the time undisturbed at home, in the via delle Rose in Ottaviano, where she did her embroidery and tended her rose garden.

The Cutolos' lawyer, a tall, jocular figure called Paolo Trofino, with a voice shot to hell by cigarettes, and long hair swirling around his shoulders, describes Rosetta as 'associate director' of the NCO. Raffaele, he insists, has always made the decisions.

Trofino has managed to maintain this line through no fewer than nine murder trials. Rosetta Cutolo was cleared, on appeal of the murder of drug dealer Francis Turatello – who was hanged by a fellow prisoner inside a Sardinian maximum security prison; the prosecution alleged that Rosetta had given the order to the murderer's wife, who passed on her instructions during visiting hour. Rosetta was cleared, again on appeal, of ordering the murder of Giuseppe Salvia, deputy governor of Poggioreale prison in Naples. Salvia had denied Raffaele Cutolo the perks he was accustomed to in prison – he was used to receiving visitors at all hours and having his meals brought in to him. Cutolo sentenced him to death for over-zealous exercise of his duties. She was also cleared of the murder of Vincenzo Casillo, Cutolo's right-hand man. Casillo was suspected of embezzling money, and died in a car bombing. A few days later, his girlfriend was buried alive in a cement pillar: Cutolo wanted her silenced because he deemed she knew too much about the organisation.

Rosetta has always had a love-hate relationship with her brother. 'Their relationship is very stormy,' says Trofino. 'They often have rows. She thinks he talks too much. She wishes he wouldn't give interviews.' Trofino only agreed to defend Cutolo in the first place if he gave up pretending to be mad. 'He has delusions of grandeur, that's all, like Napoleon, or Hitler. I will say one thing for sure. He's not normal.'

When Rosetta gave herself up to the police in February 1993, after ten years in hiding, the papers described her as looking like a dowdy housewife. The Italian press describes almost anything in a skirt as *bella* – it helps keep the readers interested – but Rosetta, never. At 55, her grey hair was neatly trimmed and curled, her famous 'eyes of ice' had melted with age. The police chief who went to arrest her said later that as he opened the door, she burst into tears.[22] (Her lawyer, who was also present, says she was perfectly calm and resigned.) The

police claimed she had given herself up because she was afraid
her enemies were trying to kill her. Others said that, faithful to
the last, Rosetta had been sacrificed to her brother, that her
capture was part of a bargain between Cutolo and the
magistrates, but on this subject her lawyer reserves comment.

Cutolo's toughest opponents among the Camorra clans united
against him were his former allies, the Moccia clan. The
Moccia brothers were a force to be reckoned with, partly
because of their ruthless nature and deadly firepower, but
chiefly because of their mother, Anna Mazza.

'Of all the people I have come across in all these years – and
I've come across quite a few – none of them has given me the
feeling that I get from signora Mazza,' says Giacomo Travaglino, a young magistrate in Naples. 'She is the kind of woman
that, if she decides something is going to happen to you, it will
happen, no question.' Travaglino, who is responsible for seizing
the assets of Camorra families, was once shot a caustic remark
by Anna Mazza during a cross-examination. He subsequently
found a bullet hole in his bedroom window.

Anna Mazza's husband Gennaro Moccia was an old-style
camorrista, boss of Afragola, a small town in the Naples
hinterland. They were wealthy, and had good relations with
the rising star Raffaele Cutolo. A bitter territorial feud with a
rival clan came to a crisis when, on 31 May 1976, Moccia was
shot in the face and died at the wheel of his car. The family was
decapitated, and the remaining members had to fight or run.
They decided to fight.

Their first target was Moccia's number one rival, Antonio
Giugliano, who was charged with his murder, and then, to the
family's disgust, acquitted. A few days after the verdict, on 29 May
1978, Giugliano was walking through the old Naples courthouse
in discussion with his lawyer. People were pouring down the
staircases and criss-crossing the cobbled internal courtyard;
defendants chained together were taking halting steps towards the

cells. A young lad ran through the crowd, a pistol in each hand, and shot Giugliano several times. Carabinieri brought the boy down with a shot in the side. He was Antonio Moccia, aged 13. He was dragged off and interrogated, but he was too young, by a matter of weeks, to be prosecuted, and they had to let him go. The next day they arrested his mother.

'Up to that point, Anna Mazza had been just the wife of a capo,' says Travaglino. 'That day, she became a capo in her own right – one of the most dangerous, certainly one of the most bloody.'

Interrogated by the police, she denied instructing the boy to avenge his father, but showed no remorse for what her son had done. As prosecutors later pointed out, the boy had merely 'avenged the murder of his father in the only way acceptable to, and recognised by, his culture'.[23]

The Moccia clan had fired the first shot in a war for control of the territory. Within a few years, the Moccia brothers and their troops had systematically wiped out the Giugliano family. 'Their strength,' comments Travaglino, 'lies in the fact that they are pitiless; they stop at nothing.' Having defeated the Giuglianos, the Moccia clan turned on its former allies, the Magliulo family, and picked off one after another until the last remaining members packed what they could carry and cleared out of town.

'They are serious killers, but none of them would have moved a muscle without the word from la signora Mazza. We are talking about young men with long-playing records for murder. None of them would have lifted a finger if their mother had not told them what to do.' Travaglino laughs, with his back to the glass wall of the conservatory.

The high-rise office of Saverio Senese, Anna Mazza's lawyer, commands a view over the Naples harbour into the sunset. Across the water the outline of Capri is as faint as a gauze backdrop. The waiting room is full of the debris of tedium: piles of unread magazines reduced to shreds by constant flicking, free-standing ashtrays overflowing with butts; plants suffocating in corners.

Anna Mazza arrives in a blaze of dyed red hair and a pair of huge dark glasses. Her substantial form rounds the door like a woman going into battle, clasping her Gucci handbag in one fist and gesticulating with the other. Her lawyer, a sprightly little man, hops about like Willy Wonka and is gone. The Black Widow of the Camorra, as she is known, stays on her feet, shouting at me about the injustices to which her sons have been subjected. She is in designer mourning: below the wide black frames with gold and diamanté clasps, her mouth is daubed with mulberry lipstick; she wears a long black jacket armoured, unnecessarily, with shoulder pads; tailored black trousers, lace tights and shiny pumps. Her fingers are jammed with thick gold rings. She fires accusations against high-handed judges, vindictive carabinieri, and libellous journalists. The list begins with the carabiniere who wounded her son in the courthouse all those years ago. (He is, she tells me, very sorry.)

'The day after my son shot Antonio Giugliano in the courthouse, the police interrogated me; they said I had forced my son to commit this terrible crime. I told them the only thing my son did wrong was to shoot that son of a bitch in a decent place. He should have butchered him in a filthy back alley like he deserved.

'Since that day I have been persecuted by the law.'

The Moccia clan had the right credentials to rise in the Camorra: a bulletproof car and a friendly relationship with Raffaele Cutolo. 'I knew Cutolo,' says Anna Mazza. 'Everyone did. My sons were in jail, and in those days being sent to Poggioreale prison was a death sentence. Cutolo was running the place. It was war inside those prison walls, the violence was terrible. I used to get cartons of cigarettes for Raffaele Cutolo so he would protect my sons; I gave them to his sister Rosetta. If I took her gifts for him, he would make sure the boys weren't killed. I didn't have much choice.'

The deal with Cutolo didn't last, because the Moccia brothers failed to show him sufficient deference. A defector later revealed that Cutolo was displeased when the Moccia boys planned a murder without consulting him, and disdainful when they botched it.[24] So the family threw in its lot with the growing alliance against Cutolo, and Anna Mazza's eldest son Angelo became one of the leaders of the Nuova Famiglia, the army of Camorra clans united by loathing of the self-styled Messiah. 'There were three of them,' says Anna Mazza, proudly. 'The most powerful bosses of the whole Naples area: Carmine Alfieri, Alfredo Galasso and *my son* Angelo.'

Angelo turned the family into an efficient and imaginative killing machine, controlling an extortion racket that brought in millions, and raking millions more off the building and public works contracts which they scooped through their links with local councillors.

The Moccia family, according to Judge Travaglino, moved as one, directed by the iron will of the matriarch. 'There was a close tie, a common interest which originated with whatever the mother decided . . . Those boys took the path they did because of who their mother was.' When the Black Widow was banned from southern Italy, she moved to Formia, near Rome. Angelo, who was then on the run from the police, went to join her. Police noted a sharp increase in the crime rate in Formia following Signora Mazza's arrival.

In November 1987 Vincenzo, Anna Mazza's favourite son, the most handsome of her dark, strapping lads, was ambushed in Afragola by two carloads of men from the rival clan, and died in a storm of bullets. As soon as she heard about her son's death, Signora Mazza broke her parole and drove straight home. Twenty-four hours later the body of Vincenzo's killer was found, naked and mutilated; he had been crucified and tortured with electric shocks. The Black Widow was already on her way back to Formia. One after another, the men who had ambushed Vincenzo Moccia were eliminated as the Moccia boys took their revenge. Anna Mazza had sworn to make the Magliulo family pay for her son's death 'until the last generation'.[25]

Since their father was murdered, the Moccia boys have defended their territory with staggering ferocity. They are driven by vendetta, before which potent machinery the laws of

the state are as irrelevant as shadows. Anna Mazza's role, now
that all her sons are in jail, is to justify everything they have
done in the name of revenge. She believes they were right to
act and, by the same logic, it was wrong for them to be
punished. She is up to date on their cases, comes in for daily
conferences with her lawyer, and follows the legal polemics in
the news. As she talks, she produces bundles of yellowed press
cuttings from her handbag and smooths them out on the black
leather sofa for me to read.

She has been under investigation since her adolescent son
was found in the courthouse holding a smoking gun, but
magistrates have had a hard time making charges stick. They
sent her to prison, and she was released by a judge who was
subsequently convicted of corruption.[26] They sent her into
internal exile – the first woman to be punished in this way for
mafia crimes – and she obtained certificates describing her
alarming state of health, a rare condition which could only be
cured in her local hospital, a private institution near Afragola. 'I
don't know what kind of doctors they are,' laughs the
magistrate Giacomo Travaglino, 'but I wouldn't go to them for
anything worse than a cold. Signora Mazza swore blind they
were the best cardiologists in Italy.' Travaglino, who confis-
cated any of the Moccia family assets the law could get its hands
on, became convinced that what the family owns in Italy is
only a small proportion of their total wealth.

Anna Mazza recently moved to Naples to be nearer the prison,
and spends her days seeing lawyers, taking advice, talking to
magistrates, attending trials and appeals. In all this she is powered
by righteous indignation. She chose Saverio Senese as her lawyer
twenty years ago, when he had established a certain notoriety by
defending Red Brigade terrorists. His courage impressed her. She
wanted a lawyer who would go to war.

The day I met her, Anna Mazza, proud mother of the third
man in the Camorra's ruling triumvirate, was trying to rescue her
son from a life sentence, by claiming he has had a change of heart.
'I'm not saying my son isn't a criminal, but he's being persecuted.
He's being held in solitary confinement, in a maximum security

prison, so I'm only allowed to visit him once a month. When I see him, he's behind a thick glass barrier. I can't even touch him . . .' Her mouth distorts and wobbles. She takes a roll of lavatory paper out of her Gucci handbag and tears off a few sheets to dab at her eyes. She removes the immense dark glasses to reveal eyes as small and hard as bullets.

She has tried to play the maternal card before, without success. She told magistrates: 'I have always followed my sons' progress closely in everything they do, whenever I have seen that they needed a mother's love.'[27] As her sons have confessed to over a dozen murders, this assertion threw an interesting light on the benefits of mother love.

But Anna Mazza remains convinced that she has the moral upper hand. She explains that the Moccia family protected and assisted the people of Afragola. 'Those people love me. They loved my husband. You ask them: they'll tell you that when the Moccia family lived in Afragola, there were no drugs; there was no crime. Whenever I go back they come to me and say: "Signora, please come back, what are we to do without you? There's no one in charge here now." '

One of the many times the Black Widow was banned from living in Naples, she took herself to Codogné, a prosperous Italian town where there is strong support for the Northern League – the party which aims to split from the backward, mafia-ridden south. Protesters appeared under her window, chanting 'Mafia scum go home' (according to Judge Travaglino, she organised the demonstrations herself). 'We do not want your undesirables,' the placards read. 'Take back your murderers, your extortionists, your armed robbers.'

'They sent me to have my meals in an old people's home,' Anna Mazza recollects. 'It was disgusting, the conditions in that place were dreadful. All the patients stank of urine, they were so sedated they could barely sit up, and the place was filthy. I went to the director and said: "Is *this* how you treat your old people?" '

2. The Women Who Want To Be Boss

For Brenda Colletti, the mafia was better than the movies. Her husband Philip was an ambitious small-time hit man on the fringes of the South Philadelphia mob, and she longed for him to make the grade, to become a made member. She loved the rules, the secrecy of it, the sense of danger. She loved the way it felt like being in a team: us against them.

What she couldn't stand was when they were all together in a restaurant and the men would get up and go off to another room to talk. Even more galling was the time she finally got to meet John Stanfa – the Old Man, the Sicilian capo of the South Philadelphia mob – and he scarcely gave her a glance.

'He didn't say anything to me because I was a wife. A woman. Women are low class . . . they're like . . . they're the next thing to your pet dog. It was like "Hey, how ya doin'?" and then all the men went out to talk. And the women got to stay behind – ooh, they were bimbos! they were only interested in talking about their beauty salons, talking about their nails . . . you should have seen the make-up. I just didn't fit in . . .

'Afterwards I used to ask my husband "What did you talk about?" I told him I'd love to get involved. He'd say "You can't, you're a girl." I said "I'd love to, it'd be a thrill." I really wanted it. I've just never been a regular girl. Never interested in getting my hair all fancy, never interested in clothes. I always usually hung out with guys.'

I had met Brenda Colletti at a railway station in New Jersey in a blizzard; the snow was two-foot deep and my train had been delayed by over an hour. She was smiling, and a small crowd congratulated us on our meeting: she had made friends with half a dozen people in the time she'd had to wait. She was wearing a short wool jacket, sweatshirt and jeans, and her long shaggy auburn hair was loose. Her car was full of cardboard

boxes that contained her worldly possessions; I perched in the
back and we drove slowly through the snow to a vast roadside
restaurant with dark wooden booths and low table lamps.

Since the days of dining out with gangsters, Brenda's life had
taken a nosedive. With a long list of charges from possessing
firearms to murder hanging over them, in February 1994
Brenda and her husband had agreed to turn state's evidence.
Two years on, Brenda, aged 30, was homeless and living in fear
for her life, her husband was in prison, and her son was living
with her parents-in-law on the other side of the United States.
She had been caught pocketing a packet of sleeping pills in a
drugstore – she said she had been planning to take them all. As
a result of the shoplifting charge, she was booted out of the
secure accommodation arranged by the FBI for state witnesses.
'I went back there after I was discharged. They had changed the
locks and left all my stuff just lying outside in the rain.'

Brenda and Philip met under the neon glare of Dunkin'
Donuts late at night. She had just finished work as a go-go
dancer in a Philadelphia brothel. The brothel was owned by a
family of six brothers with mob connections, and as a sign of
great privilege, they used to let Brenda help count the takings.
'In that kind of world, for a woman to be allowed to do
anything was a big deal. I think that's when I first started getting
my thrills being around people that I knew were connected.
That's when I thought "I want to climb higher and higher – I
want to be in the mob", because women aren't in the mob.'

She was in the middle of getting a divorce, so it was almost a
year before Philip moved in, and not long afterwards he started
working for mobster Raymond Esposito, one of Sicilian capo
John Stanfa's soldiers. 'Raymond used to drop by or we would
go to his house. I didn't like him at first – he had watched too
many *Godfather* movies. He is one of those guys who does all
that stuff – kisses on both cheeks and you gotta kiss my ass . . . I
wasn't going to kiss nobody's ass – except for the Old Man,
John Stanfa. That was different 'cause he was the boss. You had
to treat him with respect.'

The Collettis' kitchen table became the meeting place for a

small group of aspiring mobsters. Philip bought Brenda a pistol and took her to practise shooting at a Philadelphia gun club. There were guns hidden about the house, out of reach of their little boy Paulie, and the basement was used as a firing range. 'The next people in the house had to dig the bullets out of the wall. We were just bad people.'

Before he could be sponsored for initiation, Philip had to kill a man. His first opportunity arose when he was given the order to eliminate the capo John Stanfa's main rival, Michael Ciancaglini, known as Mikey Chan. Philip and his cronies put together a four-pound bomb, rigged up a remote control detonator and made elaborate plans about how best to hit the target. Night after night, Philip took out the bomb in its component parts. Night after night he came home despondently saying, 'It didn't go off.' In the end, Brenda, only half joking, offered to do the job herself.

'Everyone would be round at our house, talking about hunting and plotting murders.' They enjoyed the fragile companionship, knowing that one moment they could be having a beer with their best friend and the next they'd be trussed up in the boot of a car. How did they know? They'd seen the movies. 'There's a saying,' Brenda recalls, 'it's from a *Godfather* movie but everyone always said it – "Keep your friends close but your enemies closer".'

Brenda Colletti got her break the day her husband got his, on 5 August 1993. Philip and his sidekick John-John Veasey happened upon their target as he came out of a South Philly clubhouse, and shot him dead. They left his companion wounded in the street. Brenda was at home when she got a call from her husband, in a state of high excitement, telling her to 'clean the house' and get over to his parents' place as fast as she could. She did as she was told, hid all the firearms in the woodpile at the end of the garden, and drove across town. When she got there, she had to help them dispose of the getaway car. John-John set fire to the car with petrol and burned his hand badly. They couldn't take him to hospital in case someone linked his injury to the burning car, so Brenda administered ice packs in Philip's parents' back garden.

Two days later, after the trio had rehearsed their alibis, Brenda reported the car stolen, and the police took her in for questioning. 'It was a thrill. They had a good cop and a bad cop, just like on TV. All the psychology head trip. I loved every second,' she recalls, laughing. After four hours of grilling they released her without charge. It was her finest hour.

'When I came out I saw Philip. He was nervous in case I had told them something. I just told him "Nah, I handled it."

'After that, people talked to me totally different. They didn't treat me like just a wife any more. It was like, "Damn! she's cool!" you know: "She's all right for a girl." People trusted me more. It was so weird, I felt like I had a sex change or something. When we went out to dinner, I was introduced to people. There was like . . . these big union reps, they're powerful people. And I'm getting introduced to them, and all the other wives are just stuck at the table talking about their fingernails. I'm meeting all these connected people. It was really cool.'

Brenda shakes her empty cigarette packet and reluctantly accepts one of mine.

Life changed for the Colletti family. Philip had killed a big man, and Brenda had covered up the crime. The old Italian men in the restaurants and clubhouses of South Philly would stuff ten, twenty, a hundred dollar bills in their little boy's fist. They never paid for a meal in a restaurant. 'We only went to gangster places – gangster-owned. Every place we went there was someone that was connected. We would never go anywhere normal. We would never go *here*.' (She scowls across the restaurant at the waitress, who is watching in disgust as her only customers smoke cigarettes and swig bottles of beer.) When Brenda and Philip walked into a place, people would send drinks over to their table. Brenda, a nobody from a hick town of 500 inhabitants in Massachusetts, had arrived.

A week after the murder, the gangsters talked about how to eliminate the dead man's second-in-command. Someone came up with the idea that Brenda should put on her slinkiest, most alluring dress and go to a nightclub with the target. While he was distracted, she would slip a few milligrams of cyanide in his champagne. A syringe of cyanide was procured for the purpose and concealed in a block of wood out on the back patio. Brenda's ambition was on fire. 'If I had got him, as far as the family would have seen it, I'd be like . . . hey – I'd be an untouchable woman. Then I'd have said now you've gotta hire me out, I'd be one of those contract killers . . .'

But Brenda's husband didn't go for the nightclub seduction-and-poison scenario, and the subject was dropped. A few days later, Philip got arrested for possession of firearms. The police had failed to nail them on the stolen getaway car, but they had not given up. Mafia boss Raymond Esposito summoned Brenda Colletti, and asked her if she would tell the police the gun was hers. She had no criminal record, and as a woman, was unlikely to get more than a caution. She agreed to do it, and was brought before the Old Man himself. 'John Stanfa's son had been shot in the face, so we went to find him at the hospital. He called me aside and we went to a corner in the hallway and we were just talking about it and I told him what I was considering doing, and he just thought it was the greatest, and he patted me on the cheek and told me I was a smart girl.

'I left the hospital, I was just on cloud nine. That's the first time I ever got to have a meeting with the Old Man. And that was it for me. 'Cause I've never known a woman that was able to have a private meeting with the boss. Especially in South Philadelphia . . .'

Brenda's moment of triumph didn't last. Philip's bail was paid by Stanfa, but he didn't get 'made'. In recent years, the US Cosa Nostra has become less and less bound to the Sicilian family hierarchy and moved towards a meritocracy: new members are selected on the strength of their ability to bring in money, and their willingness to kill.

Philip Colletti, son of Sicilian immigrants, wanted nothing more than to be accepted as part of the family. He had killed a man for the mob, he had qualified, but then nothing happened.

He grew resentful, and then frightened. He and Brenda both slept with a gun under the mattress on their side of the bed. 'I was a little nervous about the guns. Our son Paulie was four by then. He knew what a gun was. They were always around, everybody always had guns around the house. We basically tried to keep them out of his reach, we had shelves on top of the cabinets, or they were in the basement where we had a lock on top of the door . . . The only time they were within his reach was when we went to bed. We kept them under the mattress, so all you had to do was reach under and grab it. It's at night when they come for you so we figured we'd be ready.'

Over the winter of 1993, there were no more private meetings with the Old Man, and FBI agents came to call with increasing regularity, chucking their little boy Paulie under the chin, leaving a friendly word and a contact number in case the couple should want to cut their losses and collaborate.

The FBI agents knew it was just a matter of time. Second and third generation Italians in the US mafia have started using their money and influence to send their children to college and set them up in legitimate business, forcing La Cosa Nostra to recruit new members outside the traditional families. There are many young men like Philip Colletti, who are fascinated by La Cosa Nostra, and study how to become a part of the organisation, but when it comes down to it, they are not prepared to sit in jail for years in the service of a criminal tradition, an ideal of honour, that has no real significance for them. Organised crime investigators have found increasing numbers of young mob associates, disillusioned with the organisation or facing imprisonment, knocking on their doors, offering to collaborate.

After the murder of Michael Ciancaglini, the FBI were watching Philip and Brenda closely. Philip was arrested three times: each time he was released after a week, but the couple knew the Feds were following their every move. 'We had so many charges hanging over us, we knew they were going to get us sooner or later.' On 3 February 1994, Brenda and Philip Colletti agreed to become state witnesses.

Philip went to jail, and Brenda, the streetwise, city-smart mafia moll, went into the witness protection programme. She had been given an alias for her own safety and was living somewhere in a wholesome little town in Arkansas. But the city girl in her trouser suits and high-heeled shoes decided country life was not for her. She just didn't fit in. 'People would stop me and say: "Hi y'all, how ya doin'?" I'd tell them it was none of their freakin' business.'

She left the programme and was guarded by FBI agents for the duration of the trial of South Philadelphia mafia boss John Stanfa and his associates. Two weeks before the trial began in October 1995, the brother of one of the witnesses was murdered. Taking the stand was a terrifying ordeal for Brenda: not only was she a target, but her private life was exposed for all to see – her personal history, her work in the brothel, her violent fights with Philip, everything.

Brenda's self-esteem had been badly knocked while she was being prepared as a witness, and she had had an affair. 'Before you take the stand, the prosecution starts cross-examining you, and they go over your whole life. They have to know the worst so no one can use it against you in court. When they went over the details of our relationship, the violence and stuff, I began to think, what am I doing with Philip? And I met this other guy.' The court was treated to an answerphone recording of Philip's voice, calling from prison, threatening to kill the man who was sleeping with his wife.

Brenda made it up with her husband, but she rarely gets the chance to visit him. Even with a plea bargain, he is unlikely to get out of prison within five years. In the meantime, she lives on her wits and her friends' sofas. The woman who wanted to be the first female member of La Cosa Nostra gives me a lift back to the station in her car full of boxes and bags, the car where she has often slept when she had nowhere else to go.

The testimony of Brenda Colletti and her husband helped convict John Stanfa and his mob in November 1995. But she has no rancour for the people against whom she testified, she says: she just wanted to get Philip out of prison. 'Everybody in

South Philly knows about the mob and everybody knows who everybody is. And it's accepted. It's what makes it South Philly. If there was no mob, no gangsters in South Philly, South Philly would suck. It would be just another slum. It's what South Philly is about.

'It was fun. In all honesty, I don't believe there's anything wrong with the mob. The only thing that makes it bad is that people get killed.'

The mafia's initiation rite, in which new members are solemnly sworn in, has always been an exclusively male affair. The pseudo-religious ceremony is documented as far back as the 1870s, but was first described in detail by Joe Valachi, an American mafia member who became a collaborator in the late 1950s. The initiate's finger was pierced, and the blood spilt on the image of a saint, which was then symbolically burned. As the saint's picture was consumed by flames, the novice passed it from one hand to the other, reciting a litany of rules, with the climactic invocation: 'May I burn like this saint if I ever betray my brothers.'[1] The symbolic shedding of blood and burning of the saint's image are intended to fill the new recruit with terror should he ever step out of line; it also gives him the feeling that he is part of an ancient and sacred tradition.

The initiation rite for the Sicilian Cosa Nostra has been described by a number of defectors, and the similarities with the American version are striking. (The US Cosa Nostra was created by the first waves of Italian immigrants, based on the Sicilian model. In 1943, when the American liberating forces called on the mafia's help for their landing in Sicily, some of the Italo-American ways were reimported to the motherland.) These accounts include a set of commandments dictated to the new recruits: Do not touch another mafioso's woman; do not steal; do not live off immoral earnings; do not kill another man of honour, except where absolutely necessary; never report anything to the police; never breathe a word about Cosa Nostra to anyone who is not a member. The code of honour states that a member of the mafia may not be divorced, may not be homosexual, may not be related to a member of the police. The Sicilian mafioso Salvatore Contorno, who 'repented' in his prison cell in 1984 and became a collaborator, adds to this list one essential qualification: he must be a man.[2]

Women feature in Cosa Nostra's rules and rituals only as moral and security risks. Deputy chief prosecutor in Palermo Guido Lo Forte says: 'In terms of the rules of the organisation, no woman can be a member. It is also true that a man of honour may not talk about the organisation, may not divulge the organisation's secrets, not even to his own wife, or his own mother or his own daughter or his own mistress. If he did, he would be committing a serious violation of the rules, punishable by death.'[3]

With this institutional health warning, women are placed firmly outside the action. Brenda Colletti was out of luck: a woman may not be a made member of Cosa Nostra. There is perhaps only one exception, recorded in the 1940s by a Sicilian doctor with mafia connections. The doctor describes an occasion when he lunched with Don Calogero Vizzini, a mafia boss who helped the Allied forces land in Sicily and was rewarded with extensive administrative powers. The don 'brought along a pearl-encrusted mistress, a woman of the old nobility who had persuaded him to make her the first female member of the mafia'.[4]

The first Sicilian mafioso to repent – literally – and reveal details of the organisation to the police was Leonardo Vitale, who turned himself in to the police in 1974 after a religious crisis. Vitale's father died when he was a boy, and he became very attached to his uncle, a man of honour. His honesty about why he longed to join Cosa Nostra as a lad is chilling. A nervous, emotional man, he was subjected to a battery of psychological tests so that investigators could determine whether he was of sound mind or whether his revelations about the honoured society could be dismissed as the ravings of a madman. In one of these sessions, Vitale was asked how he could kill another man: 'I did it to show I was brave,' he replied. 'I also did it as a protest against my own nature, because God made me full of conflicts . . . I didn't feel like a real man. Killing was my way of proving that I was a man.'[5] (Vitale paid a high price for his honesty. He was pronounced insane, and his evidence dismissed. He was shot dead shortly after being discharged from a mental hospital. Later, mafia defectors endorsed everything he had said.)

One of the cornerstones of mafia culture, *omertà*, is a masculine virtue. The word has come to denote the law of silence that forbids anyone to speak about mafia business, and divides mafia communities from the 'civil' world, but the origin of the word is *omu*: Sicilian for 'man'. It denotes the strength required to maintain silence in the face of fear, or pain, or death – a quality associated with manliness.[6]

The notion of what it is to be a man was defined by Sicilians according to the harsh conditions of life on the island, under wave after wave of foreign invasion and, later, colonisation by the Bourbon kings. 'According to Sicilians,' explains Henner Hess, acute observer of mafia culture, 'to be a real man means knowing how to command respect on your own terms, being capable of defending your property single-handed.'[7]

The status of a mafioso is also determined by his capacity for violence, for it is violence, or the threat of it, that allows him to defend his territory. Protecting his 'property' included his family: a man who could not protect his wife from danger was of no use to anybody.[8] A student of mafia folklore observed the phenomenon back in the nineteenth century: 'The term *omertà* [means] "manliness", that is, being manly, serious, hard, strong . . . The basis and the potency of *omertà* is silence; without this, he would not be a man; with it, he maintains his unchallenged superiority, and remains a closed book before the judiciary.'[9] Many mafiosi are also members of another secret, all-male society, the Masons, who have an initiation rite remarkably similar to the mafia's.[10]

The formal exclusion of women was quite deliberate, not just for security reasons. 'Secrecy, *omertà* – the defining characteristics of the organisation,' says magistrate Teresa Principato, one of the dozen specialist anti-mafia investigators working in the eye of the storm in Palermo, 'are designed to defend it, in the first instance, against women. The mafia's cohesion, this tight unity amongst a group of men, can only be achieved if women are kept out. There are two ways of doing this: on a formal level, mafiosi defend themselves against women by forbidding them membership of the organisation. On a deeper level, they exclude women by defining the true characteristics of Cosa Nostra as typically masculine qualities, and by ruling that any emotional attachment must be broken.'[11]

Brenda Colletti, in her ambition to be a mobster, describes herself as a tomboy who has never seen the inside of a beauty parlour. Her acute thrill at being involved in covering up mafia crimes is largely to do with crossing the line between female and male worlds, from the life of the call girl to that of the hit man. But Brenda's husband thinks differently: he doesn't want her to get involved in the poisoning plot. He commits the crimes and she takes the blame: that's the division of labour in the Colletti household.

Some historians have described the mafia as a highly structured, quasi-military organisation, in which there could be no room for women.[12] But as the organisation's business has widened, it has collected a flotsam of workers, lookouts and go-betweens, people who will hide guns or drugs or men on the run. Far from being a security risk, a woman like Brenda Colletti, who could pass as an ordinary suburban mom, is indispensable to cover up for the mob.

Recent events have forced the Sicilian Cosa Nostra to become less formal and rule-bound. Since 1992, when a new law laid down measures to protect state witnesses, the number of Italian mafia defectors has grown to over a thousand. The risk of betrayal has led to a tightening of security within Cosa Nostra: there are fewer formal meetings, and members have limited access to other associates. The initiation rite seems to be failing in its purpose — that is, to intimidate new recruits into unquestioning obedience — and has therefore fallen into disuse.

Since Cosa Nostra has abandoned many of its formal rules, women, no longer excluded on principle, have better access to positions of influence – and influence, as we shall see in later chapters, is usually connected to money. The mafia is nothing if not pragmatic. If the clan needs her, a woman can have a role in Cosa Nostra. All it takes is a strong character and a bit of intelligence.

The Camorra, which has always had a looser structure than Cosa Nostra, has seen many more women rise through its ranks. Rosetta Cutolo, sister of the charismatic Camorra boss Raffaele, had the brains, but more important, the force of personality to run the organisation while her brother was in jail. Anti-mafia prosecutor Antonio Laudati describes her as 'the first feminist criminal'[13] because she managed to command respect and fear in her subordinates. But perhaps the greatest mark of Rosetta Cutolo's intelligence, and the reason she survived when he turned against every one of his former allies, is that she did not try to take her brother's place: she remained in the background, taking care to give the impression that she only ever acted on his behalf.

One young woman who never got a chance to play an active role, but whose behaviour attracted police attention with her charisma and intelligence, was Tatiana Imparato, daughter of the Camorra boss Umberto Mario Imparato of Castellammare di Stabia, a small town in the hills near Naples. 'She has a very hard personality,' says a member of the Naples flying squad. 'She is utterly single-minded. The minute she set foot in the police station, she behaved like a mafia boss – it was her manner, her whole way of thinking.'

Imparato senior was an unusual figure in the Naples criminal hinterland: he had gone to university in Milan, where he met a school teacher, a woman from a respectable middle-class family, and married her. He came home four years later, a graduate, a trade-unionist, with a wife from the Veneto. But before long, he was approached by the local mafia boss, and agreed to join his organisation.

Imparato's wife, Elisa Cafali, whose upbringing in a wealthy northern region of Italy had not prepared her for life in the Naples ganglands, tried for years to persuade him to return with her to the north, but the situation was beyond her control. Her husband became a respected member of the local mafia, and their teenage children both worshipped him. The boy, Davide, began working for the Camorra, acquiring and transporting guns; meanwhile the girl, Tatiana, drove around in fast cars and used her father's name to get whatever she wanted.

But in the early 1990s Imparato fell out with the capo over a sum of money. The organisation split into two groups and the former allies immediately began picking each other off. Imparato, wanted by the police and hunted by his mafia enemies, went into hiding in the mountains. One afternoon in March 1993, Umberto Mario Imparato was surrounded and gunned down by police among the rocks and pines. His daughter, who may have been on her way to see him, was quickly on the scene screaming: 'Bastards! you've killed him. Let me see him, let me see him for the last time.'[14]

At 23 the camorrista's daughter had abandoned her degree in agriculture and signed up to study law. 'We're going to need a lawyer in the family more than a farmer,' she told her mother.[15] But it would take more than that.

A month after her father's death Tatiana was arrested for extortion. She was charged with taking a kickback from a developer for a building contract, and forcing the same developer to sell apartments to her at a violently reduced price. The victim, who had reported her personal and unfriendly calls, lost his nerve on the witness stand. The prosecution looked on helplessly as their star witness declared under oath that he had never seen the defendant before.

Tatiana was immediately released, and returned to Castellammare. By this stage, most of the clan's associates were in prison, and the men who had followed her father were reduced to a straggling band, without the military strength to carry out a revenge killing. In August Tatiana's brother was shot, and lay in agony in hospital for a month before he died.

Tatiana, with dark eyes and a thin, hard face under long

black hair, was undaunted. She revealed her strength of
character in an interview for the television programme *Rosso e
Nero*. Giving her interviewer a look to freeze blood, she said:
'My father was very proud. And I am very proud.' She
portrayed her father as a lone and valiant figure, fighting against
the state. 'He was on the other side, and I am on the same side
as him: I am his daughter. I believe in justice,' she said darkly.

It would be nearly impossible, according to one Naples
magistrate, for an intelligent woman born into a mafia family to
remain aloof from criminal culture. 'A woman like Tatiana
Imparato, born in a mafia environment, grows up with a
particular mentality and assimilates the mafia's distorted sense of
justice: the justice that says everyone has a right to survive, in
whatever way they can ... It's their own particular form of
justice, against the state and for their own people.'[16]

After Tatiana's father and brother died, she faced a choice
between staying in Castellammare and avenging her father, or
going north with her mother. 'She's a strong woman, a very
decided woman, she's not afraid of anything, but she faced a
serious conflict,' said the Naples police commissioner. 'She
thinks partly with her father's mind – the mind of a camorrista
– and partly with her mother's – the mind of a woman from a
decent family, a teacher. If she'd had a chance, she would
probably have taken over. But the Imparato family is finished,
there's nothing left.' Tatiana has since moved to northern Italy
with her mother.

Neapolitan women play a full and active part in society, perhaps
more than women from any other region of Italy, and the
criminal underworld is no exception. When a Camorra boss is
killed, it is not unusual for his widow to step into his shoes.
This is not about honour or membership of an organisation: she
must defend her family's position. If she fails to establish herself
as leader in his place, her children will be in danger: the family

must assert its position or risk being driven out, or wiped out, by the opposition.

The Camorra is constantly changing and evolving as alliances between families shift and break up, and is less rigid than the Sicilian Cosa Nostra. Women in Camorra families frequently find themselves answering the family's needs, stepping into the breach when the boss is in prison or in hiding. But the role they assume depends on their force of character, and the rivalries that already exist within the family.

'Women do not have a subordinate role in the Camorra clans. Quite the reverse,' says the magistrate Giuseppe Narducci, deputy chief prosecutor in the Naples Anti-mafia Department, who believes the judiciary has paid too little attention to the criminal role of women. 'In some families women are at the very top. There are women who take decisions to commit murder, in exactly the same way as men do.'[17]

But the mafia does not exist in a world separate or sealed off from the rest of the population, and prejudice is applied in equal measure. A woman who tries to rise through the ranks of the organisation and makes a mess of things is liable to receive the same treatment as an over-promoted female executive who is bullied out of the boardroom.

One woman who made a clamorous mess of things in her self-appointed executive role is Carmela Palazzo, known as Cerasella, 'cherry brandy'. A fiery, headstrong and flirtatious woman, she set herself up as the boss of her family in her brother's place, but lacked the discipline to sustain a managerial role and was punished for her audacity.

Born and brought up in a house without electricity in a Naples slum, Cerasella could barely read and write. By the age of 12, she was pregnant. The boyfriend duly married her, probably under pressure from her brothers, but a couple of years after their child, Alfredo, was born, he left her. In the overcrowded neighbourhood families climbed over each other to get by, and Cerasella's brothers proved more ruthless, and

more successful, than most. They started doing armed robberies; once they had weapons and a stash of money, Vincenzo
Palazzo made contact with a group of Nigerians who were
importing speedballs – a mixture of heroin and cocaine.

Speedballs were wildly popular in Naples at the time, and
Palazzo quickly became a big shot in the Naples drug culture.
The Mariano family, who ruled Naples' teeming Spanish
Quarter, made a hostile takeover bid for the young dealer. He
was invited to leave his original group, and join the Mariano
clan. If he didn't go, they would kill him.

Vincenzo Palazzo was forced to share his drug profits with
the Mariano family, but his old group fought back. During the
battle that followed, one of his brothers, Francesco, was killed.
Shortly afterwards, Vincenzo was arrested for possession of
firearms including a machine gun. Police also found a quantity
of heroin and cocaine cocktails.

Cerasella was devastated by Francesco's death, and Vincenzo's arrest left her short of cash. After her first husband left her,
she had lived with a series of men, and her four children had
three different fathers but no support. When her brother was
taken off the scene, the distribution of speedballs dried up, so
Cerasella decided she would take over. She was not new to the
business: brother and sister had been living in the same house
and had talked about deals every day; she had helped him count
money and stash it, and she knew where his guns were hidden
and how to get them. She went to see her brother Vincenzo in
prison and he gave her permission to take on the job. Her
control of the speedball trade made her leader of the family,
much to the irritation of the various family members who had
been queuing up to take Vincenzo's place while he was in
prison.

For four months, Cerasella controlled the supply of speedballs in Naples. She would ring a hotel near the main railway
station, the sleaze centre of the city, and get the owner to make
an appointment with the Nigerian suppliers. She would meet
them in a small, dingy room in the hotel and hand over
payment; once they had the money, they would give her the

packets of capsules, which she would then sell on to the family's dozen or so pushers.

But according to a carabiniere who was investigating the Naples drug trade, Cerasella overreached herself. She certainly had the guts to take over leadership of the clan, and her brother had given her his authority, but she was disorganised. Dealing with cash profits from drug deals requires clarity and efficiency. Cerasella was all over the place. Things began to deteriorate when she started selling the drugs on to other groups in the Naples area. She lost the clan's monopoly, and began to lose money; after a couple of months she was down about £20,000.

What happened is not entirely clear. Either she made a mess of the business and lost track of the money she was owed. Or else she was framed by members of her family who refused to accept a woman as leader. She was accused of stealing the clan's money. 'There was a stormy meeting in the prison visiting room,' says Judge Maurizio Fumo, prosecutor in the Naples Anti-mafia Department. 'I don't know for sure what happened, but a bunch of disgruntled relations stormed in to see Vincenzo Palazzo, accusing his sister of stealing. Cerasella went wild, screaming and shouting, brandishing her list of who owed her money. One of them tore it out of her fist and said they were going to take care of the debt, since they couldn't trust her to do it. Someone slapped her, someone else threw a punch – the whole place erupted.'

This humiliation in front of her brother was too much for Cerasella to bear. She had always been short-tempered; now she felt aggrieved and isolated. She contacted the carabinieri and said she had some information that might interest them.

'Maybe she did it to get back at her relatives and her brother for her humiliation,' says Judge Fumo. 'Maybe she was afraid they would discover that she had stolen some money. She told us she had a moral motivation: her eldest son had become a drug addict, and she wanted to save him. But she also wanted to avenge her murdered brother by sending his killers to prison.'

Cerasella's collaboration would give the carabinieri plenty of gossip for the mess. 'She was completely out of control,' remembers one of the carabinieri seconded to protect her. 'We had to take turns staying with her in a safe house while she was interrogated by the magistrates. It was unbelievable. She was always making innuendoes and passes – she needed the attention. One time she was walking along the street with one of the guards. They were pretending to be a normal couple out shopping. She dragged him into a lingerie store and started pulling all this really sexy underwear off the hangers, holding up suspender belts and crotchless panties, saying "Do you like this one, darling?" He wanted to die.'

In spite of her uncontrollable behaviour, Cerasella was an invaluable witness. She had a good memory, and knew a lot about the workings of the Mariano clan. On the strength of her statements, police staged a blitz in January 1992, in which forty Camorra suspects were rounded up, including seven women charged with drug trafficking. It was a lively trial. The women had screaming matches in court, and on one occasion a defendant took off her shoe and threw it at a TV news camera.

Cerasella ran away from her guards a number of times. Once they found her living with a wanted criminal – which didn't help the magistrates who were trying to present her as a credible witness. The carabinieri became more and more frustrated with her, and when she accused one of her guards of rape they finally withdrew their protection.

Judge Fumo, who spent many weeks trying to extract a coherent story from her rambling recollections, was depressed by how things turned out. 'Cerasella's story is sad, really. She gave her guards the runaround when they were supposed to be protecting her, and they got fed up. In a way she deserved it, but she was an important witness and now she's in a real mess. She is from a Camorra family, she grew up in an environment where you commit crimes in order to survive. She is proud, but she's got no education, no qualifications, she's not fit for any other kind of life . . . you wouldn't believe how ghastly the neighbourhood is where she is from, and yet she wouldn't dream of lowering herself to do a manual job . . . Obviously the only thing she's qualified to do is deal drugs.

'One brother's dead, and the other's serving twenty years, thanks to her. Her lover's in prison, so is Alfredo, her oldest boy; her other children are God knows where. She's pretty bitter about the way things have gone.'

3. Naples Loan Sharks

Don Peppino Roberti, known as *capavacante*, 'empty head', is most embarrassed to be disturbed at his lunch. He bolts down to join me at the bar, wiping olive oil from his chin. Short and dark, with a face that looks as if it has been punched, Don Peppino yoked himself to the Giuliano clan by marriage, and is a martyr to the infidelities of his big-breasted, blue-eyed wife Erminia.

We join his father-in-law, Pio Vittorio, a man with pale blue eyes and a pale blue suit, with strands of hair dyed purple slicked across his big bald head. A kindly man with a broad smile, Pio Vittorio is the patriarch of the Giuliano family, father of Luigi, 'the king', Ciro, 'the baron', and Carmine, 'the lion'. As we arrived, Pio Vittorio was talking earnestly to one of his grandsons, a red-faced young man with bloodshot pale blue eyes.

Sitting at a table outside Don Peppino's bar, circled by traffic and gypsy girls begging, we talk about the pleasures of Naples, drinking short strong coffee. Another friend of the family arrives, a big man with brutally cropped hair and an impressive scar from mouth to ear. It reminds me of the *sfreggio*, the knife slash to the face traditionally inflicted on the loser of a duel, or used in nineteenth-century initiation rituals for young mobsters joining the Camorra.[1] (During this era in Naples, it was also traditional for a man to slash his woman's face in the same way as a mark of proprietorship, so no one else would want her.) He kisses my hand. Erminia, Don Peppino's wife, known as Celeste on account of her remarkable blue eyes, drops by. Celeste, dressed in tight denim dungarees over a tight pink T-shirt, flashes blue in my direction and disappears into the bar.

There are always three or four young men hanging around, waiting to run errands for the Giulianos. It's a safer means of

communication than telephones and keeps down unemployment. Everybody fiddles with jewellery and lights cigarettes as
Don Peppino sends one of the boys on a mission. While we
wait for the boy to return, the man with the scar talks about
Mussolini.

'A man,' he says, 'much admired by Churchill.'

We light cigarettes and wait. The Giulianos hold court at
Don Peppino's bar. At least one of them can usually be found
there. It means there is always a lot of hanging around.

The boy returns with the message that Donna Carmela is in.
Don Peppino takes me to meet his sister-in-law, wife of the
man known as '*o re*, 'the king' of Forcella. Luigi Giuliano, the
king himself, is currently in prison and, according to Naples
police detectives, his wife Carmela Marzano is acting head of
the clan in his absence. She has always denied this allegation.

The first family of Forcella lives in a first-floor flat at the
junction of two busy market streets, with flower and vegetable
stalls below the balcony and a clear view in several directions.
At the entrance is a little grotto, a sanctuary to the Madonna
stuffed with artificial flowers. There are notices written in
orange felt pen requesting the carabinieri to leave them in
peace. The steel door of the apartment has the initials 'C' and
'L' hand-painted in pink. Luigi's picture on the wall, hand-
tinted, shows his pale blue eyes gleaming under a jutting brow,
cartoon cheekbones and raven hair mussed up like David Essex.
No one, in a city where infidelity is almost universal, believes
she has taken a lover through all the years her husband has been
in and out of prison.

Carmela Marzano and Luigi Giuliano are the axis on which
Forcella turns. People bring them their problems, come to
them for advice and work. The locals even dress up in
matching costumes for Carnival, in a show of neighbourhood
unity rather like serfdom. Naples police maintain that all the
local businesses – the man with the tripe stall, the flower lady,
the corner bar – pay the family protection money.

Luigi, also known affectionately as Loigino, became head of
the Giuliano family over twenty years ago. He is a legendary

figure, with his pale blue eyes under a shock of black hair and a fondness for fancy shirts. It was he who founded a temporary coalition of Camorra families to defeat the dangerous upstart Raffaele Cutolo in 1978. In the war that followed, hundreds of people were killed, many of them stabbed to death in prison. In one incident a member of the Giuliano family sent radios into the prison as gifts for his men. Inside each set was taped a cut-throat razor.

During his long career, Luigi Giuliano, once the principal importer of contraband cigarettes, has been arrested many times, on charges ranging from theft to drug trafficking and murder. Every time police came to arrest him, the people of Forcella poured out of their houses, blocking the streets, baying their disapproval, and physically preventing the police from taking him away. The only charge that stuck was mafia association, for which he got ten years. He has served much of his sentence between hospital and his own home, since he suffers from a congenital heart condition, and has a bypass. When he was acquitted of murdering a policeman in 1987, the streets of Forcella were filled with people cheering and letting off firecrackers.

The family's fortunes have taken a dive in recent years. In 1988, Vittorio Giuliano, Luigi's nephew, died of an overdose. The boy's father, Nunzio, renounced the Camorra and started a new life helping addicts. Luigi, with a number of trials still pending, declared he too had had a religious crisis, filled his house with bibles, and took up writing romantic songs and poetry. Carmela, in an interview with local journalists, began to spread the message that the Giuliano family was no longer actively involved in organised crime, but by this stage law enforcers had the bit between their teeth. They were determined to nail Luigi Giuliano, and in the meantime targeted his wife. She was arrested for drug trafficking in March 1996 but released shortly afterwards, then rearrested in July for extortion and, again, released without charge.

'Since I married a Giuliano my life has been hell!' Carmela Marzano stands with her knuckles on the table, gold hoop earrings swaying, long brown hair falling loose over her arms. 'I've been persecuted by the police and magistrates. I've been arrested again and again because of who my husband is. My sons get arrested for any stupid little thing. We are persecuted because our name is Giuliano. My sons can't get an honest job because the state won't employ them. I wanted to open a shop, but the police won't let me have a licence.'

Carmela commands respect. Even the police talk about her with frank admiration. 'Her husband is a king,' says a member of the Naples flying squad. 'But she's the one who wears the trousers. When he is in prison she does everything. People feel the boss's authority in her presence. She's smart, too. She commands authority in the neighbourhood, mainly because she shows a lot of respect for others: when we go to arrest someone and a fight breaks out, she'll get right in there and try to cool things down.'

'The Giuliano women are famous, everybody knows they are the real strength of that family,' adds Naples prosecutor Antonio Laudati. 'When husband and wife are both free, the man's role is dominant. The boss's wife can never be a boss in her own right, but when he is in hiding, or in prison, she invariably takes his place – that's the rule.'[2]

Since the Camorra is not hierarchical and rule-bound like the Sicilian Cosa Nostra, status in the organisation depends largely on charisma, and strength of character. Neapolitan women, as a senior carabiniere comments, are generally tough and outspoken, and an ambitious camorrista is likely to choose a wife with a powerful personality: 'The camorrista is a show-off, an exhibitionist, he's probably got other women. The woman he marries has to be tough. When her husband is in prison, she decides what he needs or doesn't need to know, and quite often interprets his instructions to suit herself.'

At 13, when she married Luigi, Carmela already showed the signs of a strong character, and she has trained all her life for the role of first lady. The couple have had six children; one died of heart disease at an early age. Gemma, their beautiful, petite daughter, married her long-term boyfriend six years ago. 'He was offered a job in Rome,' she told me, 'and I told him he had to choose between me and the job. We got married right away.' Gemma's wedding was celebrated the day after Naples won the football championship in 1990. The Giuliano family had courted Maradona, at the time Naples' star player, and gained a lot of kudos and not a small amount of money from the connection.[3] The Argentinian striker was guest of honour at Gemma's wedding, which caught the full glare of publicity.

The notorious Giuliano twins, now 24, have taken full advantage of their position. According to a police source, the boys began to abuse their power in the neighbourhood, eating and drinking in local bars and restaurants for free, trying on clothes and walking out of shops without ever paying for anything. It was the woman in the dry cleaner's who finally cracked. The twins always demanded that she do their clothes right away, and never paid. Eventually she reported them to the police for extortion. 'Don't you love it?' says the police commissioner. 'The boss's son goes to prison because he doesn't pay for his laundry.'

Carmela dismisses the incident as another example of the persecution of the Giuliano family. 'It was all a dreadful misunderstanding.'

When the king is in prison, his wife brings him news, keeps the family together, remains a strong reference point for the neighbourhood. Forcella is a small area but the Giuliano family is rich; their economic power allows them to maintain tight control of the territory. They have a small army of boys at their service twenty-four hours a day, who run errands for them, spy for them, watch and intimidate outsiders.

Marzano is also a protester: she fights vociferously against any perceived injustice in the legal system. In 1994 she organised a demonstration with a number of wives of detainees outside the notorious Poggioreale prison, demanding an end to lengthy periods of imprisonment without trial. Donna Carmela is not afraid to confront the outside world, and she is flattered to be approached by the foreign press. Like Pupetta Maresca, who attracted a lot of media and police attention, and managed to draw fire from her brothers, Carmela Marzano takes centre stage to deflect attention from her husband.

'I am a very humble person,' she says. Although her face is still handsome, after six children she has barrelled out, and her stomach stretches the grey tracksuit. Her fingers swell round fat gold rings. 'My whole life has become one long trial, just because I married a Giuliano.' Her dark eyes meet mine with friendly ease. A man in a pale green suit is hovering on the balcony, waiting for me to go. 'He's my lawyer,' she explains affably. 'I'm sorry I can't talk now, I'm under house arrest.'

As Judge Giovanni Falcone explained, local businesses who pay dues to the boss tacitly acknowledge the mafia's rule. 'Practised in a systematic manner, extortion is an effective way of consolidating control of the neighbourhood – this is, of course, the primary objective of every "family". Extortion ensures not only a considerable income, but also concrete recognition of the mafia's authority.'[4]

Of Naples' 1.1 million inhabitants, official figures state that around 30 per cent are unemployed, but tens of thousands of these have some kind of unofficial employment. The Camorra is always on hand to offer people illegal work: anyone who needs the money can sell contraband cigarettes or bootleg cassettes; others are employed as lookouts for criminal families, or as debt collectors, collecting protection money door to door.

Loan sharks thrive in this precarious economic climate, where people live from day to day, without saving or planning for the future, just trying to keep afloat. It is an insidious way of gaining possession of territory in the city, according to Father Massimo Rastrelli, the priest who crusades against the practice: 'Usury is a labyrinth with no way out. The result is usually the takeover of a whole neighbourhood. The people who get caught in the loan shark's trap, suddenly find they have lost their fundamental rights.'[5] According to Father Rastrelli, at least

20,000 businesses ended up in the hands of money-lenders between 1994 and 1996.

Neapolitan women, more emancipated than their Sicilian sisters, have traditionally stood in for their husbands as debt collectors when the men were in prison, but they also command authority in their own right. The chaos of everyday life in poverty and squalor has produced a city of vociferous women who know how to battle for survival. Marco Monnier, recording the mores of the city in 1862, at the time of the unification of Italy, describes with horrified fascination the women who collected protection money: 'The wife of an imprisoned camorrista presented herself at contributors' doors, and obtained their payments without the slightest trouble. Even the toughest working class city dwellers trembled before this villainess's skirts. They knew that one day her husband would get out of prison, and armed with his stick, would demand to know why they hadn't paid up. Indeed, the wife of a camorrista was a powerful figure in her own right.'[6]

One particularly successful female loan shark is Teresa Deviato, widow of the boss of the via dei Tribunali. Her domain runs along the top edge of Forcella. To reach it, you climb through narrow gloomy streets, sunless as the bottom of a tank, while high above, towards the distant strip of sky, lines of washing wave like flags.

The via dei Tribunali leads straight through the old heart of Naples, from the back of the bustling piazza Dante, to the old courthouse. The traffic is backed up end to end in single file, and locals pick their way around the cars between grocers' shops, fruit and vegetable stalls, and small, dingy shops selling lamps and books and buckets. Shopkeepers stand in the doorways, gossiping with each other or staring at passers-by. Every so often, the street widens to form a small square, into which a church has, by some miracle, been squeezed.

Just a few steps off the main drag, an old, four-storey house dominates a little courtyard with a long name, the Vico Storto Purgatorio ad Arco. The house belongs to wealthy widow Teresa Deviato, a pretty, blonde woman aged 43. The one time

I met her, she was wearing jeans and a short-sleeved pink blouse, looking like a Home Counties housewife. Her streaked-blonde hair brushed her shoulders; pink lip pencil dragged at the corners of her mouth.

Vincenzo Saetta, her favourite ('Enzuccio' for short), was the leader of a gang of armed robbers, which specialised in holding up banks and post offices. The house was the nerve centre of operations; money and guns were brought here to be hidden or disposed of. The old house is a warren of split levels and landings, attics and recesses, lavishly decorated and expensively furnished. The floors are marble and each of the three mirrored bathrooms contains a jacuzzi. In this luxurious setting, a small microphone planted in the kitchen allowed investigators to eavesdrop on a singular family life.

In one conversation,[7] the speakers referred to at least five firearms – all of which were apparently on the kitchen table at the time. Investigators identified the voice of Deviato's six-year-old daughter, complaining that *she* wanted a go with the gun.

The bug was near the television, which often made it difficult to decipher what was being said. But on 3 May 1995 it did pick up a conversation between Teresa Deviato and a friend known only as Patrizia.

'I've been very patient with these guys, honestly, you wouldn't believe how patient I've been,' Deviato was ranting. 'This bloke was supposed to give me 500,000 lire [£217] a month, and he couldn't meet the payments . . . the cheques and IOUs went backwards and forwards, and he still owed me 17,500,000 lire [£7,610].'

'What did you do about the rest?' asked Patrizia.

'I was actually in prison when he was supposed to give me the money,' Deviato said. 'But I wasn't about to let it go. He told me: Listen, I can't give you more than 500,000 a month. I was furious. I said, So what do I have to do, do I have to beat the shit out of you to get my money back? So I went to see him, I said, listen, I said. Listen, you are a shit, you know why? because I [*inaudible*] I can't accept as little as 500,000 a month, and you haven't even paid me the interest on that. If you borrow money, and you make someone wait for that money, you're going to have to pay for it . . . Well Patrì, I'll tell you what. Listen, I said, that's it, I said, I'm sending my boy over to pay you a visit.'

'Quite right!' agreed Patrizia.

'Because, I said to him, because you haven't been straight with me!' Deviato went on. 'Anyway I sent my son Enzuccio round to his place . . . [*inaudible*] and my boy put a gun in his mouth. He was crying and carrying on, and Enzuccio says to him: It's no good crying. You've got two days to give me the money. You've got to give me that money, and you've got to give me the keys to the shop. I don't want the shop, do you understand? No: I want the shop *and* the money. It's been four years we've been playing this little game. Now it's time to settle up.'[8]

The winter of 1994–95 was boom time for the Deviato family. The robberies brought in up to 200 million lire a time (£87,000), and the gang was doing two hits a week. With the help of her son, Enzuccio, Teresa Deviato's extortion racket took a slice from the income of local businessmen. Late one night, the hidden microphone picked up two voices calling numbers – not a card game, it seemed, but Teresa and her sister Maria sitting at the kitchen table, counting out banknotes in bundles of millions. The counting was rapid and businesslike: they got to 84 million lire (nearly £37,000) and started again, counting up to 49 million lire (about £22,000), and dividing up payments as they went.

The bug was in place over a period when she was making good money, but Teresa Deviato's family was falling apart. Her son Marco was a heroin addict, who lived part of the time with his father in Viareggio. As in most cultures where the real wealth comes from drug dealing, the attitude to drugs among Camorra families is ambivalent: to have an addict in the family is deeply shaming, since it shows they are not in control. At the same time, one of Teresa's sisters, Anna, was in trouble. After a string of well-publicised infidelities, Anna had left her husband to live with her lover. But while she was having dinner with

him in a Salerno restaurant, a man walked through the door
and fired at them. Anna was wounded in the shoulder, and her
lover was killed. Her husband, Domenico Silvestri, one of the
gang of bank robbers, was arrested on a murder charge, but his
wife could not, or would not, positively identify him, and he
was acquitted. (He was later convicted of armed robbery.)

Teresa had learned to cope with the family troubles alone
after her second husband, Tonino Capuano, was gunned down
in the street near their home in 1991. (They did not actually
marry, but in the amorous disorder of Naples these things are
academic: she is always known as his widow.) Capuano was
boss of the via dei Tribunali, an old-style *guappo*. He kept
control of crime in the area and declared war on drugs – this
meant that nobody was allowed to deal drugs in the neighbourhood, for which the local residents were grateful – while he
carried of his drug dealing elsewhere. He was adored. Every
sunless front room the length of the via dei Tribunali had a
poster of the boss on the wall. When he died, the local people –
who had been forced to pay him protection money when he
was alive – wore lockets containing his picture, as a mark of
respect.

Capuano was eliminated one January night, after he fell out
of step with a coalition of more modern-minded camorristi. He
was ambushed while walking home through Forcella, and shot
dead. The Giuliano family has never admitted responsibility for
his murder, but it is considered unlikely that anyone could have
committed a murder in Giuliano territory without their
permission.

Instead of abandoning the neighbourhood, Teresa Deviato
managed to make peace with the Giuliano family. Indeed, to
prove the family's solidarity with the dead man's widow,
Carmela Marzano, Luigi Giuliano's wife, stood beside Teresa at
the funeral in a public show of friendship. Teresa continued to
levy her tax on local businesses right next door to Forcella. As
the hidden listening device revealed, she continued to lend the
Giuliano family firearms whenever they needed them –
although she complained bitterly about their persistent

demands. Building on the respect she commanded as the wife of the boss, Teresa stepped into her dead husband's shoes, and started making serious money.

Money-lending has been carried out by women in Naples for centuries. According to historian Gabriella Gribaudi, women in nineteenth-century Naples controlled the local economy by giving loans and charging exorbitant rates of interest. 'If you talk to the people who run local businesses, they'll tell you women are in charge of the Camorra families' finances. They're very conscious of it, it's a tradition in this city.'[9]

Many women in Camorra circles earn pocket money by lending small sums and charging interest. It is not considered a bad thing. 'Money-lending is looked on as a favour to people who've got cash-flow problems,' commented Colonel Vittorio Tommasone, a carabiniere who investigated Teresa Deviato. 'Among Camorra wives, it's considered a harmless pastime, like bridge.'

Teresa Deviato has proved herself a dedicated player, and has graduated to high stakes. She came to law enforcers' attention for her method of appropriating businesses known as *strozzinaggio* or 'strangulation', and was arrested in 1992 for extortion and possessing firearms. Investigators discovered that she had taken over a number of small businesses in the via dei Tribunali, when the owners had been unable to meet her monthly payments at crippling rates of interest and had been forced to hand over the keys. Not that any of the victims had reported the crime: Teresa Deviato was known to be backed by an armed gang, so most shopkeepers abandoned their premises without attempting to resist.

Since then, things have deteriorated inside the old house in the via dei Tribunali. In January 1996, Teresa's son died of a heroin overdose. Police searched the house and found twenty pistols. Her favourite son Vincenzo was charged with armed robbery and attempted murder. In February, her sister Anna, who had taken another lover, was shot in the head by an unknown assailant. No one was charged, although the Naples newspapers accused her own 16-year-old son. She survived after a long period in intensive care, and anxiously awaits her husband's imminent release from prison. ('If you are interested in interviewing Anna Deviato,' I was told by a magistrate, 'you had better be quick about it.') On 20 March 1996, Teresa Deviato and two of her sisters, Antonietta and Maria, were arrested. Teresa was charged with mafia association, extortion and possession of firearms.[10]

The Giuliano household has also had its problems with the law. Luigi Giuliano has spent several months in prison, despite repeated appeals on account of his ill health. Nonetheless, the marriage of their youngest daughter, 16-year-old Marianna, gave Carmela Marzano the chance to prove that the family is not beaten. They still know how to throw a good party.

On a bright sunny September morning, the narrow, crowded streets of Forcella are bustling with excitement. Groups of women stand between the butcher's dripping tripe and the flower stall, clutching bundles of sugared almonds in lace kerchiefs, chattering animatedly.

It is Marianna's wedding day. No one makes any secret of the fact that the bride is six months pregnant. The Giulianos' parish church, in the shadow of the old courthouse, is decked out in palms. Women hurry in and out carrying white sprays of flowers to attach to the pews. As the small bunch of local wellwishers is joined by a noisy crowd of guests, the bridegroom, Michele Mazzarella, stands nervously at the church door. He looks like an ordinary spotty 16-year-old, who has been gift-wrapped in cream satin jacket and trousers, and forcibly given a neat side-parting. He accepts kisses from his teenage friends with a flicker of a smile.

'The bride! The bride!' Heads shiny with gel crane to look as the young bride clambers slowly out of the car. Donna Carmela hovers behind, adding a final touch of dark brown powder to her deeply tanned face. She accepts the guests' congratulations with a regal toss of her raven curls, and proceeds into the church. Marianna's huge blue eyes gaze out from beneath an expanse of white foaming lace, her round pregnant belly disguised beneath a high crinoline. She leans on the arm – not of her father, the king, but of her grandfather, Pio Vittorio, his old tanned face creased with smiles.

When the congregation, most of them dressed for nightclubbing, in miniskirts or trousers and huge boots, has moved back a little, the priest rattles on about the seriousness of marriage. 'You, Michele, will be the head of the family,' he intones 'You will have to prove that you are worthy of respect.' By the time he gets to the bit about God blessing this union with children, the priest is speechless with laughter. Two young men walk quickly up the aisle waving bags for the collection, but none of the expensively dressed congregation puts anything in them.

As the couple leaves the church, there is a deafening explosion – which turns out to be firecrackers. Everyone laughs and claps as the groom shakes a bottle of champagne like a Grand Prix winner, and sprays the guests.

On the way to the reception, with local photographer Luciano Ferrara, I ask directions from one of the many policemen along the road, who knows exactly where the Giuliano wedding is being held. We sail through the gates of the sumptuous restaurant gardens, and park Luciano's old rattletrap between a Mercedes and a BMW. We have no idea what sort of reception we are going to get. The only photographer allowed in is the family's trusted portraitist – who warns us to keep away or we'll get beaten up like the Channel 5 TV cameraman who tried to film this morning's photo session. I dodge past the various minders strolling around in dinner jackets, and head straight for Pio Vittorio, grandfather of the bride, who is standing in the garden, receiving guests with a broad smile. He welcomes us to the party with a genial handshake and, as we stroll through the garden, gazing at the floating island in the swimming pool, chatters about the last time he went skinny-dipping in the sea.

The bride sways into the garden, pulling twenty feet of train with some effort, accompanied by her young husband. The couple release a pair of fan-tail doves, and the groom cuts a ribbon stretched across their path – symbol of the virginity lost at least six months ago. The guests are given a hollow pineapple filled with champagne cocktail. Marianna, who looks remarkably like Lucy Ewing from *Dallas*, with her huge blue eyes and bouncy blonde hair, shouts at her bridesmaid, who has got the train in a twist.

At the entrance to the lavish gilded dining room, four men on their knees are opening hundreds of oysters. A compère bellows through a microphone and 300 guests in Versace and Valentino and four-inch heels totter to their seats. Men in chunky gold jewellery and shiny suits kiss each other on both cheeks, ignore the wine in ice buckets and order Coca-Cola.

When an important guest comes in, whole tables stand up and applaud, and men rush over to pump his hand. It all looks strikingly familiar. According to investigators, mafia members are compulsive viewers of *Godfather* movies; when the police raid a mafia house, they always find three or four of these videos on the shelf. Some say, perhaps unkindly, that today's mafiosi consult the movies to learn how to look, and how to behave.

One of the notorious Giuliano twins saunters by in a white tuxedo and wing collar (he has clearly found himself another dry cleaner), his hair shaved on the back and sides. I am seated next to the twins' handsome, sulky younger brother, and his beautiful dark-haired fiancée. Marianna's sister Gemma, dressed in a black trouser suit, wearing eyeliner painted on *alla* Maria Callas, tells me about her own wedding six years ago. 'It was so strange having the press battling at the door to get in. I can't understand why people are so interested in us.'

Donna Carmela flies past, flinging her high-heeled shoes across the floor in mock-petulance. She is wearing a russet silk slip under a floor-length lace dress, and moves among the tables laughing and talking. 'Yes, it's a pity my husband couldn't be here,' she agrees, and dashes off happily to welcome a new group of glossy, tanned guests.

The wedding feast begins with oysters and champagne, followed by course after course – octopus; prosciutto, melon and buffalo mozzarella; half a lobster; pasta with *pancetta* and zucchini; sea bass with prawns. And that's just the first half. One dish after another is brought and taken away again, hardly touched, by an army of uniformed waiters. During a break in the music, the compère announces a special appearance by the groom's uncle Franco, who presents the happy couple with a large silver platter, engraved with an effusive message. Uncle Franco takes the microphone and says a few words, choking back tears.

Mafia weddings are lavish occasions: a banquet for hundreds of eminent guests provides an opportunity for the boss to show off the family's wealth and power; it is also a chance for the guests to make extravagant gestures. A reception is useful for cementing alliances – for this reason, police photographers are positioned outside to record the family's influential friends. When Gemma got married, detectives walked right into the dining room to get a good look at the assembled guests.

The bridegroom's family, the Mazzarella clan, fell foul of the Giulianos in the 1980s, when Ciro Mazzarella made a bid for dominance of the Camorra, attempting to bypass Luigi Giuliano's Nuova Famiglia alliance. On one occasion, a member of the Mazzarella family was sent into Poggioreale prison in Naples to shoot Luigi Giuliano's brother Carmine, but only managed to wound him in the legs. Marianna's pregnancy has turned a teen romance into a peace bond, uniting two Camorra families who have been at war intermittently for over a decade. Strange that the king isn't here.

Bored with the younger Giulianos, who insist on speaking only in dialect, I sit down beside the patriarch, Pio Vittorio, and his blonde lady friend. She moved in with him ten years ago, after his wife died giving birth to her ninth child. Pio Vittorio tells me that although she is past 50, she is still described in the press as his 18-year-old tottie.

The compère introduces a series of top Neapolitan singers, most of them hired as gifts. When the band strikes up the

opening bars of 'La Macarena', the summer's version of the
Birdy Song, Donna Carmela is the first to run up and join the
formation dancers. The bride's great-aunt, a hefty old bird in
black lace with thick-rimmed glasses, clambers to her feet and
dances around on her own.

Everyone agrees it is sad that Luigi Giuliano cannot be
present at his youngest daughter's wedding, but no one offers
an explanation. They seem to have a sort of instinctive deafness
to direct questions. The official photographer says Luigi is in
hospital with heart trouble. My photographer friend has heard
that he is under house arrest after a drugs raid. A star crooner of
the evening sings one of the king's songs, a moving ballad
about how he misses Naples when he is away. Everyone
applauds, with tears in their eyes. Pio Vittorio, Luigi's father,
finishes off a bottle of champagne and gestures vigorously for
another. 'Yes, what a pity he couldn't be here.' He shrugs, and
smiles, and carries on telling the self-mocking tale of how he
used to try to train his hair to grow across his bald head.

The family lawyer, Anyo Arcella, makes an entrance, greeted
with kisses and cries of welcome. Donna Carmela rushes
forward and ushers him to his place on the top table. Arcella,
who has been getting members of the Giuliano family out of
prison for decades, is a local celebrity and guest of honour. Like
most of the mafia family lawyers, he is the intermediary
between the family and the outside world, their press officer
and public image adviser.

Arcella looks around him and smiles indulgently at the signs
of excess and expense, as though he were of another breed. (He
has been investigated several times for mafia association and
once convicted of aiding and abetting.)* He confides that the
reason for Luigi Giuliano's absence is that he had a quarrel with
Carmela the night before. 'When those two fight, they really
go for it. She hits him, the china gets smashed, she throws
anything at him she can lift. This time it's over a girlfriend. He

---

*Two months later Arcella was shot dead as he waited at traffic lights on his way
home from a late-night meeting with Carmela Marzano.

has a weakness for young girls, and his wife gets furious. Don't worry, they'll make it up in a day or two.'

As the evening wears on, the bride carries her vast crinoline with visible effort. Her husband follows her about, looking a little lost. He has already discovered that the Giuliano women are a force to be reckoned with.

Donna Carmela pauses for a minute to chat to the lawyer. Suddenly she beckons to me, and, as the guests laugh and clap, leads me through a brisk samba in the middle of the floor. She dances gaily between the tables, applauded by her admiring guests, the centre of attention. It's her day.

4. Extortion: The Deadly Protectors

Along the Ionian coast road in the beautiful and savage mountainous region of southern Calabria, every road sign is peppered with shot. The roads are badly cracked and pot-holed, and remain that way, according to carabinieri stationed in the area, to assist the bandits who hold up cars at gunpoint. Long stretches of coastline are undeveloped, kept clear of tourism to allow shipments of drugs and guns to be brought ashore undetected. In 1991, a group of young men were arrested in Taurianova, a small town in the hinterland, for using a human head for target practice.[1]

Calabria has always been cut off from the rest of Italy; the motorway which links Reggio Calabria to Naples and beyond was only completed in 1980. The relative wealth of the north of Italy has never reached this region, where views have become increasingly entrenched, and public servants are seen as interlopers. (In one small coastal town the men celebrate New Year's Eve by driving their motorbikes round and round the police station, shooting at the windows.) The Calabrian mafia, the 'Ndrangheta,[2] evolved in the power vacuum created by the region's hostility to central government, and the territory was carved up between local dictators.

For over forty years, 'Ndrangheta families have waged violent campaigns for control of the region. In an area cut off for long periods from state control, bitter and bloody fighting between clans left over 2,000 dead, including women and children. At one point there was a price on the flesh – per kilogram – of anyone who dared give evidence against the mafia.[3]

Prosecutor Salvatore Boemi, in his darkened office in the rubbish-strewn building site that passes for a courthouse in Reggio Calabria, feels as if he is under siege, a representative of the state abandoned to his fate. Staring across the room at the hundreds of volumes of legal reports containing evidence against 300 members of the 'Ndrangheta, he explains that the Calabrian clans have their own alternative government. 'They've got soldiers who keep an eye on anyone coming in from outside, they've got debt collectors much more efficient at collecting taxes than the state, and ordinary citizens who don't feel that the state can guarantee them a hundred per cent, who prefer to have dealings with this organisation.

'It's civil war,' he says, his grizzled beard and khaki fatigues making him look like a guerrilla leader at his desk. 'The state pretends the situation is less serious than it is. But the fact is, the mafia's government is much more powerful than the republic.'[4]

Part of the reason investigators have found the 'Ndrangheta underworld impenetrable is that entire clans are related to one another. The family is the nucleus of the organisation, the criminal cell. While hundreds of mafia defectors have given evidence in trials elsewhere in Italy, in Calabria there are extremely few, since collaborators would almost inevitably find themselves forced to give evidence against their own mother and father.

In this alternative, family-based state, women play a central role, not only as the family's moral authority, but also in an active capacity. Long-running feuds between clans force the men into hiding for long periods, and their sisters, mothers or wives automatically take over. The families, like feudal lords, assert control over their territories by collecting protection money; a female representative is respected by the local people: they know who is behind her and take pains to cultivate good relations with her.

'Ndrangheta families often forge alliances by marriage, to expand their territory. Antonino Imerti, boss of Villa San Giovanni, owes his dominant position in the Calabrian 'Ndrangheta to his marriage, a strategic arrangement which combined the forces of two families across a large area. Arranged marriages such as this protect family groups from intrusion by outsiders. It is said that Imerti's enemies began to view him as a serious threat the day he walked down the aisle with Giuseppa Condello on his arm.

Boemi's investigation of the Imerti–Condello clan focused on Giuseppa Condello and her younger sister, two key players in the clan's protection racket.

Calabria was dominated for many years by the De Stefano family. In the mid-1980s, Antonino Imerti, known as *nanu feroce*, 'vicious dwarf', declared war on the De Stefano empire. On the night in 1986 when the boss Paolo De Stefano was shot dead, Imerti was already in hiding, running from the inevitable retaliation. Police investigators quickly joined the hunt, as the De Stefano family exacted its retribution and came under intense attack from rival clans. The war escalated over months stretching into years. By 1990, the death toll was over 800. The rival groups no longer waited and planned their revenge killings: Imerti's men would get in their cars in broad daylight and go out hunting. Anyone connected to the enemy family they found, they would shoot, even if it meant firing across busy town squares and café tables.

All this time, Imerti was hiding in the impenetrable Aspromonte foothills, dodging law enforcers and mafia bullets. He set up communications with his men via radio, thinking it would be more secure than the telephone, and managed to keep in touch with members of his hit squad.

But police detectives discovered the gangsters' wavelength, and recorded hours of conversations, enabling them to identify the entire group (who attempted to disguise themselves with transparently obvious code-names). On one occasion, investigators listened as three or four of Imerti's men closed in on their intended victim. The gang maintained radio contact as the target was trailed by the wife of a hit man. On that occasion, the target slipped away. On another, police heard shots being fired as Imerti's men committed a murder live on radio.

Imerti also kept in constant communication with his wife Giuseppa Condello, who remained in Villa San Giovanni while he hid in a safe house up in the hills. She was his spy, his representative, his ambassador: they spoke to each other at least once a day, and she informed him of anything that moved in his territory.

Judging by the couple's conversations, being married to a mafia boss in hiding is not unlike being the secretary of a company director who is laid up in hospital and isn't very good at delegating. In their daily conversations, Imerti asked his wife who she had seen, who they were with, what they had said. Giuseppa was in charge of accounts: he wanted to know who had paid protection money, and how much, then instructed her how to divide it up. People came to her for favours, asking her to pass on requests to her husband, urgently needing answers. She had to remember to tell him everything when they spoke at the end of the day.

In her husband's enforced absence, Giuseppa ran the extortion racket with her sister's help. When a new business appeared, they would make contact with the owner and dictate terms of payment, then make their monthly rounds to collect the money. As Imerti himself acknowledged, women are often better than men at this work, because they can be menacing without being armed.

Everybody in Villa San Giovanni paid protection to Imerti, from the property developer down to the barber. For a small businessman in an area with no industry to speak of and very little legal economic activity, there was no alternative. This system of extortion spreads the net over a wide area. Once control of the territory is established by military strength, 'Ndrangheta families tend to infiltrate a whole area with a network of cousins, nephews, in-laws and little sisters. There are few who do not pay protection money, enmeshed in the tendrils and branches of the mafioso's family tree.

Imerti and his wife had got into the habit of living apart, and she used to tell him her every move. She reports the delivery of 'shirts' in sealed envelopes; he tells her to order 'onions' and 'postcards'. At one point her younger sister Caterina, known as 'Junior', joins the conversation and reports that she is having trouble with a delivery of 'oil'. The man who owes her money is never at home when she calls, and his wife is full of excuses.

Imerti's women are constantly present in the neighbourhood, and they exert a continuous pressure on families and businesses, but on rare occasions a little more forcefulness is required. Imerti tells Junior he will take care of it: 'Don't go back, there's no need.'

In one conversation, Giuseppa Condello reports a meeting with a local restaurateur, one of Imerti's 'clients', to whom she refers as the 'Lamp Man'. He has been approached by a rival clan who have threatened to destroy his restaurant unless he pays them. He is less afraid of the other gang than of what Imerti will do if he finds out he's paying dues to another master. Giuseppa reassures him: 'I told him you aren't a Godfather type.' The Lamp Man asks Giuseppa to remind her husband of the 'message' (payment) he has sent; at the same time, he invokes their friendship. Giuseppa makes soothing noises and offers him support, but they both know that she represents a real threat.

'What's most disturbing is not so much the fact that the industrialist or the small businessman pays the 'Ndrangheta protection money, it's the distorted relationship that the clan develops with these people,' says Boemi. 'After a while the clan becomes like an insurance company, it becomes essential for the businessman to have dealings with the 'Ndrangheta. Most people would consider those dealings humiliating and frightening, but the mafia guarantees the businessman that he will be able to operate.'

Ordinary people are forced to co-operate, in a kind of mass coercion which has become romanticised under the term *omertà*. Social relationships are based on fear, and people's moral sense is blurred by terror. 'The state tells Calabrian citizens that we must stand up against the 'Ndrangheta!' declared one of the members of the Association of Women Against the Mafia in Reggio Calabria. 'If we stand up against these people, they will kill us. How can they ask that of an ordinary person?' If this is the view expressed by an anti-mafia campaigner, it is clear that very few ordinary people are likely to say no when Giuseppa Condello or her little sister pays a call.

The evident attachment between Imerti and his wife shows that an arranged marriage can grow into a bond of mutual affection, dependence and respect. They sometimes talked for over an hour. She had morning sickness and didn't feel like eating. He was concerned about her, worried that she wasn't eating enough, told her he missed her and the children.

Imerti: How are you feeling, *bella*?

Condello: I don't know, I feel a bit weird. I haven't had any pains but I feel kind of fuzzy.

Imerti: Hey, what are we going to do with you, you've got to look after yourself!

Condello: I know, I know, I am looking after myself really, maybe too much, maybe that's it — if I let myself go a bit more, maybe I'd feel better . . . I miss you so much.

Imerti: That's good to hear.

Condello: I couldn't wait for you to call, I've been waiting since quarter to ten and I was thinking I must remember to tell him to call sooner because it's so awful waiting.[5]

She was often depressed, living apart from him, having to remember all those instructions when she was feeling nauseous and tired. 'What else? What other news?' he asked for the hundredth time. 'Um, I made a couple of pizzas,' she replied. On another occasion, after they had been talking for a while, he said: 'OK, I don't think I can remember anything else to tell you.' Happy to be in contact of any kind, she said: 'If you want, I'll just wait on air in case you think of something.'

While Giuseppa Condello and her husband discussed the minutiae of their daily routines and the clan's intimate business, police detectives listened. Their conversations were recorded throughout 1990, and the principal players were rounded up in December of the same year. In the trial of Imerti and forty members of his organisation, Giuseppa Condello was sentenced to fourteen years for extortion and mafia association. 'For once,' says Boemi, 'I had no trouble at all convincing the judge that the women played a significant role.'

According to Imerti's lieutenant, who later defected and became a collaborator, the conviction of his wife enraged Imerti more than any other aspect of the trial – to such a degree that he laid a plan to assassinate Judge Boemi.

A mafia boss accepts a prison sentence as an occupational hazard, and many continue to operate unchecked from within the walls of Italy's prisons. The moment his wife is arrested, he is in trouble. Imerti, without his military presence, and without his wife to represent him on the ground to collect dues from 'his' people, is boss of nowhere.

Across the narrow channel from Villa San Giovanni is Messina, Sicily's major eastern port, an hour's drive north of the thriving city of Catania. Until very recently, it was believed that eastern Sicily was free of any mafia organisation. One man who dared to publish revelations about the Catania mafia's links with politics and industry, the journalist Giuseppe Fava, was assassinated in 1984.

For many years, Catania has been dominated by the mustachioed mafia boss Nitto Santapaola, believed to be second only to the *capo dei capi*, Salvatore (Totò) Riina. A number of small criminal groups operate in Santapaola's shadow, making alliances and falling out, each with its own racket, fighting over scraps.

Eastern Sicily has seen the greatest number of *stidda* or splinter groups, lawless gangs of under-age criminals and Cosa Nostra rejects, which enter into contracts of a kind with the local mafia. They occasionally shoot people or set fire to buildings for the clan; in return they are permitted to operate their own scams and rackets. In Gela, an industrial wasteland on the south coast, one of these teenage gangs was headed by a young woman, Emanuela Azzarelli, known as 'Bonnie', whose fame, since her first conviction for armed robbery at the age of 18, has been amplified by the Sicilian press. One journalist describes her standing on the roof of a car, dressed in combat gear, directing her gang of thieves in a street raid – like a scene from *Fame*.

The fluid nature of the Catania mafia, like the Naples Camorra, favours women ambitious for a criminal career. 'In Naples, you have Rosetta Cutolo, who was delegated to run the organisation because her brother was in prison,' says Sicilian historian Salvatore Lupo in Catania. 'In Palermo, where the structure of the organisation is extremely formal, that could never have happened. When the boss goes to prison, the person who takes his place is the next one down in the hierarchy, never a family member. But where there is a more informal structure, as you have in Catania, the wife may suddenly be called upon to direct his affairs.'[6]

One woman has emerged in Catania as a clan leader in her own right, a woman who, despite her youth, built herself a reputation for ruthlessness. Building contractors in the area volunteered sums of money, even apartments, to keep her off their backs. She is currently being held in a maximum security prison wing reserved for mafia members, one of the few women to have been distinguished by such severe punishment.

On 27 December 1994 a curious telegram arrived at Gazzi maximum security prison in Messina, eastern Sicily, addressed to Antonino Cintorino, a mafia boss serving life for murder. The telegram was from his wife. It read: 'My love, I long for the time to pass till I can be with you. My love, don't worry about a thing, the horses are all safely in the stable, because it's cold outside. Everything's OK here. I love you more than anything in the world . . .'[7]

Cintorino was head of an organisation operating in Calata-biano, a small town between Mount Etna and the sea, near the tourist resort of Taormina. He didn't, of course, own any horses. His group was engaged in a bitter war against another group, known as the Carrapipani, for control of a lucrative extortion racket. When Cintorino had the upper hand, no one could open a shop or build a shed without giving his mob their monthly rake-off; he lent money to local businessmen at crippling rates of interest. One developer was forced to give

Cintorino and his wife a flat in a new apartment block, which they wanted to make their home.

Cintorino was arrested in 1993. But local police were dismayed to find that as the boss began his sentence, his group continued to operate uninterrupted. Tradesmen carried on paying regular sums of money to the organisation, and hungry splinter groups scavenging around the edge of his territory were kept at bay.

In a bid to understand how the organisation was operating so successfully without its leader, Catania investigators placed a bug in Cintorino's house, and tapped the telephone. As they monitored the tapes, they got an unpleasant surprise.

A series of conversations throughout January 1995 revealed that Cintorino's group was still very much in control of the area, and collecting protection money from local traders. One man, apparently a plumber, was owed a substantial sum by a builder, Martino Magro, for work on a housing development. When he couldn't get Magro to pay, the plumber appealed to the local mafia to help him recoup the money. A gang of thugs was duly dispatched to pay Magro a visit. Magro, terrified, also turned to the mafia boss, appealing for mediation. The person he turned to was Maria Filippa Messina, Cintorino's wife.

Magro's plea to Messina was recorded by police. 'Listen, I just wanted to say I was very happy to hear that the person I'm supposed to give the money to should be someone so . . . yes, I was glad, very glad, now I know what to do. Now I know the order of the day . . . well, now, you tell me what to do, and who I have to pay . . . Last night I couldn't sleep because . . . Maria, I am an important man around here, I can't afford to have any problems.'

Maria Filippa Messina was only 24 when her husband was locked up for life. Despite her youth, she decided that nothing was going to change, and that she would take his place as leader of the clan. Within a few months she had proved herself an able substitute. She got hold of guns coming from former Yugoslavia, armed her men, and continued to run the extortion racket, earning a fearsome reputation.

A later visit to the boss from the unfortunate builder, again monitored by the police, revealed that turning to the mob had driven him deeper into financial crisis. The organisation had lent him money to pay his debts, and was demanding repayment at punishing rates of interest. The builder's wheedling tone, a combination of fear and gratitude, demonstrates the extortioner's peculiar power. She is effectively offering protection from her own bully boys. And he is in no position to bargain.

'. . . I swear, it's been a month exactly, not a day over a month . . . just as soon as I can make it, don't you worry, you can be sure I'll be there . . . you know I'm more than happy to bring you the money, I can't tell you how happy I am now I know I can count on these fine young lads if I ever have any trouble.'

The mafia emerged in nineteenth-century Sicily as protector of the peasant workers against the abusive absentee landlords. But gradually the middlemen or *gabellotti* became hands-on managers, exploiting the peasants who worked for them and stealing land from the rich. Yet while they became greedier and more powerful, they managed to sustain their image as the people's protectors. A major part of the mafia's power base is the support of ordinary people. The mafia boss forces small businesses to pay protection money as a sign of feudal loyalty; in exchange, the boss is obliged to protect the businessman against threats or incursions by other mafiosi. But the businessman now belongs to the mafia boss, and if he fails to pay, his protector can destroy him.

'In the poorer neighbourhoods there is a strong belief in the mafia as protector,' explains Lupo. 'It's a belief arising from fear, or perhaps, a combination of obedience and fear. It's rather like the notion of consensus under a totalitarian regime. There is consensus, but it is achieved by coercion.'[8]

Maria Filippa Messina knew how to exploit the vulnerability of local businessmen, and her group had the necessary firepower to make sure no one refused to pay, or did anything stupid like go to the police. She also took advantage of the informal structure of the Catania mafia to make her bid for power. When she took over from her husband as director of the organisation, she had to make sure the men respected her authority. Major decisions were referred to the boss in prison, but most of the time she used her own wits (from the transcripts of conversations secretly recorded in her home, it becomes clear that she is the only one in the gang with any wits to speak of). However, not all Cintorino's men were prepared to stand by and let his wife take over. A power struggle developed between Maria and Cintorino's deputy, known as Saro, who was on the run from the police and hiding somewhere near Catania.

As she tried to take control of the group's financial affairs, and raise money for her husband's legal representation, Messina found herself blocked by an invisible rival. To protect his position within the group, Saro hung on to the ledger containing the names of businesses and how much they all paid, and refused to let her have it. She was furious. 'At the end of the month, we've got a lot of payments to collect,' she bawled at one of her soldiers. 'Seeing as he [Saro] can't get here, the rest of us are going to have to collect the money ourselves. Tell Saro to send me the ledger – if I could get hold of it, at least I'd be able to see who owes us money, so we'd know where to go.'

Since collecting protection payments is the principal means of endorsing the mafia boss's control of the area, Messina was advised by one of her associates that this was the route she must take to establish herself as leader. 'Unless you make an agreement with your husband, Saro is still the leader in his place . . . but as soon as you go out and start collecting that money, you can give the orders.'

But Saro failed to deliver, and Maria became increasingly angry. 'I just want that book, that's all . . . he was supposed to bring it over, like he said he would. I could have had it by now . . .'

She was already zeroing in on power: in the telegram about getting the horses safely into the stable, she told her husband there was a security problem, but she had already dealt with it. A very particular relationship develops between a husband in prison and a wife running his affairs on the outside: he depends on her for everything, from his clean laundry to collecting his income. He has to trust her utterly.

The rival splinter group continued to give Messina's organisation trouble, mounting a serious challenge for control of Calatabiano and the nearby resort Giardini Naxos. Police monitoring tapes understood that Messina had assumed military command. In response to the rival power bid, she planned a massacre. Her intention was to blow up four members of the rival clan with a bomb. At this point, she appeared to be acting on her own initiative. ('I will be the one to decide who is going to get it,' she snapped at one of her lieutenants.) She contacted two hit men in Catania and arranged for them to come up to Calatabiano; she organised back-up and logistical support for the hit; hired rooms, ordered vehicles from Sicily and weapons from former Yugoslavia. At the end of January she said to one of her men on the telephone: 'I'll organise the houses, and the cars, and then I'll get him [the hit man] to come down here and he can do the job himself . . . That way we can blast them out of town, and at least then we'll get a bit of peace.'

As detectives listened, these were the words which convinced them that Maria Filippa Messina was *de facto* leader of a criminal organisation. The plot to blow up her enemies, which the papers headlined FOUR FUNERALS AND A WEDDING,[9] only failed because the police intercepted Messina's men on the verge of committing the massacre. She was arrested in February 1995 and charged with being one of the leaders of a mafia organisation trafficking in drugs and arms; extortion, murder and attempted murder, and possession of firearms. She was also charged with usury and demanding money with menaces. In December 1996 she was moved into solitary confinement under emergency provisions reserved for dangerous mafiosi.

★

Cosa Nostra formally forbids its members to live off prostitution, but as with all the 'Honoured Society's' commandments,
with a certain amount of guile it may easily be broken. In the
morass of mafia sub-groups in the Catania area, the lawless
underbelly of Cosa Nostra, a couple of enterprising women –
mother and daughter – developed a racket which gave them
control of the city's sex industry.

Between 1991 and 1992 a number of prostitutes in the San
Berillo area of central Catania – behind the splendid baroque
Teatro Massimo – were approached by a woman known simply
as 'Aunt Lucia', who offered to lend them a small sum of
money. Many of the prostitutes were newly arrived in Italy,
mostly from South America, and some of them took her up on
the offer. The terms were stiff: they were expected to pay back
a certain amount every day, and if they missed one day's
payment, they would be right back to zero. Aunt Lucia's
interest rates were so high that the girls inevitably began to fall
behind on their payments, and before long they were trapped:
girls who had come to Italy to make themselves a life were
forced to stay on the streets to pay off the loan sharks.

Control of the prostitution business in Catania was entrusted
to Lucia Niciforo by her son-in-law, Orazio Nicolosi, known
as Orazio 'u Lisciu, or 'Smooth Horace', second-in-command
of the Savasta clan, which controls the oldest district of Catania.
Lucia's team included her daughter, Maria Rosa Vasta, who
kept accounts for the Savasta clan. Lucia's group would borrow
money from the clan at 15 per cent, and lend it on to
prostitutes and brothel owners at interest rates of up to 200 per
cent. Before long, the brothels were having to hand over most
of their takings to service the ever-mounting debts, and the
Savasta clan ended up controlling Catania's sex industry. In
some cases, gangsters simply moved in and took over the
business.

The debt collectors' methods were brutal. The girls began to
receive visits from men who threatened them and beat them
up. In court, witnesses reported hearing the prostitutes complaining: 'Aunt Lucia never stops threatening me, and she's

always sending her boys round. You only have to miss one day and they'll be right over.'[10] Biagia Diano, the madame of a brothel, borrowed an insignificant amount, and ended up owing Aunt Lucia 40 million lire (nearly £17,500). Lucia's thugs paid her regular calls, and on one of their visits broke her arm. When she was questioned by police, too frightened to risk another beating, she said she had fallen over.[11]

Aunt Lucia rejoiced in a fearsome reputation: one investigator described her as 'intimidating and hard – a terrible woman', and asked very particularly not to be quoted. But the greed and ambition of the individuals in the group was so out of control that they were claiming interest at impossible rates; one prostitute ended up owing them the absurd sum of 300 million lire (over £130,000) on a small loan. Although most of the girls were too frightened to give evidence, about half a dozen who found themselves with a debt they would never be able to repay were eventually persuaded to come forward.

In June 1994, Lucia Niciforo was arrested at the age of 64, and charged with mafia association, extortion, and usury. Her daughter, the Savasta clan's bookkeeper, was arrested five months later, after brothel keeper Biagia Diano testified as part of a plea bargain to get herself off a charge of living off immoral earnings.

In spite of her respectful title of 'aunt', greed made Lucia Niciforo scarcely human. The mafia professes respect for all women, but the only thing that really matters is their ability to bring in money. In this context, respect is altogether phoney. It is the mockery of human values such as trust – the extortion disguised as a loan, the offer of protection too dangerous to refuse – that, perhaps more than anything else, characterises the Italian mafia.

5. Vendetta

In the featureless flatlands of the Campania countryside, the small town of Nola is dismally quiet. Nothing moves that is not observed. Eyes behind net curtains follow you the length of the street. When you turn the corner, other eyes take up the watch. Those eyes used to spy for the Camorra boss Carmine Alfieri, who, until his arrest in September 1992, ruled this town. Nothing happened in Nola which might attract the attention of law enforcers, or interfere with Alfieri's operations.

On the edge of town, villas with palm trees, and purple bougainvillaea flying over their high-walled gardens give way to intensive farmland, commercial greenhouses and fields planted with neat rows of vegetables. Here Amalia Pizza lived with her mother, five brothers and two children on an isolated road.

Amalia had been married, but she ran away after her husband's father sexually assaulted her. Furious and humiliated, she telephoned her own father and told him through tears of rage to come and get her. When her father arrived, urged on by the dishonour done his family, but mostly by his daughter's rage, he shot the old man dead.

It was 1987, Amalia, not yet 30, was home again with her children, aged seven and nine, and her father was in prison, doing time for murder. Amalia was a stronger character than the rest of her family, and treated her brothers, whom she adored, as though they were her own children. Two of these brothers were loud and aggressive lads, desperate to be somebody and prove themselves. They swaggered around town, hanging out at the bar, bullying the younger boys and boasting about who they had beaten up or who they had got into bed. One of them announced that he fancied the boss Carmine Alfieri's daughter.

The lads were keen to be noticed by the local Camorra, hoping that if they proved they were tough, they'd be invited to join the Alfieri clan. They walked into shops in the middle of town and told the owners to pay them protection money, or they would smash the place up. When Alfieri heard about these upstarts asking for protection money on his territory, he told one of his managers to give the boys a talking to. But the brothers, when summoned by one of the boss's men, didn't turn up. Encouraged by their own audacity, a few days later they picked a fight in the bar and one of them punched Carmine Alfieri's nephew.

'They wanted to be part of Alfieri's organisation, but they didn't know how to go about it,' says a carabiniere who knew the family. 'They got it all wrong. They had no idea how big Alfieri was.'[1]

A few days after the bar brawl, the brothers received another summons to a meeting with Alfieri's manager. 'He's heard about the fight,' they told their sister excitedly; 'he's going to ask us to join.' On the afternoon of 27 September 1988, the two would-be camorristi, aged 21 and 23, set off in the car to their meeting; their 19-year-old younger brother went along with them for the ride. They were met in a wood by six men carrying guns, who emptied several rounds through the car windows and left the three boys dying among the shattered glass.

Amalia was beside herself. She was obsessed with the thought of her brothers' violent death. She went to see one of Alfieri's men, Raffaele Tufano, and asked him what had happened at the 'meeting'. He hesitated, and mumbled that he didn't know what she was talking about. She asked him to help her find out who did it, and he refused.

'From that moment she was convinced it was he who had killed them, on Alfieri's orders. She came into the station and told us we had to arrest Alfieri,' says a detective. 'But the mafia culture was so ingrained in her, she couldn't answer our questions. It was a very difficult, complex business for her. It went totally against her upbringing to talk to the police, yet she

was here, of her own volition. She was telling us who was
behind her brothers' death, yet she couldn't, or wouldn't, give
us the evidence that would prove it. She was consumed by grief
and anger – sometimes when she talked about her brothers she
would start sobbing violently and it would take ages to calm her
down. It was a long and painful process – it took about two
years to pull all the different elements together.'

After her first visit to the carabinieri, Amalia was summoned
by Carmine Alfieri's mother, who told her to explain herself.
The Camorra boss's widowed mother is a figure of great
authority, said to have an important influence on her sons.
Alfieri was in hiding at the time, and when news reached his
mother of this young woman's visits to the police, she
investigated personally. She told Amalia she shouldn't be
talking to the *sbirri*, the police (literally 'spies'), and demanded
to know what she had told them.

Amalia Pizza's need to avenge her brothers became an
obsession. She told the police she *knew* who had killed her
brothers, and could not understand why they would not act.
On one occasion she flew into a rage, screamed at the men
behind their desks that they didn't know how to do their jobs,
and stormed out of the station. But no one else would listen to
her; she had no one else to go to. Later she came back, tear-
stained, and apologised.

'She was no great beauty,' says Luigi Gay, the magistrate who
conducted the investigations, 'she was short and quite fat . . .
She adored me: when she saw me in court, she wanted to come
over and kiss my hand – which would have been a little . . .
awkward. I felt she was weak and defenceless, but when she
took the stand she was incredibly tough. She tore into
everyone.'[2]

Prison sentences for avenging dishonour are still very mild in
Italy, and after two and a half years Amalia Pizza's father was
released. She was on his case as soon as he got home: she told
him it was his duty to avenge her brothers' murder. The
wretched man, who had just done a stretch for defending his
daughter's honour, was reluctant to go back to prison. His

daughter went wild. The tiny house resounded for weeks with their screams and yells.

But Amalia Pizza's father was no match for her. On 14 April 1992, police on patrol duty in Nola watched as a car driven by a young woman drew up at the kerb, and an older man in the passenger seat aimed a gun into the crowd. Before the police could react, one of the men on the pavement fell to the ground and the car sped away. The dead man was identified as Raffaele Tufano.

'It was one of the hardest things I've ever had to do,' says the carabiniere who went to arrest Amalia Pizza. 'We had built up a great relationship with her over the months, she had finally begun to trust us, and realise that we were on her side. Then she went and destroyed her life.'

Amalia was charged with murder. Her father, who had gone on the run immediately after the killing, was arrested shortly afterwards, but denied everything. After a year on remand she was released, pending trial; her father, with a previous conviction for murder, remained in prison. She went home to her mother, who was looking after her children and her two surviving brothers. She met a man, Felice Stefanile, who seemed to like her. She thought he could offer her a chance to start again. She was still young, she didn't want to be alone. She moved in with him, leaving her children in her mother's care.

But it wasn't long before her mind went back to her brothers, so young, gunned down unarmed and helpless. She could not fail them. She had committed one murder but couldn't stop there. There were others she was sure had been involved. They shouldn't be allowed to get away with it, she told her new boyfriend. If he was a man, he would do this for her. It was his duty to avenge her brothers' murder . . .

'She went on and on at me about it,' the unhappy Felice later confessed. 'She did my head in.' When he couldn't bear it any more he started to hit her, to shut her up. It was March 1995, seven years after her brothers' death. She went on and on: revenge. He hit her more. One day he started to hit her and he didn't stop until she was dead.

The spectre of the vengeful crone exerts powerful pressure on women like Amalia Pizza: she believed it was her duty to the dead to ensure that they were avenged. 'She destroyed her family. It was like something out of a Greek tragedy,' says one of the carabinieri who knew her well. 'That whole family was doomed. She was a very strong character and she had this obsession with vendetta. She was more camorrista by nature than most of the men I've come across.'

The classic view of mafia women is of avenging angels in black veils, crying vendetta for the murder of their loved ones. It is a view enjoyed by the writer Norman Lewis, who describes a blood feud between two families from the suburbs of Palermo, in the late nineteenth century: 'By 1878 [six years after the vendetta began] a man might be approached by some enshrouded, tragic crone he had never seen before – the female head of one of the clans – who would inform him that he was now the surviving head of the [family], and that he must consider himself in a state of ritual vendetta with some cousin he had never seen or heard of . . .'[3] Lewis describes one of the constant features of the ritual, noted in different parts of Italy: 'the kissing, even the pretended sucking of the wounds, by close relations such as mother, wife or brother, followed by the spoken formula: "In this way may I drink the blood of the man who killed you".'[4]

This sort of theatrical performance sent a strong message to the rest of the neighbourhood that the family would not permit the murder of one of their own to go unpunished, and thereby salvaged their honour until such time as they could avenge the wrong (if ever). The widow's cries also awakened her son's sense of shame, if she felt he needed reminding of his duty. In Naples I sat at the kitchen table of a woman whose eldest son, aged 26, had been murdered by her former lover. She was in deep mourning, with black kohl smudged around her small eyes, flanked by her daughter and her daughter's boyfriend.

Suddenly she leapt up from the dinner table, and standing in front of her dead son's picture, howled, kissed his blurred image and wept real tears before sitting down again as though nothing had happened.

The role of a woman inciting her man to carry out a vendetta has been consigned to folklore. It adds to the mystique of mafia women, and is seldom taken seriously as a criminal offence.

In America, Victoria Gotti, wife of the notorious Dapper Don, former head of the Gambino family, has stayed in the shadows for years, but she is said to be a woman of formidable character. Although she has claimed ignorance of her husband's illegal business (she told police 'I don't know what he does. All I know is, he provides'[5]) one incident shows that she was prepared to use his methods where necessary. The couple's 12-year-old son Frank was playing in the street one day in 1980 when he was knocked over by a car as it backed into the street. The driver, a neighbour, John Favara, had failed to see the boy darting out behind him: he ran him over and dragged him several yards along the road. By the time he realised something was wrong, the child was dead.

The courts ruled that it was an accident, but Victoria Gotti refused to accept that Favara hadn't been at fault. Over the following weeks, Favara received hate mail and threatening phone calls from a woman disguising her voice. Someone sprayed the word 'murderer' on his car.[6] One day, Victoria Gotti attacked him with a baseball bat. Favara decided it was time to move house. But before he could get out of Howard Beach, he disappeared.

Later, two mob informers revealed what had happened to Favara. He had been bundled into a van and delivered to John Gotti, who strung him up, still alive, and cut him in half with a chainsaw. The killing, according to a former associate of Gotti, was ordered not by the mafia boss, but by his wife, the dead boy's mother. 'She actually ordered this man to be killed . . . His wife said, "I want this man dead," and it was carried out.'[7]

The crone crying vendetta is an image taken up with

peculiar malice by the Sicilian writer Leonardo Sciascia, who
thrilled with horror at the notion of the mafia woman spurring
on her sons to take revenge: 'How many misfortunes, how
many tragedies in the South have been caused by women,
particularly the ones who become mothers. Women in
southern Italy are terrible in this regard. How many crimes
of passion have been provoked, caused or encouraged by
women!'[8]

Sciascia reserved his fiercest criticism for mothers who bind
their sons' self-esteem and sense of self-worth to the violent act
of revenge. A Sicilian witness, Giacomina Filippello, when
asked by the court to define a mafioso, replied: 'A man who
can prove his worth.'[9] One way in which a man proves his
worth, and attains status as a mafia boss, is by avenging a wrong
done to him or his family. Until 1975, this principle was
enshrined in law: a man who killed his wife, sister or daughter
because she had been discovered having unlawful sexual
relations, received only three to seven years: murder was
justified if his honour was at stake.[10] Camorra godmother
Pupetta Maresca, by avenging her husband's death herself,
robbed her son of the chance to prove himself a man. He
became increasingly violent and thin-skinned, boasting about
how he was going to take his revenge, but he had no status in
the organisation.

One woman's desire to avenge her dead husband destroyed
her own son. Serafina Battaglia's second husband, Stefano
Leale, owner of a coffee house in the old centre of Palermo,
was a member of one of the mafia clans engaged in a long-
running feud. The battle was said to have started in 1958, over
the seduction of a young girl: the seducer had refused to marry
her, so a member of the dishonoured girl's family shot him
dead. Twenty-four men died in the tit for tat killings that
followed.

During the course of this war, in April 1960, at nine o'clock
in the evening, Stefano Leale was pulling down the heavy
metal blinds outside his shop. The rattle of the blinds drowned

out the sound of four gunmen approaching. When he turned round and finally saw the killers upon him, Leale drew his gun and tried to defend himself, but the masked assailants shot him dead.

Battaglia's son by her first marriage, Salvatore Lupo Leale, a handsome man, happily married with two children, carried his stepfather's coffin at the funeral. But as far as his mother was concerned, this was just the beginning of his duty towards the dead. A profoundly religious, powerful woman, Battaglia has been painted in the image of the vengeful harpie. 'Battaglia was a cursed woman, one of those women who incites and nurses a vendetta. After her husband's murder, every morning without fail she would scream at her son: "Get uuuuup! they have murdered your father! Get uuuuup! You must go out and kill them!" Every single morning. Her son didn't want to get up. He didn't want to kill anybody. He was married, and happy, the sort of chap who gets on with his own life and keeps himself to himself . . . But she went on at him, she bullied him and wouldn't leave him alone.'[11]

Battaglia hired a bodyguard for her son, and got them guns. Nearly two years after Stefano Leale's death outside the coffee shop, Salvatore finally agreed to give his mother the revenge she craved. He hired a hit man, but before they could execute the vendetta, his intended target heard about the plan. Some reports suggest that Salvatore's bodyguard betrayed him.[12] Early one morning in January 1962, while the snow settled on the mountains around Palermo, Salvatore was gunned down as he walked through the city, alone.

Serafina Battaglia had seen two men she loved murdered by the mafia, but there was no one she could trust to avenge her dead. There remained only one possibility: she would have to do it herself. Battaglia agreed to give evidence against the men who had murdered her husband and her son. She knew a great deal about the long-running feud between the families, and was asked to testify against a number of mafia figures. She was a tremendous figure in court: she would turn up in her black cloak and hood, clutching a huge crucifix in both hands, weeping and keening in the witness box, pointing her finger at the murderers and calling on God to do justice.

But Battaglia, one of the first people to testify against Cosa Nostra, was dismissed by the judge as an unreliable witness. 'How could you have known that information?' he asked incredulously during the cross-examination. She replied: 'My husband was a mafioso – and the Alcamo and Baucina clans used to hold meetings in his shop. They used to sit around the table for hours, discussing what was going on, that's how I got to know them. I know how important they are, their status within the organisation, the crimes they have committed. My husband used to tell me everything, I know everything. If the wives of murder victims would only talk, like me, not out of hatred or vendetta, but because we are hungry for justice, the mafia in Sicily could have been wiped out by now.'[13]

Battaglia would have been happy to obtain justice with a revenge killing, but since there was no one to do it for her, she took it upon herself to exact revenge through the law. Sadly, the law let her down. After nine years of trials, appeals and high court hearings in different parts of Italy, all twenty of the accused were acquitted – a verdict which did nothing to encourage other mafia women to come forward and testify against Cosa Nostra. Not surprisingly, other mafia women have shown a similarly ambivalent attitude to the law: as a last resort, they have tried to obtain justice through official channels, but without demonstrating much belief in the system. This ambivalence has its roots in southern Italy's ancient mistrust of the government. The environment which nurtured mafia culture was created in the absence of instruments of state to serve the people. The justice of nineteenth-century Sicily was a justice bought by the rich and visited upon the poor: 'The vendetta,' explains Norman Lewis, 'was the weapon ready to hand of the poor and otherwise defenceless in a society where law did not exist and justice meant the baron's court and the baron's torture chamber.'[14]

★

In Calabria, the blood feud is a traditional way of meting out justice. To kill someone in revenge, as part of a *faida* or feud, is not merely forgiven in Calabria. If a man is wronged and fails to take revenge, he loses the respect of his community, and his family is disgraced. 'In Calabria, there is no such thing as forgiveness,' says historian Enzo Ciconte. 'To forgive is a sign of weakness.'[15] This culture has been appropriated by the 'Ndrangheta: by assuming folkloric guise, as it has done elsewhere, the mafia has persuaded ordinary people that it is a force for justice, that it represents their interests better than the treacherous and distant state.

Blood feuds in Calabria have been known to last for decades, from generation to generation, long after everyone has forgotten the slight that caused the first revenge killing. Such vendettas usually only grind to a halt after the last member of one of the warring families is dead. Women are responsible for keeping the flame of vendetta alight, and reminding successive generations of their duty towards the dead, with theatrical displays of grief, keening over the body and swearing vendetta over the open wounds.

The 'Ndrangheta clans are built on blood lines; the region is carved up into small feudal territories divided between families. 'Traditional values are passed on, not at school, but at home, and the family home is run by women. So we can assume that the job of passing on mafia values to the next generation is also entrusted to women.'[16]

The law of vendetta does not acknowledge any other form of justice. A man who serves a prison sentence for murder will have to face his victim's family, many years later, when he gets out. A man who has suffered an attack on his family may refuse to tell the police who committed the crime, so that he can avenge the wrong with his own hands, and thus redeem his honour.[17] Such faithful adherence to the value of honour, of proving a man's worth, is inculcated in the child from its earliest days. 'In Calabria, the family is the criminal cell,' says prosecutor Salvatore Boemi. 'These people are mafiosi from the day they are born.'[18]

When a member of a feuding family gets shot, the other members shut themselves indoors and plan the next move. 'The family arms itself, they never go out, they disappear from circulation for a while,' explains Nicola Gratteri, an investigating magistrate in Reggio Calabria's Anti-mafia Department. 'The woman is the one who goes out, follows the enemy, notes his movements, and works out when they can get him. She plans a strategy and tells them when it is safe for them to "go hunting". A lot of women have been arrested for this activity, but not many have been convicted. It's easier to catch someone smuggling drugs than hatching a murder plot in her own home. It's not as if we're talking about something that happened years ago: the last blood feud killing was twenty days ago.'[19]

The murder referred to by Judge Gratteri took place in Africo, a small, ugly grey town of raw concrete on the Ionian coast, hedged in by the slopes of the Aspromonte foothills. On the edge of town is a large house surrounded by a high wall. The owner was engaged in a feud with another clan in the area, and he had taken extreme measures to make the house safe, with guard dogs, video cameras, alarms, and razor wire; on the rare occasions when he left the house, he drove a bulletproof car. Two hundred yards away there was a building under construction. Among the scaffolding and cement blocks, a marksman from the rival clan waited, peering through the telescopic sight of a high-velocity rifle. After several days, the gunman saw his target approach an upstairs window, and blew half his head off.

The traditional Calabrian blood feud was fought in defence of a family's honour, and the 'Ndrangheta's vendetta merely usurps that ideology. Feuds between 'Ndrangheta clans may be sparked off if one family tries to claim protection money on another clan's turf, or fails to respect an agreement over a drug deal. Judge Boemi suggests that a mafia clan will start a feud deliberately, as part of a military strategy: 'Behind the original act of violence which sets in motion the whole chain of killings, one group is trying to get rid of the other, to defend its territory. Two groups fought each other for twelve years for control of the profitable area around Palmi.'

'The wars go on for ten or twenty years,' says magistrate Nicola Gratteri. 'There is no possibility of a peaceful solution, because these are leadership issues. A boss cannot be seen to submit to a snub from another clan. The only way mediation can be achieved is when the offenders are brought before the boss, who executes them personally.'

A Calabrian collaborator has described how a meeting of 'Ndrangheta leaders was called in 1991 to negotiate an end to the six-year war between the major clans. The bosses came up to Milan from Calabria, each one heavily guarded, and were joined by high-level representatives of both Sicilian and American Cosa Nostra, who laid down the law. 'They said if there was one more murder, the killer's family would be wiped out – there had been more deaths in Calabria in six years than there had been in America in fifty. The killing had to stop.'[20] The only dissenting voice in this top-level mafia conference came from the widow of Calabrian boss Domenico Serraino, who had been killed in the war. 'She didn't want to hear about any peace.'

The image of blood is central to the feud. Calabrian folklore refers to blood murmuring, whispering or calling out for revenge. *Sangue chiama sangue*: the sound of blood calling blood is said to ring in the ears of the dead man's relatives. And it can only be silenced by the blood spilt in a revenge killing.

There is another way to end a blood feud between clans, and restore peace. It can be done by arranging a marriage between a girl and a boy from the warring parties. In the crude symbolism so relished by the 'Ndrangheta, the blood of the first man murdered in the feud is 'paid for' by the blood of the virgin bride. 'Women come into their own, as figures of central importance – and as goods to be exchanged – when families want to bring a feud to an end. The sacrifice of the virgin blood of a woman from the enemy camp compensates for the blood that has been spilt in the war.'[21]

★

In modern Sicily, vendetta can be seen in purely pragmatic, not symbolic, terms. The mafia boss rules by virtue of the authority he or she commands among ordinary people in the area. A family that has been wronged, and fails to respond, loses respect. Battles for control of the territory have been known to go on for years, with each side avenging its dead as swiftly and brutally as possible so as not to lose ground. In many cases what is described as a blood feud is really a strategic war.

For the would-be boss, avenging the dead is a means to obtain position – failure to do so is career suicide. In such cases, the mother who incites the son to kill is more than the avenging angel, she is a kingmaker.

One historian who espouses this view has become very unpopular among others more attached to the mythology of the mafia's code of honour. Salvatore Lupo believes that the Sicilian culture of vendetta is overrated as a motivating force for murder. 'The mafia is a great creator of myths. There is no such thing as a blood feud. The rationale of vendetta doesn't exist.'[22] A revenge killing, according to Lupo, is seldom carried out on principle alone. It is part of a military plan, executed when it suits the family's interests, and only if the clan has adequate manpower, since it may provoke further reprisals. 'If there is a pattern to vendetta, it is a pattern of war: two opposing sides confronting each other. A family that hasn't got the power to avenge a brother, has to accept his death. They can't even consider the possibility of revenge.'

From this perspective, Sicilian women play a part in mafia wars as military strategists. They command respect among the footsoldiers, and have an intimate knowledge of the territory.

Grazia Ribisi, 52, a widow from southern Sicily, is described by people who have no personal animosity against her as short, fat and ugly, with eyebrows tortured into shape, black hair cut like a helmet, and – in a part of the world where you have to try quite hard not to get a suntan – a waxy pale face. Five of her six brothers (the youngest had moved away) formed the armed wing of a mafia clan headed by Agrigento boss Giuseppe Di Caro; they were known as 'the terrible brothers', and were renowned gunmen – one of them reportedly threw a party to celebrate his 150th hit.[23]

Palma de Montechiaro, on the south coast of Sicily near Agrigento's Valley of the Temples, is a small town built of honey-coloured stone, clustered around the stunning baroque church which starred in Visconti's film *The Leopard*. But speculators have descended, under contracts arranged by the mafia: blocks of flats have been built, without planning permission, where there used to be school playgrounds and police car parks. The picturesque old town is surrounded by raw concrete villas which scramble over rocks and riverbeds, clinging to the edges of the mountain slopes.

The 'terrible' Ribisi brothers (all cursed with the same terrible potato-shaped heads and squashed noses) staged a takeover of the Palma crime industry in 1984. They murdered the ruling capo and took control of Palma in their own right, but continued working as crack hit men under orders from the higher echelons of Cosa Nostra. In 1988, at least one of the brothers was involved in the assassination of Judge Antonio Saetta, murdered with his handicapped son, who had been sentenced to death by Cosa Nostra for refusing to rig a trial.

Around the time of Judge Saetta's death, a new group of aggressive youths emerged in Palma, armed robbers and thieves, who stuck their guns in people's faces and demanded money from tradesmen already paying protection money to the Ribisi family. The brothers retaliated, and fought to assert their control. Over three years, 150 people were murdered in Palma de Montechiaro in well-publicised executions: each one fell in a public place, most of them in the full light of day.

On 6 August 1989, Gioachino Ribisi was having a pizza with his family when two men wearing full-face motorbike helmets walked into the crowded restaurant and shot him.

The 'terrible brothers'' revenge was swift: the next day a soldier from the rival clan was shot dead. Their enemies hit back in a furious gun battle in which Rosario Ribisi was shot in the legs. Rosario, the most powerful and wealthiest of the brothers, leader of the clan, was treated for his leg wounds in hospital, tended by his brother Carmelo, who kept a gun in the bedside table. On 4 October 1989, killers walked into the hospital ward and opened fire with machine guns, shooting Rosario where he lay helpless with his legs in traction, and leaving Carmelo face down on the floor in a pool of blood.

The remaining two brothers disappeared, apparently to give themselves time to regroup. The police in Palma suspected that Grazia Ribisi, who was close to her brothers and married to a member of the allied clan, was in contact with them while they were underground. Investigators' suspicions were heightened when her husband, Pasquale Allegro, was sent into internal exile 150 kilometres away on the west coast, and she stayed in Palma.

The police chief in Palma de Montechiaro talks about Grazia Ribisi as a smart woman, who, although she didn't get beyond primary school, was capable of intelligent planning. 'She may not have had an education, but she's not stupid. She's not an attractive woman, no one could call her that, but she is clever, in her own way. Ignorant, illiterate, coarse – but feared and respected. She was the only person the surviving brothers trusted. She was very cunning on the ground: she got around, found people to take messages and food to her brothers – which was a difficult task considering she had to be certain she never employed spies, or ran any risk of being followed.'

She was tailed as rigorously by the police, who wanted her family in jail, as she was by the rival group, who wanted her family dead – and she evaded both. Police were convinced that she was collecting extortion money on her brothers' behalf and the investigation began to focus on her.

'Grazia Ribisi more or less held the reins of the organisation at that point,' says magistrate Teresa Principato of the Anti-mafia Department in Palermo, who took over the investigation after the death of Judge Paolo Borsellino in July 1992.

'She ran the clan's business and managed her brothers' lives in hiding, maintaining their cover and keeping them informed.'[24]

On the strength of Principato's belief that Grazia Ribisi was the central commanding figure of the family at this point, police put a tap on her phone, and concealed a bug in her bedroom.

As the Ribisi clan came under sustained fire, the Allegro family, who were linked to the 'terrible brothers' by Grazia's marriage to Pasquale Allegro, began to mutiny. They had suffered heavy losses, and voted to protect their families from further attacks by withdrawing from the conflict. When she heard of the betrayal, Grazia Ribisi was furious. She talked to her husband on the phone, calling his relations cowards and traitors for abandoning them in their hour of need. The police, monitoring the conversation, pricked up their ears. She cursed the men who had murdered her brothers, and swore revenge.[25]

According to Palma's chief of police, Grazia Ribisi was determined to keep the family going, to revive its power and prestige in Palma, so that they could avenge her brothers' deaths. If they failed to avenge Rosario's death, they would lose their dominant position in Palma – but they lacked the military strength to do it.

As the war intensified, more members of the Ribisi clan fell. They were no longer sure where the attack was coming from, and the former allies began to turn on each other. Investigators and mafiosi were equally confused. Voices amongst the Allegro group whispered that Grazia Ribisi was getting information about their movements from her husband, and passing it on to hostile elements.[26]

Conversations picked up by the bug hidden in Grazia Ribisi's bedroom convinced investigators that she was the first to grasp what was happening. Investigating magistrate Teresa Principato explains: 'She understood that "The Hand" as she put it [i.e. the hand of death] was coming from a newly formed splinter group. She had observed a number of signs, and we heard her describe them. She deduced from a series of situations she had observed that there was a new group that no one even knew existed, who were decimating the older mafia families. We used Grazia Ribisi's information as the basis of our investigation.'

In a conversation on a telephone line monitored by police,

Pasquale Allegro's uncle, who had lost patience with Grazia's aggressive bullying, and her demand that his family come to the defence of her brothers, said: 'We've got to cut down this tree, it's the only way to stop the machine.'[27]

Investigators believed this was the proof that she was the central reference point for the Ribisi family. Remove her, the speaker seemed to say, and the rest of them will be rendered harmless. Grazia Ribisi was arrested and charged on the basis of this interpretation.

Grazia bellowed in protest as she was manhandled into the van and shouted from her cell that she had been doubly persecuted: first by killers, then by the police. Investigating magistrates found her charmless, aggressive and uncooperative, but when the case came to trial, judges disagreed with the investigators' interpretation of the recorded conversations, and in spite of her unprepossessing manner, found no evidence to suggest that Grazia Ribisi was the 'tree' that stood in her in-laws' way. To magistrate Teresa Principato's dismay, Grazia Ribisi was acquitted. 'These particular judges don't believe that women have any involvement in the mafia,' she commented bitterly. Not only was she acquitted, Grazia Ribisi was awarded £30,000 compensation for two years' wrongful imprisonment.

Grazia's husband died (of natural causes) while she was in prison, but she has returned to live in Palma de Montechiaro with her two daughters, aged 13 and 10, who go to school locally. Her house is by no means luxurious: the exterior, like all the others, is raw cement, not plastered or painted, and the interior is surprisingly simple. No one can remember a time when she didn't wear black. She wears a locket for her dead husband – just the one: if she wore one for every member of her family killed in the long years of the mafia war, she would clank like a belled cow. She is sometimes seen around town now that the war is over, and lost. She has nothing to fear, because no one has anything to fear from her.

6. The Sins of the Mother

On 23 May 1996, while most of Italy was watching a television film about the assassination of Judge Giovanni Falcone, a crack police squad swooped on a house near Agrigento in Sicily. They emerged with two prisoners: the bloated, bearded Giovanni Brusca and his long-haired younger brother Vincenzo. The brothers and their girlfriends had also been watching the Falcone film, although the drama was rather more familiar to them than to the rest of the audience: Giovanni Brusca is accused of detonating the bomb that killed the judge, his wife Francesca Morvillo and three bodyguards. Investigators had closed in on Brusca after discovering his underground arsenal containing ground-to-air-missiles, rocket launchers and anti-tank guns. Police were jubilant and emotional at the capture of the man accused of slaughtering their colleagues; they whooped and waved their guns in the air.

The first person to make a statement on the arrested men's behalf was not their lawyer, but their mother. A short woman with dyed strawberry blonde hair pushed back in an alice band, Antonina Brusca, 63, scared journalists with her cold eyes and sarcastic manner. Her husband, Bernardo Brusca, boss of San Giuseppe Iato, is serving three life sentences; her three sons, of whom one is already in prison, face charges of murder, drug trafficking and mafia association.

'I brought my sons up well, and taught them religion,'[1] she announced to journalists outside the police station where her sons were being held. She summoned the image of a God-fearing family that gives liberally to charity. God featured repeatedly in her speech: she said she only misses Mass if she is physically restrained from entering the church, and that He is a great defender of the Brusca family. She intoned: 'If the Holy

Spirit will enlighten our minds, and enlighten the judges' minds, my sons will not be convicted.'

Signora Brusca accused the police of beating and kicking her sons in custody, referring to the heavily built 28-year-old Enzo as 'the little one'. The intention was to plead the innocence of her boys, but it isn't really in her nature to plead. The image of a humble, God-fearing family wore thin, and she soon tired of it. She expressed nothing but scorn for the press and the judiciary ('communists who lock people up and throw away the key'). She referred to the assassination of Judge Falcone as a 'misfortune' and added darkly: 'It's just as well, oh yes, it's just as well, that in San Giuseppe Iato people still treat the Brusca family with respect.'

'You can always tell when things are going badly for Cosa Nostra,' remarked prosecutor Antonio Laudati. 'When there's an emergency they bring out the women.'[2] Signora Brusca came out fighting, defending her sons from the accusations levelled against them. It is a role that mafia women have always played – covering their heads with black shawls and filling the streets with their wailing when the police come to take their men away. The only difference is that nowadays, television cameras and reporters' tape recorders are on the spot to take down every word.

But while raising the cry that her children were innocent, Antonina Brusca – perhaps involuntarily – asserted her sons' criminal pedigree, reminding us that they are inheritors of a name that bears authority in their part of Sicily. 'Respect' is a word unmistakably redolent of mafia culture. She would have us believe her boys are worthy of the name – and she should know. Her husband comes from a line of mafiosi, all labourers, country people, but with a compelling ambition: to command respect. Bernardo's father, the patriarch Don Emanuele, was one of the mafiosi who joined forces with the bandit Salvatore Giuliano in the 1940s, in a bid to split Sicily from the rest of Italy. Their sons started early in the family tradition, threatening anyone in San Giuseppe Iato who failed to pay protection, torching cars, making their presence felt in the stench of burning rubber.

Antonina Brusca claims her sons are persecuted because of the name they bear, but her own words demonstrate an involuntary pride in their mafia heritage. If the sins of the father are visited on the children, who exactly is responsible?

It was difficult for Italian magistrates investigating individual crimes to secure convictions until they started treating the mafia as an illegal organisation, under the new La Torre law passed in September 1982. Until this point, women's cultural role, such as instructing children in their duty to continue a family vendetta, was considered part of traditional folklore, and not punishable by law. As we have seen, a tendency to romanticise vendetta as a part of the mafia's honourable code prevented investigators from seeing that women played an active role in mafia families' military strategy.

It is only recently, according to the Sicilian historian Salvatore Lupo, that the notion of the mafia family as a socially dangerous environment, a hotbed for the next generation of criminals, has begun to attract proper attention in Sicily. 'The judiciary completely failed to tackle the problem in a serious way. They did not consider the family important as the environment in which the mafioso is raised, and therefore overlooked the one way they could have broken the ties that bind this organisation. There are two stages to the making of a mafioso: one is his upbringing, the training he receives within the family (that is, the female side); the other is his formal entry into a (male) structure with an initiation ceremony and its own set of rules. The family aspect of his development has been badly underestimated.'[3]

The mother's responsibility in forming the character of a junior mafioso has finally come under scrutiny by investigators. It has also become the subject of intense and painful debate in the media. One of the reasons it took so long for the issue to emerge is that most Sicilians are unwilling to conceive a negative side to the relation between mother and child. Years after Leonardo Sciascia aroused fury by saying that mafia women are worse than the men because they incite men to carry out vendetta, others are taking seriously his perception of the mother poisoning her children's minds.

Liliana Ferraro, who took Falcone's place at the Ministry of Justice after his assassination in 1992, has been uncomfortably high on the mafia hit list ever since. The danger of her own situation has forced her into a degree of isolation; she is divorced and has no children, and goes everywhere escorted by bodyguards. Ferraro perceives an insidious force at work in the bond between mother and child in a mafia family. Chain-smoking little cigars in the large, homely apartment in the centre of Rome where she lives alone, surrounded by paintings and Victorian vases (presents from friends), Ferraro explains: 'It's difficult for us to understand the subtle role that women have always played – the mother working on the child's unconscious, passing on mafia values in her breast milk. Inculcating mafia culture in the children – the mafia way of thinking: the hard line on justice, survival of the fittest, how to justify their actions, no matter how terrible – this is done first and foremost not by the man, the father, but by the woman, the mother.

'It would be impossible for all these mafia dynasties to go on generation after generation if there weren't a fertile terrain in which to nurture them. This fertile ground is culture, tradition, silence – the culture of a particular environment. But that's not all. Any environment is created by people – and that includes women.

'You only have to listen to Giovanni Brusca's mother to understand that this woman, who talks to the press, and Totò Riina, the boss who will never talk, are one and the same thing. They have the same background; they have the same feelings. Totò Riina's greatest ally is Brusca's mother. It's incredible but it's true.'[4]

Riina and Mamma Brusca are not only soulmates but military allies: the two families joined forces under the Corleone flag when Riina made his bid to take over Cosa

Nostra. The family link is strengthened by the fact that Giovanni Brusca is Totò Riina's godson, his criminal protégé.

Riina's own children were brought up in segregation from the rest of the world. After narrowly escaping imprisonment in 1969, when he and the Corleone boss Luciano Leggio were acquitted of murder, Riina went underground. In 1971, his beautiful fiancée Antonietta Bagarella (known as Ninetta) was summoned before magistrates in the Palermo courthouse. (She had already run into trouble when the nuns at the school where she taught had asked for a certificate of good conduct. The police refused to issue one, so the nuns gave her the sack.) She was accused of running messages between the various exiled and imprisoned members of the Corleone mafia: Luciano Leggio, her brothers Leoluca and Calogero Bagarella, Totò Riina, and their lawyers. If found guilty, she would be sent into internal exile, the first woman to be punished in this way for mafia crimes.

On her way into court Ninetta Bagarella posed for a photo in her simple floral print dress, her dark hair falling loose down her back. It was the only picture of her the papers had on file until 1993, and it did her no disservice. She gave a magnificent performance for the crowd of journalists: 'I love him. I'm a woman, aren't I? Haven't I the right to love a man, isn't that the law of nature? You ask how I could have chosen a man like him, about whom people say such terrible things. Is it against the law to love a man like Salvatore Riina? I love him because I know he is innocent.' She was convincingly guileless: he was in hiding, so she played the lovesick fiancée who doubts her lover's affection. 'I haven't seen Riina for two years, I don't even know if he loves me any more.'[5] The Palermo press corps was in love. It was a romance that was to last many years.

Riina and his young fiancée got married in a secret church service in 1974, and she joined him in hiding, moving between a series of safe houses in and around Palermo. He consolidated his position within the organisation, forging links with industrialists and setting his rivals against each other, clawing his way to the top of the mafia's ruling body, the *cupola* or Commission.

Ninetta gave birth to four children in Palermo's most exclusive private clinic, and registered them under their real names. The most wanted family in Sicily had friends in high places to protect them, but all the same, Ninetta kept her children under close watch, occasionally taking them shopping in town, but never letting them out of her sight. Since they couldn't go to school, the former schoolmistress taught them herself.

The birth of a son and heir, the couple's second child, had been the cause for major celebrations. When Gianni (short for Giovanni) was five, his father took him on his knee in front of a group of mafia associates and admirers, and held the handle of his gun towards the boy. 'Let's see your trigger finger,' he said.[6] How they laughed.

In January 1993, Totò Riina's former driver, the *pentito* Baldassare Di Maggio, turned him in. Two days after the boss's arrest, while the papers and television news still resounded with the story of his capture and his crimes, his wife and their four children took a taxi to Corleone. They moved into their grandmother's house in the old centre of town, where the dun tiled roofs huddle together under the mountain. It was their first ever official appearance in public. The first family of Corleone had come home. Ninetta Bagarella wanted the world to know they had nothing to fear.

The children were given their first identity cards and went to the local school. This is not to say that the family started behaving like ordinary people. Whenever Ninetta went to meet the teachers, she always arrived in convoy: two cars would draw up outside the school and her people would go in ahead to make sure it was safe. The young Gianni, heavy-set and square-faced like his father, roared around on his motor-bike, shooting his mouth off, losing his temper, letting the acquiescent citizens of Corleone know that the boy was back in town. He started school, but was humiliated to find himself so much older than the rest of his class, and soon dropped out.

According to Tony Calvaruso, one of the Corleone clan members close to the boss's family, who later became a defector, it was during this period that Gianni began to attend clan meetings, and was initiated into Cosa Nostra. It was also during this period that the boss's son and heir began to suspect he was being followed. His aunts' house, where they all lived, was under police surveillance, and one night investigators heard him ring his mother and tell her he thought someone was tailing him. Terrified that he might be kidnapped, his mother told him to alter his usual route home and go to stay at a relative's house.

The suspected kidnap attempt was mentioned a few days later at a meeting called by his uncle, Leoluca Bagarella. The would-be kidnappers, it was decided, would be dealt with. 'I'll take care of it,' said the young Riina.

'You shut up,' said his uncle. 'I'll handle this.'[7]

Days afterwards, a young Corleonese, Giuseppe Giammona, was shot dead. Twenty-four hours later, gunmen shot Giammona's brother-in-law Francesco Saporito at the wheel of his car, killing his wife Giovanna Giammona and narrowly missing the year-old baby cradled in her arms. Uncle Leoluca had handled it.

Besides behaving like a junior gangster, Gianni began to assume responsibilities within the clan. In a letter to a certain Salvo, in handwriting barely joined up and badly spelt, he set up a meeting with other mafiosi and told them to send payment for a deal. 'Salvo', according to informers, was the code name for none other than Giovanni Brusca, boss of San Giuseppe Iato and Totò Riina's godson. Police found the letter when they raided Brusca's house.

One day in 1996, the 20-year-old stocky youth was having an afternoon nap when the carabinieri arrived at the family home in Corleone. He paused to push a palmful of gel through his thick black hair, and took leave of his family in silence.

For the boss's eldest son to be arrested so young was a disaster. His mother issued a letter to the press – it was the first time she had made a public statement for over twenty-five years. Aware of the fascination she exercises on the Italian public, she dropped a perfectly calculated bombshell. The letter portrayed her boy as the innocent victim of a vendetta against her family, presumed guilty because of the name he bears.

'I have decided to open my heart, the heart of a mother swollen and overflowing with grief at the arrest of my son . . . We all miss him terribly, life in our family has become a nightmare, we cannot accept that a boy of only 20, with no previous convictions, could be arrested and, after two days of interrogation, taken away and locked in a cell . . .

'Justice demands that people should know, Giovanni is a normal, open, happy, easy-going boy. He works in the fields and when he comes home in the evening he meets his friends at the bar . . . He collects compact discs, motorbike and car magazines, and knows all the makes and models . . .

'In the eyes of the world, my children were born guilty. No one considers that when they were born I (*la mamma*) was a free citizen, my husband guilty only of failing to report for probation. We have brought up our children making enormous sacrifices, overcoming tremendous difficulties, giving them every possible love and support. We have raised them to respect the family and love their neighbour . . . The motto of the Riina household is "Respect everyone and everything" . . .

'Fortunately no one can undo divine law: the commandment "Honour thy father and mother" must be obeyed by everyone, including our children, who adore us and live for us, their parents.'[8]

The letter was a masterpiece of motherly love. The words 'mamma' and 'figlio' were repeated like a prayer, as though a mother's love absolves the boy of any crime. By implication, anyone who wants to lock up the boy is attacking that sacrosanct bond. The phrase 'respect for the family', so redolent of mafia culture, passed as a bourgeois platitude. There was no mention of her husband's lengthening string of life sentences. Like Mamma Brusca, Ninetta Bagarella dismissed terrestrial law and went straight for the divine.

It was not the first time the Riina family had defended itself in this vein. After so many years of silence, the press release from the boss's household was becoming a regular thing.

After her return to Corleone in 1993, Maria Concetta, the eldest daughter, had started school at the age of 19. She was a sad figure, an ugly girl, with her father's heavy features covered in spots, consumed by longing for a boyfriend. Her classmates joked, though not unkindly, that they had to find her a mate – but who was going to knock on Signora Riina's door and say they wanted to go out with her daughter? As she was so much older than them, her classmates sought her advice: she became an older sister figure for the girls, and when she put her name up for class representative, she was elected.

Prosecutor Ilda Boccassini, famous for her outspoken attacks on the mafia's sentimental mythology, took the opportunity to ask whether Riina's daughter, now she was class rep, would publicly renounce the mafia. Maria Concetta responded with a carefully staged interview in a high-profile weekly magazine. Using a sympathetic journalist, she cleverly twisted the question, protesting that she was being asked to deny her own father.

'What am I supposed to renounce? The affection and the love that papà has given me since the day I was born? How could I stop going to see him, knowing that after every visit he counts the days until the next time? How could I help loving him? The memories that bind me to him are heartbreakingly tender . . .'[9]

She described a family life reminiscent of *The Waltons*: father coming home at six after a hard day at the office, the children rushing to the door to fling their arms round his neck, the family settling down together in front of the TV news, mother doing the ironing. The children were, she implied, vaguely aware that they were in hiding from the law (on the TV news his name would come up again and again against a backdrop of mangled metal and strewn corpses). The closest thing she describes to a moment of revelation is when her younger sister Lucia, watching her father's face flashed up in the report of a murder on the news, turned to him and said, with wonder: 'I knew it! I knew Bellomo wasn't our real name!' But in spite of the evidence beamed daily into their luxurious hideout, the

children's innocent minds were untroubled. The most important thing was that they were together.

With all its unintentional ironies, Maria Concetta's interview
was a propaganda hit for the mafia. It threw the judiciary into
disarray: several magistrates attacked Boccassini, accusing her of
unnatural cruelty, and insisting that the children of a mafioso
must be given every chance to prove themselves innocent.

When her brother was arrested in June 1996, Maria Concetta
reappeared, telling *La Repubblica* her brother could not be
guilty. She knew him, she said; they had grown up together.
One more time, the love of a woman was produced as
evidence that the man was innocent.

Boccassini was of a different mind. She pointed out that
Gianni Riina, the son of a mafia boss, had grown up in a sealed
environment, cut off from law-abiding society. The only path
ahead of him was to become a mafioso. 'If what the
collaborators say is true, this boy has been made a man of
honour. Which doesn't surprise me in the least. It's inevitable
that mafia culture, its manners and customs and its code of the
family, are more important than anything else to its members.
They subsume every other teaching or experience. It's obvious.
I don't believe Giovanni Riina was forced to become a man of
honour. Quite simply, the boy took the only career he was
offered in life. This is why I have always maintained there is no
middle way: there are no half measures between the mafia's
family-centred culture, and a sense of community, a sense of
state.'[10]

Ilda Boccassini's words were clear and uncompromising, but
Maria Concetta and her mother had taken the temperature of
the moral climate. They knew that people don't like to believe
that a woman, particularly a mother, could have a criminal
mind. Most Sicilians feel their primary duty is to the family, not
the state. In the battle for the moral high ground, the mafia
gained a significant advantage by presenting itself as the
defender of family values.

Propaganda is a powerful weapon in the war between the
mafia and the state, and the mafia had lost a few recent battles.

Since the massacres of judges Falcone and Borsellino, which made two martyrs for the anti-mafia campaign, Cosa Nostra has lost a lot of public good will. In order to function, the mafia requires the consensus of ordinary people, who regard the local boss as someone who guarantees them work, who imposes order, who solves their problems. In a profoundly conservative society, the mafia represents constancy.

The bond between mother and child is a dependable relationship more dear to a Sicilian than any other. (The attachment even has a name: *mammismo*.) The mafioso, attentive to his public profile, makes much of the relationship with his mother. It is an irony not lost on the biographer of Corleone boss Luciano Leggio, who portrays a man with a relish for killing and lust for power undiminished by a lifetime in hiding. Being one of Italy's most wanted couldn't keep him away from mamma: 'Once he came back to Corleone on the sly to see his mother, because, like all murderers, he adored his mother.'[11]

This exploitation of the familial bond to give the organisation a human face is an extreme version of the adulterous politician appearing in public with his wife and family and thinly stretched smiles. During the maxi-trial held in Palermo in the mid-1980s, an 11-year-old boy, Claudio Domino, was shot dead in Palermo. His father had won the contract for cleaning the maximum security courtroom, and the murder was widely reported as an attempt to free up the contract for a mafia firm. Sensing a PR disaster, the Commission of Cosa Nostra reacted immediately. The day after the murder, one of the defendants, the mafioso Giovanni Bontate, asked permission to make a statement in court. 'Signor Presidente, we have nothing to do with the assassination of Claudio Domino,' he announced. 'This crime offends us, but even more offensive is the attempt by the press to attribute blame to the men present in this courtroom.

'We too have children.'[12]

As hundreds of mafiosi stood in their cages to be judged, Bontate, who may have been acting under instruction from the

Commission, was attempting to bolster the saying that the mafia never harms women or children. This tired old cliché survives to this day, which is surprising, since there is plenty of evidence to the contrary. Children are sacred to Cosa Nostra until they challenge or threaten the organisation in any way. In 1948, trade-unionist Placido Rizzotto was murdered by the ambitious young Corleone mobster Luciano Leggio. The killing was witnessed by a 12-year-old boy, who was so traumatised by what he had seen, he went into shock. His mother took him to hospital, where he was given a tranquillising injection that killed him instantly. It was not a mistake: the injection was personally administered by the hospital director, Michele Navarra, at the time head of the Corleone clan.[13]

The family unit demands loyalty above the state. Liliana Ferraro has looked into the heart of mafia culture, and found there the amoral mother–child relationship.

'The mafia mother's task is to justify her children in everything they do,' she explains in her slow, rasping voice. This function, it is clear, has nothing to do with raising upstanding citizens: it is a vindication of the mother–child relationship in any circumstances.

'Giovanni Brusca, in his mother's eyes, is not a criminal. As far as she is concerned, he is merely the vessel for the family's proper and worthy values; he lives a sensible, normal life, it's others who are bad. His mother says, "Go to work". If this work means killing someone, then that is the right thing to do. These people believe they are acting out of sound principles, which is much worse than disobeying the state. They don't even believe in the state. They can't imagine any other way of life than the one in which their husbands – not police, or magistrates or politicians – dictate the rules.'

Under Italian law, a woman cannot be prosecuted for aiding and abetting a member of her family. If the family is indeed the crucible of mafia values, this should be the place to start dismantling the whole edifice. But Ferraro, hoarse with smoking and talking, holds fast to the ideal of a healthy family relationship, and to the example that must be set by what is known as 'civil' society. 'We cannot say that the children must pay for the guilt of their parents. Our culture does not allow us to say that if a child has bad parents, it will turn out bad. I reject that equation entirely.'

When Ninetta Bagarella's letter appeared in *La Repubblica*, commentators nervously praised her maternal instinct. No one wanted to fall into the trap of attacking the sacrosanct mother–child bond. 'This is the letter . . .' said Palermo's deputy chief prosecutor Guido Lo Forte, hesitantly, '. . . of a mother.' Only one magistrate, public prosecutor Teresa Principato, condemned it outright as a perfect example of mafia culture.

The most alarming aspect of the letter, according to Principato, is the systematic justification of the father's actions to the son. 'They have to put up a front, for themselves and for the children, to create an outward show of respectability. Salvatore Riina's wife has brought up the children, creating an impression of normality, while underneath, the family is completely abnormal.

'It is the mafia wife's duty to model the blood family on the mafia's principles, its phoney culture, to the extent that the two worlds begin to overlap and become indistinguishable: filial love and respect get confused with a need to defend the father's bullying and violence.

'The woman's role is to ensure the continuity of mafia values, because she is entrusted with the children's upbringing, and the children are the future of the organisation.'

Instead of the mafia modelling itself on the family, we have a family modelled on the principles of the mafia. The relationship is reversed. And this is the breeding ground for the next generation.

7. The Breeding Ground

Two things are important to a mafioso. Money and children.

The Sicilian mafia germinated in conditions of bleak rural poverty, and in many areas offered the only means for a young man to improve his financial situation. As he climbs through the ranks, the focus of his life becomes the power, and money, that his sons will inherit. Totò Riina, son of peasant stock, who rose to be head of the Commission, has acquired tracts of fertile agricultural land around Corleone for his children. Bernardo Provenzano, who grew up with Riina, sent his sons to private schools in Germany. The father creates the means for his son's social ascendance, while the mother, in charge of his moral education, makes sure he is up to the task.

In the USA, mafia members like Angelo Bruno, the gentlemanly don of South Philadelphia, have tended to use their accumulated wealth and power to send their children to college and make a better future for their families, outside the mob. Still, association with La Cosa Nostra has acquired a taint that no amount of money can erase. One of John Gotti's men, a Gambino family member known as Foxy, tried to protect his sister from ending up with a gangster. He told his associate Tommy De Simone: 'Listen, we're in this life together, but don't you ever think that you are going to take my sister out. I don't want her involved with anybody like us.'[1] (De Simone later shot Foxy dead, which probably didn't endear Foxy's sister to him.)

The short, savage South Philadelphia boss Nicky Scarfo had three sons. The eldest, Nicky Junior, wanted to be a boss like his father, and made his way in the neighbourhood, imitating his father's every move. The middle one, Christopher, wanted nothing to do with the mob life. He disowned his father, moved out of Philadelphia and took his wife's maiden name.

The youngest, Mark, was bullied and harangued by his father, who tried unsuccessfully to turn him into a mobster. Philip Leonetti, a turncoat from Nicky Scarfo's mob, said later: 'Mark wanted to work, he wanted to be a normal kid. He wanted to play sports in school, but his father said if you play sports in school, you're a jerk off. He didn't want Mark to work for anybody. He thought that was like lowering yourself. The kid wants to work, you know, what's the big deal about that? But he was on this kid like he was already a member of La Cosa Nostra.'[2]

During his father's trial on racketeering charges, Mark Scarfo tried to hang himself, at the age of 17. His mother found him and rushed him to hospital, but he remains in a coma. He had been driven to despair, between the taunts of his schoolmates who called his father a gangster and murderer, and his father's insistence that he should think, talk and behave like a mobster.[3]

Sicilians like to keep power in the family. Successive generations of Bruscas, of Vernengos, of Madonias, have continued the clan's rule. Getting rich is not the organisation's sole purpose. Besides making money, they feel the need to hang on to their power, to retain the almost divine right the clan exercises over its territory.

Over twenty years, Catania boss Nitto Santapaola – officially owner of a car showroom – built an organisation whose grip was felt in every sector of the eastern Sicilian town, from the smallest shops paying protection, to the businessmen laundering money. It was an empire unchallenged, protected at the highest level by politicians and industrialists, and continued to grow while Santapaola was in hiding, dodging a murder charge for more than ten years.

Santapaola's wife Carmela Minniti was an elegant, capable, educated woman, who brought up their three children, travelling between their home in Catania, their lawyer's office, and her husband's hiding place out in the country. Even when in hiding, Santapaola would go hunting with important local figures and entertain politicians and industrialists, but there was more to it than protecting his financial interests. Both

Santapaola and his wife were consumed with the desire to be accepted by the Catania bourgeoisie. The former shoe salesman sent his children to private schools, desperate for them to climb into the ranks of industry or the professions, to make the grade in Sicilian middle-class society.

'They had a relationship anyone would envy. Not that Signora Minniti confided in me, of course,' says the couple's lawyer, Giuseppe Napoli. A man who in another life would have been a lorry driver, Napoli is nervous, fiddles with keys and cigarettes, demands to see my press card. His brillo-pad hair sticks up from a globular head; today he is wearing a striped sports shirt with a ring-pull zip, instead of one of his famous florid ties. 'She was a beautiful woman, a cultured lady, nicely dressed, well-spoken. A sight better than most of the lot we get in here.'

When Santapaola was arrested, his wife appeared to take it in her stride; she visited him regularly and went to see their lawyer more frequently. However, when their sons, Vincenzo, 24, and Francesco, 21, were picked up and charged with mafia association, her outward composure cracked. 'She was very unhappy after her sons' arrest,' recalls Napoli. 'She was beside herself. She had kept them away from any kind of mafia activity. I have been representing these people for twenty years. She trusted me. She used to come and see me every day, just to talk about her boys, talk to someone who could offer her some comfort, anything she could hold on to. She'd come here and have a good cry, just to get some moral support.'

Leaving the courtroom one day in January 1994, Minniti burst into tears and made an impromptu appeal to the TV cameras. 'They are just two children who've got nothing to do with their father's business. I brought them up by myself, I was responsible for their education, and I can assure you that they're just two innocent children. Besides, my son Francesco isn't well.'[4]

The spontaneous interview was a hit. Journalists described the boss's wife as dignified, elegant, a mother moved to tears by love of her children. 'She knew she might be able to evoke some sympathy, to influence public opinion in her favour,' says her lawyer.

Carmela Minniti's most important task in life was to guarantee her sons' respectability; to prepare them for the social leap for which their father worked and planned. Suddenly their stock fell; they were *déclassé* among criminals. After her attempt to appeal to public sympathies as a mother, Minniti became increasingly devout, and started to make regular calls on the archbishop of Catania. Rumours began to circulate that, influenced by the archbishop, she was planning to turn state's evidence, or trying to convince her husband to do so – anything to get her boys out of prison.

On 1 September 1995, Carmela Minniti's daughter Cosima answered the doorbell at their home in Catania to a man claiming to be a police officer. When she opened the door, three gunmen pushed past her and shot her mother dead.

The city waited tensely for a revenge attack from the bereaved husband, Nitto Santapaola, known as 'the hunter', the supreme boss of Catania. Nothing happened. Rumours buzzed around Catania that if Santapaola had not taken revenge, it must have been he who had his wife murdered to stop her from turning informer. Perhaps her distress at her sons' ruin was liable to make her act irresponsibly, maybe even betray the organisation.

Speculation was put to rest by a confession from an unlikely quarter. In September 1996, a year after the murder, the *pentito* Alberto Ferone, a tall skeletal figure, former hit man, admitted that he had killed Santapaola's wife in revenge for the murder of his own father and son.

If Nitto Santapaola's elder son was being groomed to take his father's place, his career is already over. But there may be some truth in his mother's assertion that the sickly younger son was brought up protected from mafia crime.

There is a theory that mafia families try to keep one child out of the business – as usual, there are pragmatic reasons behind it. In western Sicily, one son, usually the youngest, would be packed off, probably to England, to study, and grow up unknown to the police, without a criminal record. He could then take over unobserved when all his male relations were locked up.

Carla Cottone, a middle-class graduate, proprietor of a chemist's shop in Palermo, married Aldo Madonia, like her a pharmacy graduate, and the youngest son of Cosa Nostra Commission member Francesco 'Ciccio' Madonia. Don Ciccio had amassed a fortune trafficking in cocaine with Colombia; when he was arrested in 1993, police seized 250 bank accounts, 202 buildings, and 62 commercial companies.[5] Giuseppe, Aldo's older brother, was sentenced to life for the murder of the police captain Emanuele Basile; he was also one of the high-ranking members of Cosa Nostra to have direct contact with the mafia's 'tame' politician, Salvo Lima.[6]

Aldo Madonia was arrested in January 1993, accused of working for his family. In an unprecedented move, on 29 March, Carla Cottone appeared on the peak time Maurizio Costanzo chat show to proclaim her husband's innocence. 'He has done nothing. He is paying the price for that heavy name he has been saddled with . . . Aldo has never followed the same path as his brothers and his father, he's got nothing in common with them . . . I would have no hesitation in accusing my father-in-law and my brothers-in-law of committing crimes, but Aldo is innocent.'[7]

That a wife should come to the defence of her husband was no surprise. But for her to admit that the rest of the Madonia family had a criminal past was shocking. Her in-laws were not pleased. She had acknowledged what the mafia never publicly admits, that the family was a criminal entity. In July 1993 a car bomb exploded, later discovered to have been intended for the show's host, Maurizio Costanzo – either to kill him, or to warn him against eliciting such dangerous confessions on camera.

Carla Cottone's intervention failed: a collaborator incriminated Aldo Madonia as an initiated member of the mafia clan, and in December 1995 he was sentenced to six years and six months for mafia association.

The question of whether a mafia boss and his wife could

Pupetta Maresca (*Photo Sud*)

Rosetta Cutolo, sister of Camorra boss Raffaele (*Luciano Ferrara*)

(*Right*)
Immacolata Iacone, who
married Camorra boss
Raffaele Cutolo in prison
in 1983 (*Luciano Ferrara*)

(*Below*)
Santa Puglisi murdered
in the Catania cemetery
in 1996 (*Fabrizio Villa*)

Carmela Marzano, left, at the wedding of her daughter,
Marianna Giuliano to Michele Mazzarella in Naples in 1996 (*Luciano Ferrara*)

Diego Maradona with Erminia Giuliano (*Photo Sud*)

Luigi Giuliano with his wife Carmela at the wedding
of their daughter Gemma in 1990 (*Photo Sud*)

Ninetta Bagarella, wife of Corleone boss Totò Riina. Seen here in court with her daughter Maria Concetta Riina in 1996 (*Abbaleo/Olympia*)

(*Opposite page: above*) Vincenziana Marchese on the day of her wedding to Leoluca Bagarella in 1991. She later killed herself. (*Abbaleo/Olympia*)

(*Opposite page: below left*) Rita Atria who killed herself in 1992 after becoming an informer at the age of seventeen (*Shobha/Contrasto*)

(*Opposite page: below right*) Carmela Minniti, wife of Catania boss Nitto Santapaola. She was murdered in a revenge attack in 1995 (*Fabrizio Villa*)

Women carrying Rita Atria's coffin at her funeral in Partanna,
Sicily, July 1992 (*Shobha/Contrasto*)

bring up a child to be part of law-abiding society is about to be put to the European Court, when Camorra boss Raffaele Cutolo, serving several life sentences in solitary confinement, will make his request to have a child with his wife by artificial insemination.

The personal cult of Cutolo had grown to Messianic proportions by the early 1980s, and although he is not a good-looking man, with his pinched mouth and close-together eyes, he was undeniably charismatic. Immacolata Iacone, a young, dark-eyed woman of 20, with prominent cheekbones and an aquiline nose, was visiting her brother in prison when she caught sight of him. He was twenty-two years her senior, serving his second life sentence. On 1 May 1983, divided by thick security glass, they were married in Asinara maximum security prison.

You could say she was bred to it: her father and uncle were both murdered in a long-running Camorra feud, and her 20-year-old brother was gunned down in 1992. Her younger brother, the day he was let out of prison in 1996, beat his wife savagely about the head with a hammer in front of their small children, and left her to die.

Another version of the story says that Immacolata was offered to Cutolo by her brother. The tyrannical 'professor' announced that he wanted a wife, and Immacolata was brought in like a lamb to the slaughter. 'It was an arranged marriage,' says Amato Lamberti, president of the region of Campania. 'She had never met Raffaele Cutolo. Her family brought her to the prison. Cutolo had expressed his intention of finding a wife, and there were already good relations between the Iacone and Cutolo families. The Iacone family was chosen, and the relationship increased the family's importance.'[8]

The couple have occasionally managed to steal a passionate kiss in the courtroom, as he is led between the witness box and the cells, but they have never consummated their marriage. The virgin Immacolata has become a legendary figure, waiting quietly for her husband's release.

Seven years after their marriage, Cutolo's lawyer sent a

request to the Ministry of the Interior, asking permission for
Raffaele Cutolo and his wife to have a baby. Cutolo also wrote
a letter to Don Riboldi, a famous anti-mafia priest. 'My wife
has done nothing wrong. Why should she be denied every
woman's right?'

Cutolo's first and only son, Robertino, a good-looking boy
with a Greek profile, became one of his father's lieutenants in
the Nuova Camorra Organizzata. He was shot dead aged 25,
leaving a wife and two children. Robertino had been arrested
several times before his death, although his father always said he
was too stupid to commit crimes.

Since Cutolo is in solitary confinement and may only see his
visitors through a thick glass barrier, he initially suggested
impregnating his wife artificially, but six months later, after
reports that she would have none of it, he asked to become a
father 'naturally'.[9] The authorities were appalled at this potential propaganda offensive by the charismatic former boss, and
have turned down the request again and again. Cutolo's lawyer,
Paolo Trofino, plans to refer the matter to the European Court.

The notion of allowing the boss to produce a son in his own
image, and perhaps perpetuate the terrible lineage of an
organisation that ripped the heart out of Naples, is abhorrent to
some members of the judiciary, and they will fight it all the
way. 'I don't think we want to perpetuate this undesirable line,'
said an MP and member of the Commission on Penitential
Affairs. While a surprisingly large number of high-ranking
Camorra members have defected, Cutolo is one of the last
Camorra bosses not to become a collaborator. This obduracy
reinforces the perception that Cutolo still clings to mafia ideals,
and would therefore be unlikely to bring up his own child in
any other culture.

'On the one hand you can understand there is the human
longing for a child – and a man who has married a younger
wife who wants to give her the chance to have a baby . . .'
offers prosecutor Antonio Laudati. 'But the state has to try to
prevent the mythology of a notorious criminal spreading any
further.'

In spite of people's squeamishness about challenging the mother–child relationship, there seems little doubt that most mafia parents are bound to pass on their criminal culture to their children, and their children's children. One magistrate in Calabria has come to the conclusion, after fifteen years of practising law, that there is only one way to break the mafia. 'Sterilise them.'

8. Battle for the Children's Souls

East of Palermo, beneath a frowning brow of rock, lies Villabate, a narrow strip of green between the mountains and the built-up shore. Among the trees there is a riding school, where children trot in line around a sandy circuit. Every weekend Giuseppe Di Matteo used to ride his moped to the stable, where he would spend the day grooming and schooling his two horses. At 13, Giuseppe had a passion for horses. He would sometimes wear his riding hat proudly to school, and occasionally brought in rosettes from show-jumping competitions.

On 23 November 1993, Giuseppe was drying off his horse after an afternoon ride, when a car drew up at the stable. Three men in police jackets got out and called over to the boy: 'Come along, hop in the car, we're going to see your father.' Giuseppe's father, Santino Di Matteo, a mafioso turned informer, was being held in a secret location under police protection, and Giuseppe hadn't seen him for weeks. The boy's face lit up; he dropped the brush on the floor of the yard and ran over to the men: '*Sangue mio, sangue mio*' (My blood, my flesh and blood) he chanted, climbing into the back of the car. 'Let's go.'[1]

At some point in the journey, Giuseppe Di Matteo realised he was not going to see his father. The men held his arms and put a hood over his head. When the car stopped they took him out and steered him down some stairs into a darkened room. They wound rope round his wrists and ankles and tied them to the wall. And there they left him.

Santino Di Matteo, known as Mezzanasca, 'half-nose', because of his flat boxer's features, a member of the *mandamento* (district section) headed by mafia boss Giovanni Brusca, was arrested on 4 June 1993. Di Matteo had been one of Brusca's trusted hit squad, and the boss had spent months in hiding at his house. Together they had stood on the mountainside above the motorway outside Palermo, waiting for Judge Giovanni Falcone's motorcade to approach from the airport. One of them had pressed the detonator and turned the magistrate's cars and the motorway into a tangled mess of metal and concrete.

Nearly five months after his arrest, Di Matteo decided to collaborate. He was taken to a secret location, where magistrates heard his first statements. His wife, Francesca Castellese, was brought in, and he told her what he was planning to do. 'She wept,' says the lawyer, Luigi LiGotti, who specialises in defending collaborators. 'At first she said she understood his decision. Later she changed her mind. She is very bitter. She blames him for what happened.'[2]

Di Matteo's wife was told she would be offered protection, along with their sons, Giuseppe and his younger brother Nicola. There was a high risk of a revenge attack as the news broke that her husband had decided to talk. Brusca, who had eaten at their table and slept under their roof, knew where to find them. She was invited to leave her job with the local health service, and move into a flat somewhere in the north of Italy, in a town where nobody knew who she was, where even her family would not be able to find her.

Castellese refused to go. She took the children from their house in the country up to Altofonte, a small, inward-looking, mafia-dominated town in the mountains, and moved in with her mother and her brother, the former mayor. She continued to go to work every day. By moving into the bosom of her family, she publicly dissociated herself from her husband's decision.

It was not enough.

When Giuseppe did not come home at his usual time on that November afternoon, his mother rang the stable. The stable manager told her the boy had left at 4.45 on his moped. She rang the hospitals in the area, but there had been no casualties that fitted his description. At nine o'clock in the evening a note appeared on the door of her father-in-law's house. It read:

'We've got the boy. Tell your son to keep quiet.' It warned them not to involve the police.

The next day Giuseppe Di Matteo's mother dropped off her younger son Nicola at school and went to work as usual at the health centre. Neither she nor the boy said a word about Giuseppe's absence. Staff at the school were mystified. People knew the boys' father had become an informer: if Giuseppe had been taken away for his own protection, why not take his little brother too?

The headmistress of Altofonte's middle school, Irene Iannello, is a brisk woman with bright lipstick and chestnut hair, and a voice pitched constantly at assembly volume. Giuseppe Di Matteo's picture hangs on the wall behind her desk: he is clearing a jump on his bay horse, looking eagerly towards the next obstacle. He had brought the picture in and given it to her; it was to end up on the front page of every newspaper in the country.

She talks about him warmly: a lively child, capable, bright and irrepressible. She remembers. 'After Giuseppe had been absent for three days I called his mother. She told me he was ill and would be back at school as soon as he was better. But we soon realised that he wasn't at home either. Nicola, the younger brother, wasn't well, he kept complaining of stomach ache, and he was very pale. In the days that followed, I had to call his mother a number of times and ask her to come and get him. After about a fortnight I received a visit from the DIA [the Direzione Investigativa Antimafia, the special anti-mafia police unit]. They told me Giuseppe was missing, and that his mother was refusing to co-operate with their inquiries.

'A month after Giuseppe failed to come to school, I rang his mother again to tell her I was obliged to report that he was not attending. She told me not to worry, she would get the appropriate medical certificate to explain his absence.

'I have to admit we all thought she was acting very strangely – we knew Giuseppe wasn't at home – what was she going to do with a medical certificate? We began to think she was more mafioso than the rest of them. But you know she was just very frightened. She knew the people they were dealing with, and was probably just playing for time.'

School warden and sports master Nino Bruno was shocked by the mother's behaviour: 'She knew what was happening – you know, she was friends with these people. If she had only told someone about it, maybe we could have done something.' He had tears in his eyes. 'Maybe the boy would have been found.'

When news reached the collaborator Santino Di Matteo that his son had been kidnapped, he escaped from police custody and slipped down to San Giuseppe Iato, the small Sicilian town controlled by the Brusca family, in a desperate bid to get information on the boy's whereabouts. After two days he gave himself up to the police.

On 1 December, Santino Di Matteo's father found another note under his door, with just three words: 'Shut his mouth'. With it were two Polaroids of the young hostage holding a newspaper, dated 29 November. The kidnappers knew Giuseppe's grandfather adored him, and were convinced that the old man was the weak link, the one who might persuade his son to retract his confessions, making them unusable in court.

'I wanted my son to retract,' said the old man later. 'We all did, to save the boy.'[3] But Santino Di Matteo kept talking. A videotape arrived on his father's doorstep. The old man, weeping, watched images of the boy in squalid surroundings, pleading for his father to deny everything and set him free.

In February 1996 Giuseppe Monticciolo, another member of Brusca's group, joined the growing ranks of defectors, and the details of Giuseppe Di Matteo's fate were finally revealed. On 11 January 1996, Giovanni Brusca had learned from the TV news that he had been given a life sentence *in absentia* for the murder of industrialist Ignazio Salvo.[4] In a rage, Brusca gave the order for the boy to die.

The kidnappers made Giuseppe write a last letter to his grandfather. In a wobbly scrawl, he wrote: 'I can't stand it any more. I have tried to kill myself once already. Obviously none of you care about me.'

They turned the boy to face the wall. Monticciolo held his feet, while Enzo Brusca, Giovanni's younger brother, held his arms. The third man, Vincenzo Chiodo, took a short length of rope and hooked it round the boy's neck. Giuseppe, weeping and whining, offered no resistance. After two years tied up in darkened cells, his muscles were flaccid and wasted. 'I don't think he knew what was happening until the last minute,' said Chiodo later.

When the boy was dead, the men lifted the little corpse into a vat of acid. They burned his clothes and the mattress he had slept on. As Chiodo was about to put the rope on the fire, Enzo Brusca said, 'Why don't you keep it as a trophy?' and laughed. Chiodo dropped the rope into the flames.

In spite of their precautions, the kidnappers were jumpy, aware of how serious the effects of this crime would be if they were discovered. The mafia had always made propaganda mileage out of the 'rule' that they never harmed children, and this murder would provoke a major offensive against Cosa Nostra.

Shortly after the boy's death, police found the underground bunker where he had been kept. Vincenzo Chiodo, who owned the building, went on the run. Mafia associates called on his wife a few days later, with a message for him. They told him not to worry, they wouldn't abandon him, and handed over a bundle of money to see him through this difficult period in hiding. A few days later, his wife found a note for her husband under the door. It read: 'If you get arrested and you talk, we will drink the blood of your children.' The following day, Chiodo turned up at the DIA's Palermo headquarters saying he had information on Cosa Nostra if the state would protect his family.

After hearing the news of Giuseppe's death, his mother continued to work at the clinic every day. She made no public statement. Her younger son continued to go to school.

The school headmistress organised a public demonstration in

Altofonte, and 2,000 people walked though the narrow, twisting streets holding sheets daubed with anti-mafia slogans. Instead of closing their doors, the women of Altofonte stood at their doorways and watched the procession go by. But Giuseppe's mother wasn't there.

'I saw her at work at the clinic a few days later,' says the headmistress. 'She beckoned me in, and thanked me for organising the procession. She said she had no idea there would be such support from local people. I gave her a hug.' The bereaved mother, the mafia wife, object of the community's mistrust and sympathy, began to cry. The brisk, bright head teacher, pillar of the community, patted her shoulder and gave her a talking-to. 'I told her to forgive her husband, to support him. She looked at me. She said, "Oh?" I said he needed her support, it was his son too . . . I know it was very bold of me, but . . . Anyway she didn't answer.'

The two women stood in their awkward embrace. Between them lay the yawning gap that divides mafia society from the 'civilised' world.

Santino Di Matteo, by deciding to collaborate, in the eyes of the law-abiding Catholic community had cleansed himself of the moral tar that clings to his crimes, but from his wife's point of view he had acted dishonourably and put his whole family in jeopardy. When his wife refused police protection, the law-abiding world decided she had taken a risk with her sons' lives, and condemned her.

By a strange moral alchemy, the 'penitent' mafia boss became the victim. The bereaved mother, who made no outward show of grief, was viewed as unnatural, because she failed to share her pain with the many people grieving for the death of her son. She remained sealed within mafia culture. People saw her as part of the culture that allows these hideous crimes to happen.

While the boy's mother kept her silence, his father unleashed his agony from the witness box. After Giovanni Brusca's arrest, Santino Di Matteo, addressing him in court from a video-conference screen, burst out: 'If I catch you I'll kill you with my own hands. Why didn't you come and find me, so we could have seen who had to die, you or I?'[5]

The court was shocked by the outburst, but somehow relieved. People could empathise with this expression of grief. Giuseppe's mother's silence was both mystifying and frightening.

Francesca Castellese was brought up in Altofonte, a small town which has been controlled by the mafia since the Allies liberated Sicily from the Fascists at the end of the second world war. Her brother was mayor, and she grew up enjoying the privileges guaranteed by her family's powerful position. She married a man of honour; he was well known and respected in the community. They had money and status; her children would grow up with a head start in life.

If she had left home and gone into police protection when her husband defected, she would have turned her back on all this. It is possible that Francesca Castellese didn't believe the state could protect her children from a mafia attack, but it is more likely that she was not prepared to leave Cosa Nostra. The cultural pull of the organisation, which encompassed her whole family, was more powerful than the state.

'A lot of women feel their world collapsing around them, as the number of "penitent" mafiosi increases. This is because they are willing participants in mafia culture. Within this culture, "penitence" is considered a form of treachery against the mafia. It is a secret society, an anti-state organisation, whose existence must never be admitted, even in the face of irrefutable evidence. The penitent mafioso's treachery is an act of surrender to the state. In the eyes of those who embrace this code and this culture, the mafia is innocent.'[6]

There is a dual rationale behind a woman's outright condemnation of her man's decision to repent and confess: he has both threatened the organisation and put her children in danger.

The Camorra godmother, Pupetta Maresca, who shot her husband's killer at the age of 18, moved in with cocaine dealer Umberto Ammaturo after she got out of jail, and a couple of years later, they had twins. Ammaturo became a collaborator in

1984, several years after they split up, and now she has nothing but loathing for him.

Maresca's mafia pedigree is impeccable: she was born and raised in a respected family; her brothers controlled a stake in the contraband cigarette business, and she married a mafia boss at 17. She despises the man she now calls '*that* Ammaturo' for trading in his children's safety in return for a reduced prison sentence. 'Now that Ammaturo has decided to defect, they have taken away my children in case someone tries to harm them. I can't go and see them because I could be recognised, and someone might follow me . . . I'm so frightened I'm forced to stay away from them – my own children. A man who decides to collaborate negates his feelings. Otherwise I don't know how he could do it.

'I refuse to leave here. When that Ammaturo started to talk, I said, I no longer live with this man. Everyone knows it, the law knows it, the very stones in the street know I have nothing to do with him. I said: If they want to kill me, let them kill me, but I'm not going anywhere.'[7]

Leaving home, for mafia women, means more than a change of daily routine. Guido Lo Forte, deputy chief prosecutor in Palermo, explains: 'They have to leave their environment, they have to change their culture, and their way of thinking. While they were wives of men of honour, they could command as much respect as their husbands – which suited them very well. The moment their husbands repent, the wives find themselves marginalised from their communities, but also in mortal danger.'[8]

A woman brought up in a mafia family is cradled, protected and assisted by her family in all areas of her life. She uses their connections, their influence, and their power. To have this taken away from her is like a betrayal.

Collaborators who have described the initiation rite for new members of Cosa Nostra have made it clear that no one is allowed to leave the organisation alive. In 1991, the law offered an alternative. The families of mafiosi were confronted with the possibility of subscribing to an alternative system of power: the state. For the men who have lost their power within the organisation, who can no longer trust their closest allies, to disappear into a witness protection programme was their only means of survival. But in this other power structure, the one governed by the laws of state, the wife of a mafioso finds herself in a social void. Outside the organisation she is nobody.

Material considerations play a large part in the tug-of-war between the mafia and the civilised world. In the poorer areas of southern Italy, the mafia is the only means for a man to climb, socially and financially. The mafioso who sets himself up in illegal business in order to ensure a prosperous future for his children, and then throws it all away and turns informer, cannot expect the children to be overjoyed when they find their prospects drastically reduced.

Social status is even more important to the families of emigrant Sicilians, who cling to the protocol of the old country while scrabbling for a foothold in the New World. Frank Friel, an American organised crime investigator, came up against this phenomenon while he was working with a South Philadelphia mafioso, Mario Riccobene, who had decided to collaborate.

Riccobene had given statements to the police, but was anxious about his family's reaction. He wanted to be sure of their moral support before he testified in court against his former friends and partners in crime. His marriage had broken down, and it was his girlfriend, rather than his wife, who had gone with him into the protection programme, but he still needed his family's approval. Friel invited them to meet Riccobene in a police safe house in the New Jersey countryside.

'The daughter turned up in a fury. She was violently against her father's decision. She reckoned she would be stained with the stigma of having a rat in the family – she said she wouldn't be able to show her face at the beauty parlour. Her father was facing life, but she was more concerned about her image in the neighbourhood. She told him he could not expect the family's support if he "flipped". [The American word for becoming a state witness, to "flip", has connotations of madness; while the

Italian word, *pentirsi*, to repent, has connotations of religious conversion. Both descriptions are equally far from reality.]

'When I suggested to her that the alternative was to see her father behind bars for life, she replied that he had made his decision to live like that, and that was his business. But she wasn't going to let him ruin her life.'

Friel, a family man deeply attached to his own daughters, and whose hobby is photographing sharks, was shocked by Miss Riccobene's response. 'I separated them when it became clear to me that she was giving him a hard time.'[9]

By convincing people that the organisation is always right, and that its accusers are wrong, the mafia has created amoral monsters, parents and children who attack each other in defence of the organisation's warped values.

For the children of some mafia defectors, the betrayal is too shameful to bear. Alfredo Galli, a boss from Castellammare di Stabia in the Naples area, became a collaborator, and, living under police protection in the north of Italy, began drawing a map of Camorra families for the police.

News of Galli's defection leaked back to Naples. At the time, his daughter Monica was going out with the nephew of a Camorra boss from Secondigliano — one of the few clans left with any real power. Monica Galli, 23, may have been threatened by her boyfriend, or she may have felt genuinely aggrieved by her father's loss of honour. She may have been worried that her boyfriend would leave her if he knew she was the daughter of a traitor. In any case, she felt she had to prove that she was disgusted by her father's change of heart. She took a plane to Turin, and went to visit him in the anonymous flat where he was being held for his protection. Close family members were the only visitors considered safe. On her way to the flat Monica bought a knife, and as her father opened the door to greet her, she stabbed him in the chest.[10]

Enrico Incognito was not every mother's ideal boy: self-dramatising, flamboyant, with a coke habit and a dose of paranoia, he was the charismatic leader of a criminal group with mafia links in Catania. He was scarcely on speaking terms with his mother, who saw him no more than once a month, although they lived just a couple of streets apart. In 1994, aged 30, he was separated from his wife and lived in a top-floor flat in an apartment block in Bronte, a suburb of Catania on the slopes of Mount Etna.[11]

Incognito's group had links with the top mafia family in Catania, the Santapaola clan. He was on good terms with a number of politicians, and had his fingers in several mud pies – extortion, building contracts, drug trafficking and so on. He had already made a spectacle of himself when he was placed under special police surveillance and, in protest, set fire to himself inside the courtroom. But in spite of his apparent disdain for Italian justice, Incognito had begun to consider collaborating with investigators, and had made contact with a marshal in the carabinieri to discuss terms.

But despite his name, Incognito had not quite come to terms with the witness protection programme, which would make him disappear and be reborn somewhere far away, as an invisible grey man. Before he started his collaboration, he wanted to make his mark: he decided to make a video recording of himself recounting his story.

He got a friend to set up two cameras in his flat, and for days the friend filmed him as he paced the room in bordeaux silk pyjamas, talking about his connections in the Catania underworld. The footage, which ended up in the hands of the police, recorded the events of the last day of Incognito's life.

After the filming had been going on for a couple of days, his family, all of them inhabitants of the same Catania underworld, became alarmed about the eccentric Enrico's intentions. He had a massive falling out with his brother, which he also recounted to camera, for good measure. On 24 March 1994, his mother went to visit him. He let her in, but to show her he wouldn't be swayed, he didn't interrupt the flow of his recording, and carried defiantly on. She sat quietly in his L-shaped room watching, occasionally commenting as he strutted about.

The doorbell rang and he answered the intercom. It was his

brother. 'You can't come up!' Enrico bawled into the speaker. 'I don't want to see you!' His father, who was downstairs as well, tried to reason with him, but he refused to let them in and slammed down the handset. His mother tried to calm him down.

A few minutes later the doorbell rang again, this time outside the flat, and Incognito, still declaiming, went to answer. He looked through the spy-hole: it was his neighbour. He opened the door. The neighbour darted to one side. Behind him was Enrico's brother holding a gun. He shot twice, point blank. Enrico fell. The cameras rolled.

Just as the growing number of *pentiti* seemed to be making serious headway in the battle against Cosa Nostra, an alarming number of women reacted violently against their husbands' choice – not with silence, like Santino Di Matteo's wife, but with dramatic, public declarations. Most of them forced their children to take sides against the mafia defector.

'The wife of a man of honour is bound to be immersed in mafia culture,' says prosecutor Guido Lo Forte. 'So is his daughter, so is his mother. When he decides to collaborate, the women are thrown into crisis. They find themselves faced with a choice. Either they follow the man, which means they must break with their culture, their mentality, or they stay where they are, in which case they must publicly dissociate themselves from the defector. They must openly condemn him as a liar, a traitor, an *infame*. They must do that if they are going to carry on living in their neighbourhood.'[12]

There is no translation for the word *infame*: it describes a moral void, beyond the ultimate sanction protecting the law of silence: 'A man who talks is a traitor, he is unworthy, *infame*, dishonoured, he is utterly unworthy of respect.'[13]

At the headquarters of the special unit for the protection of collaborators, Antonio Manganelli points out the conflicts that arise when a woman has to choose whether to support her penitent husband. 'Marriages take place between people profoundly immersed in that environment: a mafia wife is not just a wife, but also the daughter of a mafioso. If she goes with her collaborator husband, she has to betray her family. Very often, behind a woman who rejects her husband is a mafioso father.'

One woman who was crushed by just such a conflict was Vincenzina Marchese. A woman with delicate features and high cheekbones, she married the mafia boss Leoluca Bagarella on his release from prison in April 1991, after an engagement of fifteen years. Her credentials were immaculate: her father was Vincenzo Marchese, a powerful Palermo boss, and her brother, Pino, was Corleone boss Totò Riina's godson. Shortly after Vincenzina and Leoluca Bagarella got married, they disappeared into hiding.

In August 1992, Pino Marchese, once a faithful soldier, was double-crossed by Totò Riina (Riina had ordered him to commit a murder and simultaneously destroyed his alibi). Marchese, realising Riina would not protect him, became an informer, and gave evidence against his former protector and mentor. The shame of having a traitor in the family struck deep into the Marchese clan.

Leoluca Bagarella was finally arrested at home in June 1995. There was no sign of his wife, just a bunch of flowers in front of her picture on the mantelpiece, a sign of mourning. He was wearing a locket with her picture – another sign of mourning. People muttered that Bagarella had killed his wife, unable to stand the shame of being married to the sister of an *infame*, a traitor.

By the time he was arrested, a number of Bagarella's former allies, including the Di Filippo brothers, had begun to collaborate, and in the months that followed, investigators and journalists pieced together the events leading to Vincenzina's death. One said she had hanged herself in shame after her brother turned informer. Another said she was clinically depressed, after a series of miscarriages. A note found in the couple's home said: 'Forgive me, Luca, it's all my fault.'[14]

Bagarella was arrested with the help of his former soldiers, Emanuele Di Filippo and his brother Pasquale. Emanuele had been arrested in February 1994 and had become a collaborator shortly afterwards. Pasquale was arrested on 21 June the same year, and, encouraged by his brother, immediately decided to talk.

The Italian news agency ANSA had only just put out on the wires that two more mafiosi had defected – not even their names had been made public – when the telephone rang at the agency's Rome bureau. It was Giusy Spadaro, wife of Pasquale Di Filippo. She was with her sister-in-law Angela Marino, Emanuele Di Filippo's wife. The two women wanted to make a statement. 'Men from the DIA came to see us. They offered us protection, but we refused. Write that down. We've done nothing wrong, we are good people, we are not *"pentiti"* because we haven't done anything. We have nothing to repent . . .'[15]

The women's message was directed more towards the arrested boss Leoluca Bagarella, to protect themselves from his vendetta against their treacherous husbands, than towards civil society. In fact, they don't seem to have a clue about how civil society views legality. These women claim they have done nothing wrong, but at the same time they publicly align themselves with the mafia.

They called a press conference in their house near piazza Magione, a derelict part of Palermo still bombed out after the Allied air raids of 1943 where, until recently, inhabitants had to collect drinking water from tanks in the square. Their language was redolent of mafia culture: dishonour, cried Giusy Spadaro, is worse than death. 'They'd be better dead, it would be better if our husbands had been killed. When I heard the police at the door, I thought: They've come to tell me my husband's been shot. But no, it was worse than that. This way I am dishonoured. It would have been better if he was dead.'[16]

To prove that death was preferable to their present plight, the turncoat's sister Agata swallowed a bottle of tranquillisers.

She was whisked off to hospital and whisked home again an hour later, pale and shaky.

'Balls,' commented the Sicilian writer and politician Claudio Fava, son of the journalist murdered by the mafia. 'Playacting. They're just acting out the part that has traditionally been assigned to them. What these women are expressing is not just scorn for their husbands: it's more like a piece of theatre. They are making this dramatic flight back into the only environment they know, the only hierarchy they know: the mafia.'[17]

The dramatic spectacle of women weeping, ululating and beating their chests is a sight familiar from films such as Francesco Rosi's *Salvatore Giuliano*, in which the women in black veils take to the streets, howling and clutching each other, to protest against the police for arresting their men. It is part of a pattern of uncivil disobedience, to demonstrate that the working-class population does not feel represented by the state. It is also a bid for sympathy: in a society which regards the mother's relationship with her son as sacred, a woman's public gesture has great power.

Claudio Fava sees the Di Filippo women's gesture as a sign of deliberate recidivism, rejecting all possibility of progress, or redemption. To him, born and raised in Catania, eastern Sicily, their message is clear: We will never change.

The mafia women who refute their husbands' decision to defect are quick to haul the children over to their side: Pasquale Di Filippo's wife Giusy Spadaro, whose father Tommaso, boss of the Palermo clan of La Kalsa, is currently serving thirty years for heroin trafficking, declared that she had filed for a legal separation from her husband. 'I have told the children: You no longer have a father, you must reject him, forget all about him.'

She may be trying to save herself, and her children, from revenge attacks by the mafia. There have been a number of incidents in which the children of defectors have been beaten up at school, their families have had their car tyres slashed, they have been threatened, bullied and shunned. This sort of public dissociation may be intended as an appeal to be left in peace, to stop local bullies drumming the women out of their homes.

But there is more than fear at work; there is also loyalty. Many women brought up in the mafia environment believe that the mafia boss is there to help them. Without him they would have no one to protect them against a hostile society. And when their husbands betray the mafia and turn informer, the women fight for the children's souls.

Fifty years after Cosa Nostra took control of Sicily in earnest, the state is about to join the battle.

While Sicily was still reeling from the news of Giuseppe Di Matteo's appalling fate, a judge in the juvenile courts, Nino Scarpulla, told journalists that there was only thing to do if the wife of a *pentito* refused to go into the protection programme with her children: take the children into care. 'We must remove them; not only for their safety but to stop them growing up in the mafia environment.'[18]

Scarpulla believes that the children have no choice about whether to join or to live by the rules of Cosa Nostra if they stay within a mafia family. He proposes a moral rescue, with dawn raids, like those used to remove children from parents suspected of sexual abuse, to take the children into care.

This proposal, which naturally caused an outcry in the family-oriented south, was followed by a suggested change in the law, from the department responsible for the protection of mafia defectors. The problem needed urgent attention: by the spring of 1996 there were already 955 children under protection of 10 years of age or under, and a further 728 between 11 and 18.

'The parents of a six-year-old girl, relatives of a collaborator, refused to go into protection because they didn't know how to explain the changes, including a new surname, to their child – but also because they wanted to hold on to the traditions and culture of their family ... It's understandable that people should have such scruples, but it's difficult to see how we can reconcile them with the need to protect people who are in immediate danger of revenge attacks.

'A situation which commonly occurs is that the parents separate when the collaborator's spouse refuses to go into the

protection programme, and carries on living at home . . . The
question is whether the Protection Service will be authorised to
make autonomous decisions, and impose its decisions on the
parents.'[19]

This discussion document suggested taking the children to a
place where they would be protected not only from material
harm, but also from a dangerous moral environment. To the
majority of the Sicilian public, it was a solution only slightly less
offensive than kidnapping.

The children are sometimes caught in an unseemly tug-of-
war between the parents: they become pawns in the battle
between the two worlds – the 'moral' and the mafioso.

In 1993, the testimony of Claudio Severino Samperi caused
major damage to the Catania clan of Cosa Nostra, when he
revealed Nitto Santapaola's links with politicians.

Samperi was a rich man, he had made a fortune out of illegal
gambling dens, but, according to his lawyer, Enzo Guarnera, he
was becoming increasingly disillusioned with the pointless
brutality of Cosa Nostra. As a test of his loyalty, he was told to
kill his own brother, a man of honour who had fallen from
grace, apparently because he had betrayed his wife with a series
of mistresses. Samperi was also instructed to kill his sister, whose
promiscuous behaviour, he was told, was unacceptable. He
couldn't refuse, but tried to find a way out, and set himself up
to get arrested. He managed to get picked up in a raid on one
of his gambling dens, early in 1990, and immediately offered to
collaborate.

When Samperi began to talk, his own turbulent love life
came to light. The deputy chief prosecutor in Catania, Nicolo
Marino, describes a scene worthy of Feydeau. 'Samperi decides
to collaborate . . . we have to inform his family. His wife
arrives, and then another woman turns up – his mistress. We
have to find a place for Samperi to stay, to get him sorted out as
quickly as possible. His wife has the two children with her. We
find a little flat with two rooms. He says fine, we'll all go there.
So we, moral beings that we are, have to authorise this highly
unorthodox arrangement, with the wife and the lover in the

same flat. At one point the head of the flying squad asks Samperi, "But just a minute, how did your wife take this?"

'He replied, "Sir, my wife is only human." '[20]

After a few days of this uncomfortable situation, with the two women living nose to nose and Samperi, one imagines, sleeping on the sofa, the police organised separate apartments, and Samperi went to live with his mistress. A few days later, his wife picked the children up from school and disappeared.

Being only human, Samperi's wife, Maria Iannone, wanted revenge for this public humiliation. She took the children back to Catania, back to the mafiosi who had been betrayed by her husband, threw herself on the mercy of her husband's former allies, and went underground in his old neighbourhood. To get back at her husband, she was prepared to put the children's lives at risk. 'Knowing that Samperi would be worried in case the children became the target of a revenge attack,' says his lawyer, 'she hoped to lure him into mafia territory.' At which point Samperi would have become the target. Samperi, for his part, recognised that his wife's actions could be exploited by the Santapaola clan, who had already razed his luxurious villa to the ground, and who were now toying with the lives of his children.

Iannone's plan came out all wrong. Two or three months after her disappearance, the police raided the hideout of another mafioso, Salvatore Pappalardo, who happens to be Samperi's cousin. When they burst into his house, they found Maria Iannone with him.

She is now on trial for aiding and abetting Salvatore Pappalardo. Her ex-husband, Claudio Severino Samperi, a former mafia member, has confessed his part in mafia crimes including extortion and running illegal gambling dens, and 'repented'. Now morally cleansed, he has been granted custody of the children.

9. The Drug Trade: Women's Work

A Naples policeman reporting for guard duty at a hospital near Poggioreale prison in 1989, found a most unusual set-up. His charge was Raffaele Stolder, a camorrista charged with drug trafficking and murder, who had been moved from the prison to a private hospital room because he had kidney trouble. Although the patient was supposed to be in isolation, under 24-hour guard, the door was wide open, and police withdrew discreetly to another room as visitors came and went. Stolder's wife, Patrizia Ferriero, sometimes stayed for days; she even had the key to another room where the couple could spend the night together. 'We were constantly, constantly being told that Stolder was extremely dangerous, and that we should take extreme care,' the policeman, Rocco Santoro, was to testify much later. 'We paid no attention.'[1]

Stolder's police guards were rewarded for their enlightened attitude in cocaine, which the camorrista had brought in specially. 'Everyone seemed perfectly at ease with the situation,' said Santoro. 'I didn't feel it was my place to interfere.'

In the evenings Stolder would offer a few of his associates supper, which arrived in aluminium containers from a top restaurant. One of these associates would bring in the accounts book and, according to Santoro, the police would find something urgent to do in their adjoining room while the camorristi went through the list of deals made and payments owed. 'The police took turns with the carabinieri, two weeks on, two weeks off,' said Santoro. 'The carabinieri were incorruptible, a setback which constantly irked Stolder.' Any police who would not play ball were swiftly transferred.

After Stolder had been in residence at the hospital for two years, magistrates insisted on an examination to see whether his kidney condition was really serious enough to keep him out of prison. His wife later admitted that it was she, with the help of another of her tame police guards, Nicodemo Boccia, who successfully deceived the doctors. She procured a bag of blood from another kidney patient in dialysis, attached it to her husband's back, and connected it to the dialysis machine by a tube. When a doctor tested the blood apparently coming from Stolder, he found it contaminated. Stolder remained in his five star hospital bed.

'She's very clever, a very smart woman. Cleverer than he is, actually,' says Patrizia Ferriero's former lawyer, Saverio Senese. He describes how she not only took care of her husband's custody arrangements, she also prepared his defence – once, notably, on a charge of armed robbery in a jeweller's. After her husband was arrested, Ferriero dressed up in full mourning and went to the same jeweller's. She produced a photograph of her husband, and ordered a commemorative gold medallion engraved with his image. The jeweller, without mentioning the man's resemblance to any armed robbers, duly produced this work of art. Later, when the jeweller stood up in court and identified Raffaele Stolder as the armed robber that had burst into his shop, Ferriero pounced, brandishing her medallion: 'You never said you recognised him when I brought you his photograph! How can you say you recognise him when you have just engraved his picture on a medallion for a dead man?'

Stolder escaped from the hospital in 1989, shortly after his bogus blood test, and went into hiding. He had to disappear from Naples for a while, so he entrusted his business affairs to his wife. According to judge Giuseppe Narducci, deputy chief prosecutor in the Naples Anti-mafia Department, who led the investigation into the Stolder clan, Patrizia Ferriero was her husband's equal. His men had no problem accepting her leadership in his absence. Stolder imported large quantities of cocaine from South America, via Holland and Belgium. His wife travelled to the Netherlands on more than one occasion to contact international traffickers, and took charge of distribution. She set up meetings with Stolder's business partners, the powerful Contini clan, and divided the merchandise with their representatives – an extremely delicate task, given the volatile relations between families and the large quantities of cocaine involved.

'There are lots of women involved in the drug trade, but none of them has had a prominent, directing role like la Ferriero,' observes Narducci. 'It's a tricky and complex process: obtaining the drug – and importing weapons, because drugs and arms always come through the same channels – negotiating with the other clans. She also had to buy friends among the judiciary and the police force, who would protect her husband and block any investigations into the Stolder clan. You need someone very intelligent to do it, who has no previous convictions, and who doesn't correspond to the stereotype of the streetwise Camorra criminal. A woman, particularly a woman like Patrizia Ferriero – who is much more intelligent than her husband – fits the bill.'

Ferriero and her three children enjoyed a large disposable income, but her reputation in the neighbourhood was such that they seldom had to pay for anything. During this time her husband underwent plastic surgery to alter his features so that he could return to Naples undetected, but she continued to be, as Narducci puts it, 'the brains of the organisation'.

In the winter of 1990, Ferriero bought an apartment in via Niutta, in Stolder's Naples neighbourhood, close to the old courthouse. According to the testimony of former policeman Rocco Santoro, she supervised the construction of an under-ground bunker, with reinforced steel doors and a garage operated by remote control, passageways leading into the flat and down into the sewers. Cars would come in from the Netherlands with bags of cocaine stuffed between the door panels, which would be dismantled inside the garage. The drug would then be weighed, and packed in cellophane and polystyrene to keep out the damp. A safe under the apartment floor was used for storing drugs and arms. Ferriero had sole charge of the keys and the remote control – no one could get access to the bunker without her permission.

Before long, the policeman Santoro had developed a serious

coke habit, left the force and offered his services to Patrizia
Ferriero. 'She met me a few times and gave me little tasks to do
before she decided I was trustworthy,' he later testified. He
became her driver and bodyguard. Once they travelled to
Rome together to find a lawyer. One of Santoro's tasks was to
make sure the police in the area were paid off: Ferriero had
made contact with a number of corruptible officers, and every
month she gave him a wad of money and a list of names.

When police swooped on Stolder and his police mercenaries
in November 1991, they also raided the apartment in via
Niutta, where they found five kilos of pure cocaine, several
guns, and the underground passages which had been used as
escape routes after armed robberies. They found notebooks
containing the clan's accounts: income from robberies and drug
deals to be divided between associates, payments owed to the
families of clan members in prison; drug payments owing. The
figures relating to drugs were in Patrizia Ferriero's handwriting.[2] They also found her underwear in the apartment. She said
she met her husband there in secret while he was on the run,
but relations between Ferriero and her husband have not been
good, investigators say, since then. The couple have spent too
much time apart. 'One could understand,' says one investigator,
politely, 'that there might have been developments in the
meantime.'

It was at an extraordinary meeting in the splendid art deco
Grand Hotel des Palmes in Palermo in 1957, that the New
York bosses established a protocol for trafficking in heroin with
the Sicilian Commission. From then on, the equilibrium of
Cosa Nostra was determined by which family dominated the
drug trade. The old-style bosses who disapproved of heroin,
like the Corleone capo Michele Navarra, were soon blasted out
of the way by younger, more ambitious mafiosi like Luciano
Leggio.

The drug trade altered the scope of the organisation, as Cosa

Nostra moved into business in order to launder billions of narco-dollars. If mafia business had previously been limited to 'made' members, the drug trade opened the mafia's doors to unconnected people, foreigners – even women.

The Sicilian clans joined forces with the Zaza and Nuvoletta Camorra families in the 1970s, and created an unstoppable partnership. The Camorra clans established strong links with South American cartels to import cocaine; at one point, they were shipping a ton a week out of Colombia.[3] This sudden access to cocaine changed the Naples mafia: its members became absurdly rich and ostentatious, while cocaine abuse crept through the younger generations of Camorra families. New clans appeared out of nowhere, or sprouted from the severed branches of warring families.

The sex life of Neapolitans is famously agitated, particularly amongst camorristi, and most of the Camorra drug dealers seem to involve their mistresses in the trade sooner or later. Maria Cristina Pinto was a young Neapolitan woman, who wore a gun and a hard face. She had a weakness for gangsters, and she was just 19 when she hooked up with an ex-con and had a baby girl. In 1989, at the age of 22, she became the mistress of Mario Perrella, a camorrista from a criminal dynasty in Fuorigrotta, on the edge of the city. He was married with a family, but she was in love with the idea of herself as a gangster's moll. When the clan split, she reinvented herself as his personal bodyguard. As the two rival groups competed for the cocaine coming in from South America (both groups supplied, in true Camorra fashion, by the same person – Perrella's brother), hostilities often flared into gun-fights, and Pinto was always on the front line. According to investigating magistrate Giuseppe Narducci, she also supplied arms to the group, buying them under the counter from dealers in the area, in particular from a coke-addict entrepreneur who would exchange guns for powder.

As the war between groups escalated, Pinto's notoriety grew; she rejoiced in the name of the 'signora killer' or sometimes 'Nikita'.[4] Police reports state that she and her lover were driving through Naples when they were ambushed. Shots were fired at him; she opened the car door, gun in hand, and returned fire. Another time, apparently on Perrella's orders, she shot and wounded a dealer from the rival group. Pinto was proud of her position in the group; her prominent features enhanced her aggressive manner; being the boss's mistress, she was more than a hit woman – she was his lieutenant, his bodyguard.

Pinto's charge sheet included possessing arms, drug dealing, conspiracy and attempted murder. When a Naples carabiniere went to arrest her in December 1991, he forced the door of the apartment, to be faced with the barrel of Cristina Pinto's Colt .38.[5]

A number of women lured by tanned men and shiny objects threw themselves into the nets of the drug trade in the boom years of the seventies; they travelled to Rome, Milan, Amsterdam and New York. One of these women was Esmerelda Ferrara, a 23-year-old from the slums of Palermo, whose young man, Filippo Ragusa, gave her, as one of the papers put it, 'a baby and a lot of trouble'.[6] She was a singer with moderate success; he promised to turn her into an international star. He took her to the States; she made an album (*The Two of Us on the Grass*) and went on tour. He, the admiring boyfriend, her manager, arranged concerts in America and shipped her LPs from Sicily to the USA – which was when customs discovered 40 kilos of heroin stashed between the record sleeves. Judges later decided Esmerelda had been an unwitting victim, and she was acquitted.

The maxi-trial of 1985 turned up just four women among over 400 defendants; all of them on drugs-related charges. Women's usefulness in the drug trade lay partly in their invisibility. Until the eighties they seemed beyond suspicion, and there were rarely female customs officers on hand to search suspects. This invaluable prejudice was discovered in 1986 by a group of heroin dealers, who hit on the small unprosperous town of Torretta in the backwaters of western Sicily, and targeted housewives to be their couriers. They offered the women £12,500 to fly from Palermo to New York wearing a corset stuffed with heroin. In New York they would be met by a minder, who would take them to a hotel and show them the city, show them – the younger ones anyway – a good time. A few days later they would fly back to Italy with the money.

The women who accepted the job were not after a millionaire's lifestyle: they were offered the equivalent of a lottery win. In most cases, it was not greed that motivated them, just a chance to change – however briefly – the dreary monotony of poverty. They paid their debts, or redid their kitchens – marble floors, new units, all matching – and it was gone. They were back where they started, accumulating debts in a backwater in Sicily.

Vincenza Calì, mother of eight children, accepted the courier job more than once. On her second, possibly her third, journey, she went to the airport with her husband, wearing a corset stuffed with two and a half kilos of heroin. She had relatives in the US, whom she pretended she was going to visit. But investigators noticed that a trail of women from Torretta seemed to have suddenly felt the need to visit long-lost émigré cousins in New York. They monitored Vincenza Calì's telephone, and heard one of the children saying excitedly, 'Mamma's going to America and she's going to bring back dollars!'

Calì was stopped at the airport on 24 May 1986, just as she was checking in. A customs officer frisked her and instantly found the packets of heroin stitched into her underclothes. She was arrested and charged with drug smuggling. Her husband was arrested on his way out of the airport.

It was left to their eldest daughter, Piera Mattiolo, aged 26, to take responsibility for the family. I met her in her lawyer's chambers in Palermo; she had brought along her little niece, who played with the silver ornaments on the coffee table and then happily destroyed her aunt's make-up bag. Piera is tall and beautiful, with long black hair and dark eyes, quick to laugh in spite of her harsh experience.

She remembered the sentence being read. 'It was February 1988, and bitterly cold. The trial had gone on every day for a month. It was horrible weather. We had been waiting hours for the judges to come back with the sentence, and none of us had eaten anything all day. There was a terrible atmosphere in the court. When the judges came back, it went dark, I remember it. The sky went black and the room was in darkness.' Vincenza Calì was sentenced to ten years; her husband to thirteen.

'We couldn't believe the sentence. Everyone cried; even my father cried in the dock. It makes me sick to think about it.'[7]

For a time her mother was under house arrest, which was torture for her, since her children came and went as they pleased. They were running wild and getting into trouble, and there was nothing she could do about it. 'I'd ask where they were going, and they'd just say "Out" and laugh in my face.'[8] After eight months, she was sent back to prison and Piera found herself in charge of seven younger brothers and sisters. 'All the responsibility fell on my shoulders. I'm never off the case – I'm a mother to them all. Even the married ones still need looking after.'

As soon as the mother was in prison, the children fell apart: one is in prison for pushing drugs; two of the teenagers left home with their sweethearts, and brought disgrace on the family. Relatives were unpleasant – at first the children were billeted with aunts and uncles, but they all came home as soon as they could, after suffering hours of moralistic lectures.

Piera does not blame her mother. 'We were in real financial trouble before my mother went to America. She did it for us, to give us a chance to study, give us a better life.'

The motivation for most women couriers is the same throughout southern Italy: most of them do it not to be rich, but to survive. The mafia, with its monopoly of drug trafficking, offers a source of income for a vast number of people.

'Unemployment is the major problem of this city,' says Amato Lamberti, president of the region of Campania. 'Naples has a population of just over a million. The official unemployment figure is 300,000, but most of these are involved in some form of illegal activity. The Camorra provides people with illegal sources of income.'[9]

In the poorer quarters of Naples, people still live in the old windowless *bassi fondi*, the basements, half buried beneath the narrow bustling streets, where daylight scarcely reaches. The wealthier Neapolitans used to live at the top of these houses, where they could enjoy the air and the view, but in the basement flats a strip of neon and the light from the open fridge are the only things that illuminate the children's first communion pictures on the walls. In these crowded neighbourhoods, couples have as many as ten children in order to increase the presence, and the economic potential, of the family. Parents deal drugs; their children sell contraband cigarettes, bootleg video cassettes and soft drugs.

In an unprecedented move, a group of women dubbed the *Mamme Coraggio*, 'Mothers Courage', staged a protest in Naples. In a public demonstration, they announced that their children were heroin addicts, that the drug trade was poisoning the city; they needed help. It was a grassroots protest – the women were dealers, prostitutes, petty criminals – and they were frightened for their children.

The trigger for the Mother Courage demonstrations was when kids began to deal in their own homes. In order to stop them, some of the mothers turned their sons in to the police – an idea profoundly shocking in the south, where families tend to turn inwards to smother their problems. It looked like a revolutionary moment for Naples, but it was more a protest against poverty than a rejection of the drug trade.

'The *Mamme Coraggio* were not an anti-Camorra movement,' explains Salvatore Esposito, who runs a drug rehab project in the Naples area. 'They were demanding help for their addict children, but what they wanted were public services: rehab centres, somewhere the children could be taken, removed from their families. It didn't mean that anything changed in the inner city neighbourhoods.'[10]

In 1996, one of the mothers, Maria d'Elia, was arrested for dealing drugs in Naples and placed under house arrest. She was not the first of those historic protesters to get picked up for pushing, driven by poverty or addiction.

The problem is not confined to Naples. Sicilian mafia researcher Anna Puglisi reports that mothers in the poorer parts of Palermo have been known to send their children to school with packets of drugs to sell. 'The mothers of these children, when the teachers asked them about the drugs, said it was the only way they could make enough money to get by.'[11]

One Palermo matriarch set up a family business dealing heroin on a large scale, employing three generations – down to the children who ran around the streets looking for buyers. Angela Russo was born in 1908, the daughter of a Palermo mafioso, a man of respect whom she admired and adored. Every son his wife bore him sickened and died, and Angela, the oldest of five girls, was the nearest thing he had to an heir. He took her hunting, and she learned to shoot at his side. She grew up commanding, as she herself says, respect and authority (later, when she was accused of being a courier, she spurned the idea. Impossible, she said, *she* was the boss: 'I have always given the orders, why would I start running errands for others?')[12]

During the winter months of 1981, police conducted an assiduous surveillance of several families who formed a network distributing heroin and cocaine across Italy. One of these was the Coniglio family, headed by Salvino Coniglio, who directed operations, drove a BMW and was constantly flying to Milan and Rome. His mother was Angela Russo, now 74. They lived in the centre of Palermo, four generations from great-grand-mother Angela down. The house was the venue for meetings and appointments; there were phone calls day and night, with people leaving messages in code. The matriarch guaranteed her son, raised capital to buy the drugs, arranged deliveries.

If Salvino fitted the drug dealer stereotype, his mother and the other women in the household were above suspicion – with no previous convictions, they came and went as they pleased. The old lady often served as the courier, travelling by

train to the mainland in her loud black and white checked coat
with her battered suitcase – until investigators heard Salvino say
on the telephone: 'I'm sending you my mother. Look after her,
she's elderly – put her up in a nice hotel. She'll be wearing a
black and white checked coat.'

'Sure enough,' says the carabiniere who arrested her,
laughing until he nearly chokes on his cigar, 'we picked her up
in that terrible checked coat, carrying a kilo of heroin from
Palermo to Salerno.' Eight members of the family were
arrested, including four women from three different generations. Grandma Heroin, as she became known during the trial,
charged with trafficking in class A drugs, played the ignorant
housewife. 'When we arrested her,' the carabiniere guffaws
behind his huge desk, 'she said: "Cocaine, what's that? a
detergent?"'

'A detergent!'

Before the judge, Grandma Heroin exhibited sterling mafia
characteristics. She refused to answer magistrates' questions;
when her son Salvino, who appeared to be the brains, however
scattered, of the family business, became a collaborator, she
called him *infame*. 'Traitor, madman,' she screeched across the
courtroom: 'Judas, good-for-nothing. Crazy, he's crazy. Your
honour, he was struck down with meningitis at four years old,
and the doctor warned me he would always be sick in the
head.'[13] When Salvino lost control, his mother threatened to
kill him. In a typically mafioso formula, she invoked her right
to do so: 'I made you and I can destroy you.'[14]

The 'Ndrangheta, the Calabrian mafia, has increased its drug
trafficking in the last decade, expanding its operations across the
world in order to fund its territorial wars back home. In the
early stages of a historic trial of 150 Calabrian drug traffickers,
which is still in progress, a number of women have been
accused of working at the nerve centre of operations.

In July 1992, police arrested a Calabrian drug trafficker,

Emilio Di Giovine, in Portugal. He was already well known to Italian and Spanish police after a series of dramatic prison escapes, and his narcotics operation spanned Europe from Morocco to England, and across the Atlantic from Colombia to Milan. His English ex-wife Patricia Reilly and their daughter Marisa were arrested in the UK after an international police operation. Bank records at Nat West and Coutts showed that Marisa Di Giovine had deposited amounts of up to £900,000 a time; her mother was acquitted, but she was convicted of money laundering.

But it was not until the following year that the full story emerged of a massive network of drug dealers, led by Emilio's mother, 62-year-old Maria Serraino, which had been supplying funds and arms to her uncles in the 'Ndrangheta for over a decade. Emilio's sister, Santa Margherita Di Giovine, known as Rita, was arrested in Verona on 31 March 1993 at the age of 36, in possession of a thousand tablets of Ecstasy. Almost immediately, she turned state's evidence. Over the following months, she testified repeatedly as a prosecution witness against leading members of the Serraino clan, as well as her mother, her brothers, and her ex-husband.

'It was very frightening for her,' says prosecutor Maurizio Romanelli, who questioned her at the Milan courthouse. 'She only managed to go out there and talk by a huge effort of will. Her whole family was there, and there was real tension in the courtroom. She was giving evidence on a video conference, but she was so anxious, it actually made her ill. The Serraino family had announced they were looking for her to kill her.'[15]

In spite of her nerves, on 9 May 1996, the witness took the stand. She began by telling how, in 1963, her mother had packed up her eight children, left her family in Reggio Calabria and moved to Milan. When Rita was 12, her parents took her out of school. 'They said it was better if I stayed at home and worked. They said that as I was a girl there was no point in me going to school anyway. They were importing contraband cigarettes at that time, and me and my sister used to be sent over the border into Switzerland to pick up the cartons.'[16]

While her children sold contraband cigarettes, Maria Serraino began dealing in stolen goods. Gypsies and drug addicts brought her car radios, televisions and videos, gold watches and anything else they could carry. Rita was a teenager, living in her mother's flat with her boyfriend, when she started selling heroin to the addicts who came to the house. With the money they got from the mother in one room, the junkies would buy heroin off the daughter in another. Rita learned to weigh out the powder, and cut it with other substances to make it go further. 'We had incredible rows because my boyfriend used to rip off the kids and put less in the packets, so I used to put more in.

'When my mother found out we were dealing heroin she was furious. She didn't want anything going on behind her back that she didn't have control over. From then on, when the addicts brought her stolen radios and stuff, she paid them in heroin.'

The family moved into a block of flats on the outskirts of Milan, and spread out into four or five apartments in the building, which was gradually adapted to the Di Giovine family's needs. In her mother's kitchen there were holes beneath the skirting boards and under the radiator, where she kept guns. The neighbours were paid to store drugs. One couple had a loose tile in their bathroom, which could be removed to reveal a deep, narrow hole. Rita was the only one with arms long and skinny enough to reach down inside, and she used to be sent round to fetch a packet of heroin, or a gun. Another woman living in the block would take incoming phone calls for them because her line was clear of police taps. Much later, when Rita was dealing on her own, she kept packets of heroin inside a box of washing powder, on a shelf in her neighbour's bathroom.

Rita described working with her father, emptying bottles of shampoo and bubble bath, and packing them with bundles of heroin sealed with Sellotape, before pouring the shampoo back in. She told how her brother Emilio went underground after committing a murder in 1981, and how, soon afterwards, cars began to arrive from New York. When a new car appeared, Rita would work in the garage with her father, taking off the doors or the wheels. Inside would be a hundred cellophane packets, each containing a kilo of heroin.

As the family expanded its numbers – there were twelve brothers and sisters – and its operations, they took over a square in Milan, the piazza Prealpi. No one else could deal drugs or collect protection money on the piazza. Rita testified that two men were later murdered for failing to respect the family's dominion.

They attracted riff-raff from Milan's teenage junkies, who worked for the family like indentured slaves. A lad called Mimmino, who lived with Rita's mother and helped her with housework, slept in a lean-to in the back garden. They used him to try out new shipments of heroin: his reaction to the hit would tell them if they could cut the stuff any further (he died of an overdose). Rosolino, a heroin addict with AIDS, lived in the attic at Rita's brother Antonio's house, and did the housework in return for his daily fix.

Rita's version of the power structure in the Serraino–Di Giovine family was perplexing. She portrayed her eldest brother, Emilio, as the boss of the family. By the mid-1980s he had couriers bringing him cocaine from France, Spain and Germany, and Ecstasy from Holland; he was also shipping large quantities of hash to England. Only the two brothers, Emilio and Antonio, seemed to make any serious money – they drove fast cars and lived in luxurious houses; Antonio invested in restaurants, bars and shops. Rita and her mother worked constantly and did stretches in prison; at one stage Rita was banking £40,000 twice a week, but neither she nor her mother seemed to enjoy a lifestyle in line with the sums of money they were turning over.

At the beginning of her collaboration, as she later admitted, Rita tried to shield her mother, but it gradually emerged that Maria Serraino, the mother of this drug empire, the family's link to the powerful 'Ndrangheta clan back in Calabria, was the backbone of the operation.

Maria Serraino's house was the centre of operations: every transaction, every meeting, every pick-up, took place in the matriarch's flat. There was so much heroin about in Maria's flat that the neighbour's dog started behaving strangely: its owner was convinced it was drugged by the fumes.

When rival gangs threatened Emilio's safety, it was his mother who had a bodyguard sent from Calabria to protect him. When a young associate was threatened by the brothers, he turned to their mother for protection. When another dealer was caught luring clients away from the piazza Prealpi, the matter was reported to Maria Serraino by the associate 'running' the square. Rita, who was round at her mother's house, as usual, recalled: 'My mother told him: "All right, don't worry, we'll have him killed." Then she asked [her neighbour] to bring her the pistol she had hidden in the bathroom.'

At this point in the examination, the witness was interrupted by shouting from the defendants' cage. Maria Serraino was calling names from the dock.

'Did someone say "Ugly whore"?' enquired the judge.

'I think I heard the word "Dishonoured", your honour,' replied the prosecutor.

Maria Serraino was given a warning not to disrupt the court by intimidating or insulting the witness. 'But it's my daughter, your honour,' she cried, before she was escorted out of the courtroom.

'The mother looks much older than her years,' says magistrate Maurizio Romanelli. 'She tried to get off by pleading ill health, and attended most of the hearings on a stretcher. But she is very sharp and knows how to be intimidating. She often screamed across the courtroom that her daughter was a liar.'

Six of the defendants, including Maria Serraino and her sons Antonio and Emilio Di Giovine, were indicted for mafia association. They were accused of supporting the Serraino clan (and their allies, the Condello–Imerti family) in the mafia war in Calabria, by sending them a steady supply of drug profits and weapons of all kinds.

Between 1985 and 1991 the war between the Serraino–Condello–Imerti alliance and the De Stefano clan was being fought in the mountains and the cities, with heavy casualties. Rita Di Giovine described how she used to go down to Calabria for her summer holidays, and remained close to several of her uncles and cousins. Three of her uncles were killed in the war – one of them, Domenico, was shot dead just a few minutes after she'd left him. She was particularly fond of Domenico: 'If he had to go out, he would travel in a bulletproof car under armed guard, or go out with his wife, wearing a wig and a false beard, with dark glasses . . . He told me he had killed someone in the war . . . He was an expert shot. He absolutely loved guns.'

Rita had handled some of the weapons procured by her brother Emilio. 'There were machine guns, rifles, all kinds of guns, and bulletproof jackets – it was unbelievable, the stuff he had. There were bazookas – one of them was used to blow up a bulletproof car. They were all sent down to my uncle in Calabria. My aunt was the courier.'

The family's control of piazza Prealpi in Milan was exercised with the military strength that characterised the 'Ndrangheta clans. They drove around in bulletproof cars, and always carried guns; there were frequent shoot-outs between rival groups.

Everybody who came into contact with the family seemed to be part of the ever-growing empire. Rita married a Calabrian called Salvatore Morabito. 'He had just moved to Milan, and my cousin had told him to look us up. He was clean, he had a respectable job – it was just what we needed. He started doing trips to the States for my brothers, carrying heroin. I remember when he came back from America on his third trip, I went to collect him from the airport with my mother – that's when our relationship started.' Rita had three children. The oldest, Massimiliano, worked as a dealer on the square from an early age.

In September 1987, Rita Di Giovine and her husband were arrested together and sentenced to six years each for trafficking heroin. On appeal the sentences were commuted: Morabito was put under house arrest in Calabria, and Rita was released.

She was able to commute between Calabria and Milan, to carry on business as usual.

The family had a number of public officials on its payroll. While Maria Serraino was under house arrest in Milan, she got talking to Ezio Dorigatti, the carabiniere who had been sent to make sure she was complying with her bail conditions. He started moaning about how poorly paid he was, and before long he had accepted a monthly stipend from the Di Giovine family. He kept guns for them at his house, and let them know when an arrest warrant was coming down.

Other carabinieri gave the family information about investigations being conducted by their colleagues, and in exchange they were showered with gifts: 'jewellery, gold bracelets and necklaces, watches, champagne, liqueurs, anything we had in the house'. Rita went to see a carabiniere who had information on an investigation into one of her brothers. 'I took off the chain round my wrist – it was a chunky man's chain, solid gold – and gave it to him.'

In classic mafia style, Emilio managed to get himself moved from a prison cell into a clinic in Parma, on account of some mysterious illness. 'Anyone could go and see him,' said Rita. 'He lived very well, he had everything he asked for, all the women he wanted, dinners with champagne, caviare, lobsters . . .

'I was living in Milan, but every evening I had to drive over to Parma and take him money, or gifts for his girlfriends. I was working for him at that stage, keeping his accounts, keeping records of the heroin I had sold and what money was owing.'

While the family refused to work with anyone who took heroin – 'You couldn't trust them, everyone knew that' – there was a lot of coke whooshing up banknotes. Rita's sister Angela was married to a cocaine dealer who consumed a good deal of the merchandise, and lay in bed for days at a time. Rita herself relied on slimming pills, which contain amphetamine: 'Enough so you can do the normal things you have to do in a day.'

The drug trade had its hideous price. Two of Rita's sisters and a brother died of heroin overdoses. Maria Serraino, grieving for one of her daughters, announced that she didn't want to deal in junk any more. 'Emilio said, OK, we'll start doing hash. There's not much of it around at the moment so we can make a lot of money, and it doesn't kill anyone.' So the dead girl's mother started dealing hashish to salve her conscience, and carried right on dealing heroin as well.

The more money the family made, the more poisonous the atmosphere became. 'Emilio never trusted any of us. He bought a counting machine – the kind the banks use – for the money, but took it away as a punishment.'

The brothers argued about poaching each other's clients. The neighbours argued about who was getting more business from the Di Giovine family. Mother and sons accused each other of stealing.

A final blazing row with her brother Antonio hastened the end of Rita Di Giovine's criminal career. In early 1993, she was robbed of 12 kilos of top-quality hash and 3,000 Ecstasy tabs. She had gone to a bar to meet the client. After waiting nearly all day, she went back to her room and found someone had broken in and stolen the lot. Antonio got nasty. His Dutch Ecstasy suppliers were after him for money, and he didn't believe Rita's story about being robbed. She had always hated Antonio, and was frightened of him. She tried to raise cash by selling all her gold jewellery, but no one would take it, and in the end she just gave it all to Antonio's wife. She sold her car – but was still well short of what she owed her brother. On 31 March 1993, Rita was arrested in possession of 1,000 tabs of Ecstasy. She had stolen them from Antonio to try to pay her debt. She had reached rock bottom.

Since her arrest, Rita Di Giovine has testified in trials all over northern Italy, and the case against her family is still in progress. In May 1996, in a Milan court, the prosecutor asked Rita why she had decided to talk. 'I just couldn't go on living that life,' she replied. 'I couldn't stand it any more.' Her brother Antonio and her mother listened from behind bars.

'Being arrested saved me.'

10. No Such Thing as a Businesswoman

The court is called to order. The judge enters, followed by his two assistants. Two lawyers, one or two journalists and the small handful of spectators stand up. The defendant rises slowly and painfully to his feet and draws himself up to his full height. This show of respect serves to demonstrate how pitifully reduced he is by his spell behind bars. His suit, which looks as though it were made for a much larger man, hangs off his shoulders. His long white beard, once so distinctive, is straggly and yellowing, and his curly black hair is plastered back on his neck. After eighteen months in prison, Giuseppe Mandalari, at 63, is showing the strain.

Mandalari is an accountant. Not a brilliant accountant, according to investigators, not the best money could buy, but he has very particular talents. He is a Freemason, which means that apart from offering his clients advice on the setting up and renaming of companies, he can also offer them excellent contacts, especially in politics and the judiciary. His clients include some of the top names in Cosa Nostra: Riina, Bagarella, Vernengo, Badalamenti. Magistrates maintain that Mandalari, by laundering the proceeds of crime, has materially contributed to the operation of the organisation, and that he has also on occasions in the past used his influence to affect political decisions, and the outcome of trials. A respected member of the middle class, Mandalari is, according to the prosecution, an important link between Cosa Nostra and the law-abiding world.

There is confusion in the courtroom. A functionary bustles up to the bench and says something to the judge in a low voice. The judge, white haired and paternal, scrutinises the prisoner over his gold-rimmed half-moons. 'You're not well? Can we get you something? Some water?'

The prisoner, looking more like a case for a stretcher than a glass of water, nods with exaggerated gratitude.

'In view of the defendant's poor state of health,' the judge pronounces, after long deliberation, 'in future, he need not climb the stairs, but may take the lift.'

Mandalari's wife, Maria Concetta Imbraguglia, is his co-defendant in the trial, charged with conspiracy and mafia association, and helping to run the financial affairs of high-ranking members of Cosa Nostra. They were arrested together in December 1994, but she was released from prison three weeks later. She sits in court at the far end of a long table and examines him intently, occasionally asking him something in a low voice. They are not allowed to talk to each other, so they steal a few words like naughty children separated in class.

'He looks terrible,' she tells me while the court is in recess, awaiting the arrival of the couple's lawyer. 'That suit used to fit him.' She is small and neat, looks young for 58, with an intense, intelligent look, short brown hair and light hazel eyes which hold mine steadily. Her manner is sure and confiding. We sit on a marble bench in the vast echoing second-floor lobby of Palermo's law courts, a building made for giants, in which ordinary people strut about, Lilliputians trying to make their presence felt.

The police arrived at dawn in the middle of winter at their home in viale Strasburgo, the fashionable modern residential area of Palermo. 'I never thought they'd come for me. It was a real shock. We watched them turn the house over – they searched it from top to bottom, opened everything . . . They weren't particularly unpleasant about it, just very thorough. Then they opened the cabinet where we keep my daughter's collection of costume dolls. My daughter died five years ago, of cancer. She was 19. I hadn't touched any of those dolls since she died, they were exactly as she left them. At that point I snapped. I couldn't bear to let a lot of strangers rifle through my daughter's things. I pushed them out of the way, and said I would take the dolls out myself one by one if they wanted. They said it was OK, and left them alone.

'They took us to the police station, held us in separate cells. I didn't know what was going to happen to me, I just cried all day. At half past eight in the evening they took me to the women's prison.

'It was horrible – I still can't bear to think about it. I haven't slept properly since. They weren't unkind, they realised I wasn't a bad person and took reasonable care of me – not that I was given any privileges, good Lord no.'

After three weeks, a request for Imbraguglia's release on the grounds that she had been working for her husband and therefore did not, alone, constitute a danger to the public, was accepted. Since then, she has made her weekly pilgrimage to court, just to catch a glimpse of her husband.

Maria Imbraguglia, who had graduated from accountancy school, first went to work for her husband in 1971 – just the two of them with a secretary, Francesca Camarda. Among their clients in the early days were the mafiosi leading the heroin trade with the US: Gaetano Badalamenti, boss of Cinisi, who had secured himself a large slice of the contraband trade by the early 1950s and moved into drug trafficking; Luciano Leggio, represented by his ambitious lieutenant Totò Riina; and the top heroin importers in Cosa Nostra: the Madonia and Vernengo families. A number of properties registered to Mandalari's companies were at the disposal of Cosa Nostra, principally for the use of mafiosi in hiding. When police raided one such apartment, they found little bundles of sugared almonds wrapped in white netting, and thank-you notes: the place had been used by the up and coming Corleone boss Totò Riina and his wife Ninetta Bagarella, on their secret honeymoon.[1]

In the 1970s the heroin trade began to yield such uncontrollable quantities of money that Cosa Nostra had to reinvent itself as a financial empire. Capital was needed to cover shipping costs and risk, while the sudden founts of wealth required imaginative reinvestment to disguise their source. Mandalari could fix anything. Companies appeared overnight which looked great on paper but which lacked the infrastructure to function in any useful way. One company, whose books showed that it had fulfilled a series of major earthworks contracts, owned exactly one lorry, and was staffed by people woefully unequipped to build anything more complex than a sandcastle. Mandalari's political contacts ensured that these shadow companies were awarded building contracts.

These heady days ended in 1974 when Mandalari was charged with aiding and abetting the mafioso Leoluca Bagarella, Corleone boss and Riina's brother-in-law. Photographed with his arrogant stare and his little goatee, Mandalari was exposed to the public as Cosa Nostra's accountant, a title confirmed by a number of important collaborators including Tommaso Buscetta, who described him as a key figure in the organisation's economic activity.[2]

Maria Imbraguglia's life with the mafia's accountant has been punctuated by periods of enforced separation. For a stretch of internal exile, he went to stay with her sister in Genoa. 'My brother and sister had both moved to Genoa; it was a city my father had spent time in – he worked on the ships. My husband went to live with my sister and her family, which was a good arrangement, but you know, you can stay with people for a bit, but after a while it begins to get too much – you're sleeping on the sofa, they want their sitting room back, it's all a bit awkward . . .' He suggested she and the children move to Genoa: they could start again, leave Sicily for good, put these troubles behind them. But she held back, too attached to her home town to leave. 'It's my one major regret. If we had moved then we could have started again. My husband would have set up in business with a clean slate and none of this would have happened. But I told him I didn't want to go. It was my decision.'

During the 1970s, as its business interests widened from prostitution to contraband and drug trafficking, the mafia employed a motley workforce: 'The network could not consist entirely of mafiosi: there were Tunisians, Americans, Neapolitans, Marseillais, Chinese, chancers, men of honour, men of dishonour, women, bankrupts and bankers.'[3] The volume of new businesses meant that the mafia was forced to bring in people from outside the organisation to register companies, including women. Women, the mafia's accountant discovered, were ideal: on paper, they became invisible. The lists of directors of companies, subsequently seized, reveal that a mafioso would rope in every female member of his family, including his mother-in-law, to disguise his own involvement.[4] Several of the companies registered by Mandalari show his wife and the secretary as sole shareholders.

It is a murky area for law enforcement: many of the women listed are just names on a form with no active involvement; at the same time, Cosa Nostra also moved in to take over entire departments of legitimate, functioning companies for the purposes of recycling money, and drew in yet more people to its operations: 'Those named by judicial reports as intimates or accomplices of major heroin traffickers include clerks, officials and managers of [banks]; members of the professional middle classes; and directors of public agencies.'[5]

Recent investigations into money laundering in Italy and the US have begun to focus on women. 'Women play an important role in white collar crime,' says Naples investigator Antonio Laudati, now at the national Anti-mafia Department in Rome. 'They work in the stock exchange, in business, in banking . . . they're often better at this kind of work than men, because they are more capable and less visible.'[6]

Antoinette Giancana, daughter of the Chicago mobster Sam Giancana, describes an organisation set up by Italian Americans, which operated very much like the Masons. Called the Italian Welfare Council of Chicago, this charitable fundraising organisation boasted the great and the good among its membership, including congressmen, union officials and judges. The organisation offered access to this impressive network, and packed enormous political clout. Among the council's unofficial directors was Sam Giancana's wife, Angeline DeTolve.[7]

Far from the rigidly arcane society it is depicted as, the mafia is capable of great elasticity – when it serves its purposes. To function as a business in the 1990s, it cannot be exclusively male. 'Cosa Nostra reflects the macho culture that exists

elsewhere in society, nothing more,' observes Umberto Santino, at the Giuseppe Impastato research centre in Sicily. 'On
the contrary: the mafia is comparatively progressive. Look how
well Riina, an uneducated peasant, understands international
business. The mafia has to be able to develop, to change with
the times. It has developed in step with – if not faster than – the
rest of the world.'[8]

For years, the mafia took advantage of a society which didn't
care to admit that women were capable of criminal behaviour.
Hundreds of companies registered in women's names were left
untouched. But 1982 saw a major breakthrough for investigators with the passing of the Rognoni–La Torre law. This law,
named after its authors, made it possible for investigators to
seize assets believed to belong to a mafioso, even if they were
registered under another name.

The law was long overdue. It had been held up by a series of
objections from interested parties – and by fear. This fear
proved well founded when its creator, Pio La Torre, was shot
dead with his driver Rosario Di Salvo in April 1982.

'Defectors have admitted that this law has caused the mafia a
lot of problems,' says Naples magistrate Giacomo Travaglino.
'That's why Pio La Torre died. If it's a law worth passing, in
Italy someone always has to die before it gets through.

'The mafia ethos dictates that the man of honour accepts
prison as part of life – in the sense that they are part of a
criminal association, constantly at risk of losing their liberty.
The criminal knows it goes like this: he commits a crime, he
gets arrested. No problem. What he will not tolerate is when
the unwritten rules of the court system are overturned, and the
authorities start threatening to seize his assets. Because those
assets are the reason he commits crimes in the first place.'[9]

The new law defined the crime of mafia association.
Magistrates could prosecute someone for contributing to the
general aims and operation of the mafia over a period of time.
This suddenly brought into play all the women who had
knowingly acted as *prestanomi* – who had allowed their names

to be used as company directors for money-laundering operations – who had previously been untouchable.

As soon as the La Torre law was passed, the machinery went
into motion for a massive round-up. On 1 March 1983 police
knocked on the door of Mandalari's home in Palermo at dawn,
with a warrant for his arrest on charges of mafia association. He
glowered at photographers through a full beard as he was led
away.

After the trial he was once again banned from Sicily, so he
chose the closest possible point, Villa San Giovanni, in
Calabria, which has a direct ferry crossing to Messina. His wife
used to go and join him when she could, taking their little girl
on weekends, and staying for months in the summer during the
school holidays. 'It's a ghastly place,' she smiles, 'there's nothing
there. My husband took up fishing just to have something to
do. I used to go with him, he would fish and I'd sit and read.
My son would take work over to him from the office in
Palermo.'

Then their daughter got cancer. Maria took her to Paris for
chemotherapy, a week at a time. After three years of painful
treatment, she died. Her mother was lost. She stayed indoors,
shut herself inside the cool darkness of the house and hid with
her grief from the world. After a few months, her husband tried
to coax her out of her misery, and suggested she return to work
for him.

'At first I didn't really do anything. I just used to go and sit
there for a bit of distraction. Then I started answering the
phone, almost automatically, really.'

She knew the clients of old, and picked up the ropes very
quickly. Her husband's client list had grown with his beard, and
all sorts of people came and went. At one point Mandalari lent
a room in his office to a gynaecologist, who used it as a
consulting room for the wives of top men of honour.[10]

'She was always there in the office, while clients came and
went,' says Maurizio Delucia, investigating magistrate for the
prosecution. 'She is on the board of a number of companies. If
you are on the board you have to know what's going on. It's

possible for someone to be on the board in name only, but it is very unlikely in this case. We put taps on the phones and found out that she played a full part in running the company. She had an autonomous, decision-making role. The phone taps tell us that she knows her husband's mafia clients and his politician friends personally; when they rang up and he wasn't there, she was always in a position to give them an answer or make a decision. Her role in the firm is the same as his: she knows that you have to present accounts in a certain way to make it look as though the money has followed certain channels.'[11]

Some of their former clients have recently defected; they confirmed that whenever they called, if her husband was out of the office, Maria Imbraguglia would deal with their business herself.

Police put Maria Imbraguglia under surveillance throughout 1992 and 1993. 'It's a bit creepy to think that we were under investigation all that time,' she says; 'you know, the sort of phone conversations you have . . . once or twice I must have talked to friends about their private lives, perhaps we might have talked about something her husband did, or what one of us had been doing, and then afterwards you realise that someone was listening . . .'

Maria Imbraguglia claims ignorance of her husband's business. She insists she had no active role in running the companies on whose files she appeared as board member. 'I didn't do anything. My husband knew what I thought, he voted for me at meetings. My husband put me on the board because he thought it would look good on my c.v.'

She did share his interesting, influential friends: her husband is sociable and well liked, and the couple were sought after. 'My husband is the sort of man who gets on with everybody. He can talk in an erudite way to a cultured person, and chat spontaneously with someone more simple. He is very well educated, he has philosophical thoughts which I don't pretend to understand, but I admire him for it.'

The house in viale Strasburgo, Maria Imbraguglia tells me, which was repossessed with her husband's other assets, is coming up for auction, and she is having to look for a smaller place to rent. She misses her husband dreadfully, she says, her eyes reddening and filling with tears, because without him it is so hard to cope with the loss of their daughter. When they were together, they could talk about her, comfort each other. Lips trembling, she fumbles in her handbag for a tissue. With shaking hands, she takes out of her wallet a photograph of her daughter, and holds it out towards me.

Maria Concetta Imbraguglia has been working for her husband's firm since the early 1970s: it was twenty years before police began to investigate her role in the business. Although the La Torre law handed investigators a new weapon to help dismantle the mafia's business empire, few have considered women sufficiently important to use it against them. For a long time, magistrates were unwilling or unable to recognise women as capable of independent intellectual activity – in this regard, law-abiding society lags behind Cosa Nostra. Less than a year after the La Torre law was passed, Palermo mafia boss Giovanni Bontade and his wife Francesca Citarda were tried on the grounds that companies owned by the couple were used for recycling drug money. Among others on the same charge were Anna Maria Di Bartolo and her husband Domenico Federico, a builder closely connected to the Bontade family.

Both women were acquitted. The sentence, while acknowledging the women's family connections to Cosa Nostra, ruled women out of any active role in mafia business:

> . . . A woman who belongs to a family of mafiosi has not yet achieved such emancipation and autonomy that she can escape the subordinate and passive role she has always held relative to her 'man', so as to take part, on equal terms – or indeed, of her own free will – in the activities of the male clan members.
>
> . . . It is customary in this region, and in most cases

perfectly legitimate, for a businessman to register a commercial licence or a business partnership in the name of a woman – particularly his wife. But one may not necessarily conclude from this that the woman is a knowing participant in the day-to-day legal and illegal business of her husband's firm, particularly when one considers that women lack even the most basic financial knowledge, and that they are by nature and tradition strangers to the difficult world of business.[12]

This sentence, so affably patronising, effectively granted women in business immunity from prosecution, on the grounds that they are too stupid to commit crimes. By stating that women are slaves to their husbands' will, the judge also implied that they are not responsible for their actions. Neither, presumably, would they be expected to make a moral decision about what their husband does for a living. The sentence was viewed not only as an insult to women, but also as an invitation to men to continue to profit from the 'subordinate' position of their wives.[13] The verdict is all the more surprising when one considers that in 1983 the mayor of Palermo was a woman, Elda Pucci, and the name of Margaret Thatcher was not entirely unknown in Italy.

Cosa Nostra soon proved it was not of the same opinion. On 28 September 1988, Giovanni Bontade woke up early in the morning to hear someone ringing the doorbell of his concrete castle in Villagrazia, a suburb of Palermo. He opened the door to a couple of friends, and showed them into the kitchen where his wife, Francesca Citarda, who had been woken by the knocking, was preparing coffee. While they were standing around chatting, the early morning guests put down their coffee cups, pulled out their guns, and shot the couple dead.

Although people continue to repeat the old axiom that the mafia never harms women, they also say that the mafia never kills without a motive: it's messy and tends to alienate public opinion. Bontade could easily have been shot as he stood alone on the doorstep. Francesca Citarda was meant to die. Either she was directly involved in her husband's business interests, or at the very least, she knew too much about them.

Mafia security demands that there should be no written records, and although there have been notable exceptions (such as Camorra wife Patrizia Ferriero's famous cocaine ledger), most business is done in people's heads. Supergrass Tommaso Buscetta told the Palermo court: 'No one will ever find lists of members of Cosa Nostra, or contracts of any kind, or receipts for payment.'[14] This way of doing business demands not only a good memory, but a high degree of trust.

When a mafioso is in hiding, he depends on his associates to keep an eye on his business affairs, to keep him informed, and act in his best interests. In some cases, he can trust none of his associates as well as he can trust his wife. And of course, she has the added advantage of attracting little attention from investigators.

Saveria Palazzolo, wife of the Corleone boss Bernardo Provenzano, is a handsome woman, always smartly dressed in elegant suits. Now nearly 60, unlike other mafia wives she doesn't dye her hair, or wear extravagant quantities of jewellery. She and her two sons live modestly in Corleone, although her husband has made millions trafficking heroin. She drives a Fiat Tipo – not, as people like to say, a Mercedes sports car. To look at her, one would not guess how powerful her husband was.

Provenzano, one of the Corleonesi's most efficient killers (known as 'u trattori, the tractor, because nothing could stand in his way, and where he passed, he left nothing unturned), has been in hiding since 1969. There has been no sign of him for some time, and rumours have begun to circulate: some say he is very ill, suffering from cancer. Others describe him as perfectly healthy, controlling Cosa Nostra from behind the scenes. Yet others say he has left Sicily, and is biding his time, probably in the USA, until it is safe to return. There is one published photograph of him, taken when he was a fresh-faced youth in the 1950s, in which he looks bold and untroubled, with his hair slicked back over his round head, and strong jaw jutting fearlessly towards the camera.

Provenzano and Riina got their criminal education at the heels of Luciano Leggio, unstoppable leader of the Corleone clan. They were both young and ambitious, and as a murderous team were known collectively as 'the Beasts'.[15] Leggio, who was in some doubt as to which of the young guns to promote as his deputy, commented: 'Provenzano shoots like a god, pity he's got the brains of a chicken.'[16]

When a warrant was issued for his arrest on a murder charge in 1969, Provenzano went into hiding. His wife went with him, but since she was not wanted by the police she was free to come and go. During this period, she took over her husband's financial affairs, and managed his various companies. Members of the western Sicilian Cosa Nostra, even when they become immensely wealthy, typically remain in their territory and invest their money locally, rather than taking it abroad. They seldom go far from home because if they lose touch with the situation on the ground, if their presence ceases to be felt, they lose their power base. So Provenzano stayed in the neighbourhood, and since he couldn't walk into a bank without getting arrested, he entrusted his business to his wife.

Capable and clever, Saveria Palazzolo seemed to take pride in her double life. When police questioned her about her husband's whereabouts, she claimed not to know where he was. Not long afterwards, she appeared in town, visibly pregnant. 'When they saw I had a big belly they sent for me,' she told her local priest. 'They asked me, "How can you tell us you don't know where Provenzano is hiding, given your condition?" And I said, "Wait a minute, can't a woman have a baby with anyone other than her husband?" '[17]

Provenzano has to trust his wife as much in sexual matters as in business. Someone doing illegal business has no guarantees, no security, and seldom so much as a shopping list written on a piece of paper. Mafia historian Pino Arlacchi explains why the organisation is based on, or imitates, the family: 'To find people who respect agreements, who will not make off with enormously valuable goods and capital in situations where it would be very easy to do so, and who will reveal nothing to the authorities if captured, the mafia has had to turn to those who are bound by obligations of kinship – either natural or artificial.'[18]

In 1983, a warrant went out for Saveria Palazzolo's arrest. Carabinieri arrived at the door of her house in Cinisi, east of Palermo, but she was nowhere to be found. As usual, she was one step ahead of the law: she had gone underground, and was not to be seen again in public for ten years. The order for her capture was later commuted to house arrest, but she remained in hiding.

At this point, she was forced to suspend her business deals, but before her disappearance, Palazzolo had made a number of significant investments, buying shares and taking a major stake in a construction company. When questioned by the Guardia di Finanza, she had claimed it was her money, but inspectors – observing that she conducted no kind of money-making activity whatsoever[19] – contended that she was investing on behalf of her husband. Since he was unable to do business in person, they maintained, it was up to his wife to invest the proceeds of his drug trafficking in real estate, which she did – with the help of her financial adviser, Giuseppe Mandalari.

In her absence, Palazzolo was charged, alongside Mandalari, with mafia association and recycling mafia money. She was found guilty and sentenced to three years, although law enforcement officers still had no idea of her whereabouts.

The trial had some comical moments. Called to account for the first time in living memory, several of the accused gave interesting versions of how they earned their millions. Francesco Aglieri and his wife, Laura Brambillo, who were accused of investing 100 million lire (over £43,000) from heroin trafficking, said the money was her savings. 'The accused is a manual labourer,' the prosecutor observed drily, 'while his wife, to boost their modest income, works as a nanny.'[20]

Years later, Saveria Palazzolo was granted an amnesty. In 1992, as soon as she was a free citizen, she reappeared in

Corleone with her children Angelo, 14, and Paolo, 9. She announced her presence to the police, and declared she had come to settle for good. The boys, serious and well-behaved, bore little resemblance to tractors or other pieces of farm machinery, and spoke English and German fluently. They had no identification papers or birth certificates – as far as the Italian population register was concerned, Provenzano's sons did not exist. It emerged that they had spent the intervening years living with an uncle in Germany, studying at private school. They had made the transition into passable versions of middle-class boys, and their mother had brought them home in triumph to Corleone and made them legitimate Italian citizens.

Economic gains have not always meant fast cars and flash suits. For the Sicilian mafioso in particular, getting rich means leaving his peasant stock behind. The children may be sent to England or America – not as penniless immigrants but as university students – study law in Milan, and move into bourgeois society. 'The climbing is not hurried, it is done in successive waves, one generation after the other, till the highest pinnacles are reached.'[21]

Money and children, said to be the two things most prized by a mafioso, are inextricably linked, because his children's prosperity is the mobster's greatest reward. Saveria Palazzolo has given her children an education and an upbringing which will prepare them for the next rung of the ladder.

11. Women Take the Stand

On 25 September 1979 Judge Cesare Terranova brought his wife a cup of coffee in bed and went downstairs to meet his driver, Lenin Mancuso. Seconds later, Giovanna Terranova heard shots and ran down into the street, but a policeman shielded her from her husband's shattered body. Cesare Terranova, who had been a member of the Anti-mafia Commission, had recently returned to Palermo, after seven years in parliament, a highly respected criminal court judge. His murder was to become one of the first of many 'illustrious crimes' in a bloody war between the mafia and the state.

Nothing had prepared Palermo for this offensive. Between 1979 and 1982, judges, politicians and police chiefs were cut down in a series of top-level assassinations. The killings shocked the city out of its inertia. Giovanna Terranova remembers: 'I was thrown into crisis by my husband's murder, I lost all my strength, my will to live. I never went out – I simply couldn't summon the energy to leave the house. In the end I sought out other women in my situation, partly because I needed not to feel alone any more, but also because it seemed my grief was not just my own pain, it was something shared by society as a whole, by everyone who wanted a future for this country. I owed it to Cesare to do something.'[1]

Giovanna Terranova lives in an elegant apartment in Palermo, lined with books from floor to ceiling, full of objects lovingly collected with her husband, and a grand piano in the drawing room. Her black servant, in a livery jacket slightly too short in the arms, brings tea in a silver pot. Giovanna has never been afflicted with the bitterness that has hardened so many mafia widows. She fills the room with grace.

After her husband's murder, Giovanna Terranova filed a civil case, alongside Lenin Mancuso's family, in the trial of Corleone boss Luciano Leggio. But Leggio was acquitted – a result which left her profoundly disillusioned with the legal system, and she dispatched a protest to the president about the blatant inadequacies of the prosecution service, which received wide publicity. For the government, it was a stinging indictment from the widow of one of Italy's most respected judges.

Meanwhile, Giovanna had made contact with the widow of Gaetano Costa, the attorney-general who had courageously signed arrest warrants for a number of powerful mafia drug traffickers, and who was shot dead in the centre of Palermo in August 1980, as he walked out to buy a newspaper. In April 1981, Giovanna Terranova and Rita Costa collected 30,000 signatures on a petition pledging commitment in the fight against the mafia, and led a delegation of mafia widows to Rome, to demand action from the state. 'The mafia has grown with the consent of civil society,' says Giovanna Terranova. 'Society has been – if not compliant, certainly passive. I realised that we had to rebel.'

By the end of 1982, the women's initiative had attracted a lot of attention but very little concrete response from the institutions of state. The first real test came with the opening of a mafia trial in Palermo, at which the Women's Anti-mafia Association applied to bring a claim for damages. The application was turned down. This form of civil protest was new to Sicily, and Palermo magistrates – with notable exceptions such as Giovanni Falcone – were not comfortable with the notion of ordinary people claiming legal redress against organised crime.[2]

But the women's movement had begun to tap a new source of strength. Rita Costa explains: 'Women's mentality had undergone a change. They were looking for freedom. If a woman didn't agree with her husband, she told him so. She no longer accepted everything in the name of marriage. In Palermo, freedom also meant getting away from the crushing, bullying mafia. Women weren't going to be bullied at home, and they weren't going to be pushed around in public life either.'[3]

As Cosa Nostra's assassins continued their murder campaign, the association made several applications to file civil cases, all of them rejected. It was not until the maxi-trial of 1985 that the association changed tactics, and encouraged wives and mothers of mafia victims to come forward, and claim damages. In an unprecedented reach across the social divide, they called on women from mafia families to sue their loved ones' killers, and campaigned for a state subsidy to pay their legal fees.

One of the first women to seek legal redress against Cosa Nostra was Michela Buscemi, whose brothers lived and died on the fringes of organised crime in Palermo, and were murdered by the mafia. Michela, who had grown up in the slums of the city, had watched her brothers getting sucked into the mafia quicksand, but her attempts to haul them back to safety had failed.

Michela's brother Salvatore Buscemi lived down at the port, in the mafia-run neighbourhood of Sant'Erasmo, where fishing boats came in before dawn, and unloaded their catch of contraband cigarettes.

Michela drives through the dilapidated neighbourhood, where the bombed-out edges of the city slums have been razed to the ground and 20-storey council blocks have been built in their place. In between these cement towers, the shabby relics of the old neighbourhood are hugger-mugger, rearranged to accommodate any demand: a few breeze blocks jammed together with cement and a shard of corrugated iron makes a roof extension; a front door, with the help of a sledge-hammer, becomes a hole in the wall big enough to drive a van through. Michela parks her car in front of the building where Salvatore and his wife Benedetta lived, on a spit of land which juts out into the sea. She points out their flat on the first floor. She remembers looking out across the inky water from their balcony.

He was a big man, always getting into fights. 'Once people knew he could land a good punch, he got a reputation for it. If any friend of his got in a fight, they'd call Salvatore to sort it out.' Salvatore was desperate to be accepted; he would buy anyone a drink, and get into a punch-up to defend someone he hardly knew. 'The neighbourhood changed him,' says his sister. 'He went from a fearful, clinging boy to a violent man, quick to lash out.'

The contraband cigarette trade is a staple in the poorer quarters of southern Italy. It's the economic grey area, the fringe of organised crime, where unemployed youths can scratch a living selling packets of imported Marlboro and Merit on street corners. It made the mafia rich in the 1960s and has brought in a steady trickle of income ever since, with every cigarette seller paying a levy to the local boss. Salvatore Buscemi started buying cartons off the boatmen and selling packets of Marlboro on the street corner – without seeking permission, and without handing over any 'duty'.

'I told Salvatore he would get into trouble selling cigarettes without permission, but he wouldn't listen. "What else am I supposed to do?" he said. "Everyone else does it here." He knew he was dealing with the mafia, but he didn't realise how big it was.

'We were very close, we sought each other's advice about everything. My mother had so many children and I was the eldest, I practically brought up my brothers and sisters myself. I was so worried about Salvatore. We used to come over here on Sundays, I'd bring the lunch and we'd be together for the afternoon.'

One evening in April 1979, Salvatore was eating dinner in a local trattoria with friends when two masked men came in and opened fire. Salvatore was shot in the jaw and the stomach, and died in a pool of his intestines on the restaurant floor.

Rodolfo, one of the younger brothers, just 18, adored Salvatore. He followed his footsteps in everything – he even married his wife's sister and moved into a flat in the backstreets of Sant'Erasmo, a few streets up from the port. 'I was dead against Rodolfo moving here,' says Michela. 'I knew his wife was involved with *those people* . . .' He lived at the end of a narrow lane in a little three-sided courtyard, crowded with doors and balconies and windows jostling for a look-in. As

Michela points out Rodolfo's balcony, a woman leans out of an upstairs window and stares.

Rodolfo made it known that he was determined to find out who had killed his brother. Vincenzo Sinagra, a mafioso from the neighbourhood who later became an informer, warned him to keep quiet. 'I used to beg him, "We've already lost one brother, I don't want to lose another," but he said he had to make them pay for Salvatore's death. Sometimes he was really scared. He had a wife and a baby, and his wife was five months pregnant.' One night in May 1982, Rodolfo was visiting Benedetta, Salvatore's widow, when Sinagra called up for him. Benedetta later said the phone rang and she turned away to answer it; when she looked back, Rodolfo was gone. He was never seen again.

After Rodolfo disappeared, Michela used to drive around, looking for him. 'I saw him everywhere. I'd see someone in the street who had hair like my brother's, and call out, "It's him! it's him!" But it wasn't him.'

Much later, Vincenzo Sinagra revealed that Rodolfo had been taken to a windowless cellar in an alleyway in Sant' Erasmo, where he was tortured, strangled and dissolved in a bath of acid. But the acid was poor quality; after several hours the dead man's body still swam in the smoky water. The killers bagged the remains and tied it to a lump of concrete, then took it out in a boat and dropped it over the side, into one of the deep crevasses in the marina.

The building where Salvatore and Benedetta lived is now empty and falling to bits. The front door has been bricked over. Shutters bang in the wind. Over the road, the fishmongers are hosing down their stalls in front of an old apartment block teeming with people. Behind the house, down a little blind alleyway, is the mafia's torture chamber. Outside, vans and pick-ups come and go, loading up with painters' and decorators' materials, fishing gear, cases of soft drinks. Fishermen store their salted fish in the cellars locked behind metal shutters. Behind one of these doors is the 'chamber of death'. Balconies and roof terraces look inwards over the little courtyard. Now the windows are gaping and glassless, the doors nailed shut.

Rosetta took her little girl and went to see Sinagra to find out what had happened to her husband. He frightened her away. 'What are you, nuts?' he said. 'Is this your daughter? So you live round here then?' After her baby was born, Rosetta, grieving for her husband, starved herself to death.

In late 1985, when Michela heard that she could bring a case against Cosa Nostra, she decided to take the stand against her brothers' murderers. Her mother initially agreed to support her. 'But my brothers and sisters ganged up on me, and persuaded my mother not to do it. My mother rang me to tell me she was pulling out, and I could hear them all talking in the background. My mother made a statement to the papers saying I was mad, and that whatever I did, I was on my own. She was frightened of the mafia, but what was there to be afraid of if we had stuck together? They couldn't have killed fifty of us.'

Michela confided to a local police officer that her brother's widow Benedetta probably knew who had killed him. Benedetta was duly summoned, but refused to answer questions. Not long afterwards, a bomb exploded outside the bar where Michela and her husband worked. She remembers the night she spent, eight months pregnant, picking up shards of glass off the pavement. 'It was a warning. Benedetta must have told someone I had gone to the police.'

Michela Buscemi went ahead and testified in court. Only she and one other woman, Vita Rugnetta, whose son had been found strangled in the boot of a car, represented victims from the margins of mafia culture, young men summarily executed for some minor infringement of Cosa Nostra rules. All the other plaintiffs were the widows and children of public servants. The courtroom was a specially constructed bunker, with cages around the outside walls, from which hundreds of mafiosi looked into the court. 'When I walked past the cages they used to swear at me, call me horrible names. They used to call me a whore . . . I had to get up in front of the judges and the mafiosi in their cages, and say who had killed Rodolfo and why.'

Before the trial ended, it was decided that the national fund to pay the legal expenses of plaintiffs would be given to the families of public servants, not to women like Michela Buscemi. Embittered by the indifferent response of the press and the state, anti-mafia campaigner Umberto Santino wrote: 'These women's conduct should have been welcomed as a significant step, a precious example for the many people who have not yet come forward, to encourage them to follow suit at the next opportunity. Instead, they were isolated and rebuffed.'[4] The women's lawyers waived their fees, but the only funds forthcoming were raised by the tiny Impastato Centre,[5] and the Women's Anti-mafia Association.

On 16 March 1989, when the mafia trial was at the court of appeal, a voice on Michela Buscemi's answerphone said that if she didn't withdraw her evidence, her six-year-old daughter would be dead before Easter.

'She came to ask us what she should do. She was actually prepared to look for a way to go on,' recalls Giovanna Terranova. 'She is extraordinarily brave. We had to persuade her that she couldn't risk her children's lives.'

'I was seething with grief and anger the day I had to go to court and announce that I had to stand down,' remembers Michela. 'I felt like I had betrayed myself. The judge looked at me and said, "Signora, what if we all gave up at the first sign of trouble?" '

This dismissive response burned in Michela Buscemi's heart as much as her rage at having to withdraw her case. Since then, she has made a mission of her stand against the mafia. She has talked in schools, given lectures, and written a book about her life. Her emotional eloquence has moved audiences all over the world. But while others debate political tactics and attend conferences, Michela Buscemi is living on the edge of poverty. Since she testified against the mafia, no one will employ her husband. After years of unemployment, he has lost his confidence, and spends most of his time at the kitchen table, smoking cigarettes, watching foreign film crews come in and out to record his wife telling the story of how she fought the mafia and lost.

'These women who have escaped from the mafia environment they were brought up in, are completely exposed,' says Giovanna Terranova. 'They come from families where people obtain justice by themselves. Instead, these women decided that the right thing to do would be to seek justice from the state – and they have paid for it heavily. Their families have rejected them and they have lost their livelihoods.'

Giovanna campaigned for state funding for women who took the stand against the mafia, but the Women's Anti-mafia Association was split by a faction who believed the funds should only be for families of public servants killed in the exercise of their duties. The association nearly foundered on the conviction that Sicily is divided between mafia and 'civil' society. Rita Costa is still unyielding on the subject: 'Michela Buscemi's brothers were killers. I don't want to make a class issue of it, but they got themselves into that mess. I am the wife of a man who died defending the laws of a democratic society. Even killers have a right to a defence: just don't expect me to do it.' The issue drove a wedge between Signora Costa and the rest of the women's association. 'These people are married to killers,' she says crossly. 'They are the mothers of killers. Why should they be given public funds?'

One only has to look at the story of Pietra Lo Verso to see why. After attempting to sue her husband's murderers, Pietra was ruined, and her sons, with no legitimate means of support, turned to crime.

In a run-down tenement block on the edge of Palermo, at the top of a stinking staircase covered in graffiti, Pietra Lo Verso opens the door cautiously. She is short and round, with a missing tooth and a rasping voice. Her sandy hair is scraped back in a thin ponytail.

She shows me into the best sitting room, the room that, even in the poorest houses, is scrubbed and polished every day until the floor shines, full of ornamental kitsch, sugar statues and wedding presents, the room that no one ever sits in. On the dresser there is a gilded clock embraced by painted shepherd-esses and topped with a fake Fabergé egg, with its Guarantee of Quality label still hanging from one gold spike.

Pietra had met her husband Cosimo Quattrocchi when they were growing up in Sant'Erasmo. They ran away together as teenagers; he became a moderately wealthy Palermo butcher. She denies he ever had dealings with the mafia, but from her account, every aspect of his business, from his licence to the animals he slaughtered, depended on the help of 'friends'. In the end he was the victim of a cartel which he tried to circumvent, and got caught.

'My husband called me one day,' recalls Pietra in her rapid, husky voice, 'and said "I'm bringing some important guests home for dinner." I rushed out and bought seafood and prepared a lavish meal. When they arrived there were five of them, and my husband introduced me to a tall, distinguished-looking gentleman called Fisichella. He and my husband became good friends after that. My husband called him "Uncle Ninu". He was always very nice to me whenever he phoned.'

Over the seafood pasta, Cosimo Quattrocchi had entered a pact with the Catania horse dealer: the connection guaranteed him protection, but from then on, he was not allowed to do business with anyone else. Antonino Fisichella started sending him butchered meat, in contravention of the by-law which rules that any meat has to be slaughtered locally, and he had to take it. When his licence was suspended, the meat kept on coming.

'My husband telephoned Fisichella to try and stop the deliveries. I heard him on the phone. His hands were shaking. He said, "Uncle Ninu, you've got to believe me. I've had my licence taken away. If you carry on sending me meat I can't sell, you'll ruin me." Poor man, he was really scared.

'A few days later, my husband came home looking very pleased with himself. He had gone to see Fisichella to sort things out, they'd gone to a restaurant and talked it all over.

They were friends again – Fisichella even gave him this.' She points to the ornamental clock.

But once the immediate crisis was over, Cosimo was afraid to do business with someone he couldn't quite trust. He went to see a horse breeder in Bari, on the mainland, and arranged the first delivery of foals. While he was away, Pietra had a call from Fisichella. 'He rang at 8.30 in the morning, and asked where my husband was. I told him "He's gone to Bari." What could I say? I didn't think we had anything to hide.'

Pietra's feisty, defensive tone falters for an instant. 'I sometimes think that if I hadn't told Fisichella that my husband was in Bari, everything would have been all right.'

The night in October 1984 that the foals were due to arrive, Cosimo didn't come home. At about 2 a.m. the wife of one of his employees rang up, saying she hadn't seen her husband. Pietra told her not to worry, the foals might have turned up late. The following morning, she sent her young nephew down to the stables. The boy found eight men lying dead in the straw. Cosimo Quattrocchi and every one of his employees had been gunned down.

When the men accused of the slaughter – which became known as the piazza Scaffa massacre – were brought to trial, Pietra was the only relative of the murdered men to come forward as a plaintiff. 'My husband was innocent. He didn't deserve to die. I had to do something to clear his name.' In court, she was brought face to face with Fisichella, and was asked to identify him. 'He stood right in front of me and said, "I've never seen this woman before in my life." "What do you mean?" I said. "You've eaten dinner in my house. I can even tell you what you had to eat." He said he'd never set eyes on me before. In front of all those people. He said I was mad.'

The judge considered this tiny woman ranting about her innocent husband, and concluded that her story was a wild exaggeration. Antonino Fisichella was acquitted.

Pietra had managed the butcher's shop herself after her husband's death, but after her court appearance, customers started shopping elsewhere. After watching fridges of unsold meat go bad week after week, she closed the shop.

The front door bangs shut, and Pietra nervously signals me to put away my notebook and tape recorder. 'Now the children are grown up they don't let me speak to the press. My sons wouldn't let me go to court a second time. They don't want to hear any more about it. They say "Mamma, our father is dead, there's nothing we can do about it." I've always had arguments with them about it. They say I ruined their lives by going to court.'

Pietra has a ferocious manner, and in full flow she's relentless and raucous, but she lives in fear for her children. 'They've got involved with people – you know, they're just kids, the police are always coming down on them and their friends . . . they hang out with drug dealers.'

After the trial, two of her sons were arrested for possession of hash, and one of them was charged with carrying a gun. The publicity surrounding their arrest raised a public outcry at Pietra's plight, and she was quickly given a job as a cleaner with the local council. The financial support Pietra had been counting on as a state witness was withheld, because her husband had a minor previous conviction. Pietra felt 'civil society' had abandoned her. She retreated into her family and severed all contact with Palermo's anti-mafia movement.

The drama of the widows' grief focused attention on the slow, fumbling and sometimes corrupt criminal prosecution system. One of the first women to register as a plaintiff in a murder trial was Felicia Impastato, whose son was assassinated in 1978 after conducting a relentless anti-mafia campaign. Nearly twenty years after she risked everything by suing the assassins, the evidence to convict the killers is still buried deep in the secret pockets of the legal system.

Felicia Impastato's home in Cinisi, just outside Palermo, was a battleground. Her husband was a mafioso closely connected to the local Cosa Nostra clan, the Badalamenti family. Her son Giuseppe was a Communist and vociferous critic of the mafia's grip on the local economy. Giuseppe was a thorn in the mafia's side – and a sore embarrassment to his father. Felicia was stuck in the middle, defending her son, and fending off a violent husband.

Now over 80, she is still smart, with an agile wit and a sharp sense of humour. Her white hair sets off her heavy black framed specs as she sits at her kitchen table, a tiny old bird shut in a dark house with her memories, tilting at the enemies all around her.

'They killed my son because of his politics. Not because he was a thief, a poof or a bastard.'[6]

As a teenager, Giuseppe Impastato, known as Peppino, was in the front line of gang fights between Communist and Fascist groups. On one occasion, his mother pitched into the mêlée and pulled a Fascist thug off her son by his hair. The first time she saw Peppino on a political platform, she was driving past with her husband. Peppino was shouting into a megaphone, but his father, with a selective blindness which he sometimes deployed to protect himself and his son, looked straight at the protesters and remarked merely how young they were.

He was not permitted to feign ignorance for long: one of his friends dropped in soon afterwards to warn him about his son's activism. Felicia, hiding behind the door, listened. 'If it was my son,' the mafioso was saying, 'I'd be digging his grave for him.'

'He would always come home in a fury, after listening to his mafia friends telling him what they were planning to do to his son – he'd tell me exactly what they'd said, just to frighten me out of my wits. I was always there with my heart in my mouth. When I could hear my husband at the door, I used to have a rush in my stomach and had to go to the lavatory.'

Her husband would shout and smash plates, working himself into a violent rage. She would shut all the doors so the neighbours couldn't hear. She was never cowed before him, but screaming over her husband's bellowed threats never assuaged her fears. 'When it got really bad I should have packed my bags and taken my sons and left – but where would I have gone? What would I have done?'

Felicia married in 1947, but although she knew her husband was a mafioso, she claims she didn't really understand what that meant. 'It's not as if people talked about those things then. It was only later I realised what an evil bunch of gangsters they were.'

Peppino's political voice grew more insistent, with his own slot on a pirate station, Radio Aut, on which he broadcast reports from the town he dubbed 'Mafiopoli'. While her husband railed against this misguided Communist boy, Felicia found she agreed with her son. 'I heard about the things they did. I told my husband, "If you bring one of your mafioso friends to this house, I'm leaving." From then on, no one ever came to this house. His friends would come to call for him, but they'd wait outside. They knew I didn't want them here.'

As a mafioso conscious of his standing with the local boss, Luigi Impastato could not afford to tolerate this insubordination in his own family. To salvage his honour, he threw Peppino out. 'He got rid of Peppino's books,' recalls his mother. 'He knew that if the books were gone, Peppino would go too.'

Peppino went to live with a relative, but his mother found a way round the unnatural ban – every day, while her husband was out at work, she would cook lunch for her son. 'I wasn't going to have my own son banned from this house – but I was always nervous in case his father should find out. I used to have everything ready by the time Peppino walked through that door at twelve o'clock. While he ate, we would talk. I could talk to him. My husband never talked to me about anything.'

Peppino's father never came home at midday. His mafia friends had forced him to throw his son out of his house, but he turned a blind eye to this sacred ritual. 'He was a cruel, violent man, but deep down he loved his son.'

Still, Luigi Impastato was a man of honour, and none of his Cosa Nostra associates would have laid a hand on Peppino while he was alive. But after her husband died in a car crash in

1977, Felicia's nights were filled with fitful images of death. Now there was nothing to protect her son.

On 8 March 1978, some American cousins were staying. Felicia had prepared dinner, and they were waiting for Peppino before they sat down to eat. 'But he never . . . he never came.'

Peppino Impastato finished work at the radio station and was on his way home when he was ambushed and knocked unconscious. He was tied to the rails of the Palermo–Trapani line with a few pounds of explosive strapped round his waist. The murder was designed to look like a terrorist's bungled attempt to blow up the railway line.

Peppino's friends and colleagues scoured the hedgerows and the grass on the embankment, collecting the shreds of his body in black plastic bags. Amongst the fragments, they found his hands intact – proof that he could not have been holding a bomb when he died.

'How could they do that to him?' says his mother, still bewildered by the pain, fifteen years on. 'How could they have tied him like that . . .? They had to pick him up in plastic bags, all in little bits. How am I supposed to live with that?'

The trial of the unknown killers of Peppino Impastato opened in 1978. Felicia's younger son Giovanni came home one day saying the family could bring a claim for damages. But Felicia wouldn't hear of her son appearing in court. 'I will do the talking,' she told her son. 'They wouldn't hurt an old woman.'

The trial, in spite of the efforts of Peppino's colleagues and supporters, sank into the bog of judicial corruption and cover-ups, and there were no convictions. Years later, new pieces of evidence still trickle out about the murder of Peppino Impastato, but there has never been an arrest.

Felicia Impastato lives alone with her disturbing memories for company. Only her son Giovanni and his wife are regular visitors to that house. 'Nobody comes here any more. Since my husband died no one comes to visit. They know they're not welcome. I stood up for my son, and they didn't like it one bit.

Well that's too bad. I will defend my son until they close my eyes.

'Everyone said Peppino was crazy. Now they say we need a hundred like him. Now that it's too late.'

When she's expecting her son Giovanni to drop in for lunch, Felicia Impastato lays the table in readiness. If he doesn't walk in the door right on time, she clears the things away. She can't stand to have the place laid and waiting for a son who might never come.

12. Life with the Supergrass

It must have been an unnerving sight: Calogero Ganci, the tough, 20-stone bearded hit man, standing at the door of his prison cell, bellowing that he wanted to see his wife.

Despite Ganci's criminal pedigree – his father, Don Raffaele, was the patriarch of a mafia dynasty closely allied with the Corleonesi – three years in isolation in a maximum security prison had cracked him. He had agreed to collaborate with the investigators, but before he made a statement, there was something he had to tell his wife.

Isabella Anselmo was brought in, and the couple were shown into a room where they could talk. Prison guards stood silently at the corners of the cell as the big man shook, covered his face with his hands, and sobbed. 'Isabella, forgive me,' he blurted out. 'It was me that killed your father.'[1]

She shot to her feet, took a step back and stared at him, tears rolling down her face. 'How could you hide it from me all this time? How am I going to tell the children that their father killed their grandfather?'

His father-in-law had belonged to a mafia clan under attack by the Corleonesi, and Ganci had been ordered to set the trap. For the young mafioso, then in his early twenties, it was a test. He was the only one the old man trusted, and he had to prove that his loyalty to the organisation was stronger than any emotional ties.

Ganci was the number one hit man for the Corleonesi throughout the mafia war of 1980–82, when Totò Riina, in his bid for domination, mounted a spectacular attack on the Palermo clans. Ganci's confessions were staggering. He had carried out over a hundred hits and was author of many of the 'illustrious crimes' of Palermo's darkest years, including the 1982 shooting of General Carlo Alberto Dalla Chiesa with his wife Emanuela Setti Carraro, and the assassination of Judge Rocco Chinnici, founder of the anti-mafia pool of magistrates.

The assassin's decision to 'turn' was, according to his lawyer, the result of months of thought. He had been arrested with his father, which made his decision to collaborate all the harder: he would be giving evidence against his own family. But three years in isolation had given him a lot of time to think.

Ganci's lawyer, Lucia Falzone, is young, clever, pretty and ambitious. One of the few legal experts specialising in the defence of mafia defectors, her case load grows by the hour, and Falzone works late into the night seven days a week.

Breaking off from work on a Sunday afternoon, in Caltanissetta, central Sicily, she was chain-smoking, and had covered her bad skin with pale foundation when everyone around her already had the beginnings of a summer tan. The traffic roared around us as we sat stirring drinks in the dry, dirty wind.

Falzone's admiration for her client was unnerving. She described him as well read, intelligent and courteous; if he hadn't been a mafioso, he could have been a successful businessman. He was more modern-thinking than most mafiosi: he had chosen a female lawyer, for a start, which shows something of a progressive attitude.

Ganci was disgusted and disillusioned with Cosa Nostra, and in particular, with its leader. Totò Riina's despotic dictatorship required more of his footsoldiers than they could stomach. 'The younger generation, now in their twenties and thirties, are angry. They feel betrayed. They find the rules of Cosa Nostra oppressive; instead of becoming free and powerful as men of honour, they are subjected to tyranny. They are told to commit more and more dreadful, senseless crimes, and they no longer feel that the reason for these assassinations has anything to do with them. In the early eighties, during the mafia wars, they knew who the enemy was, and they knew they had to kill or be killed. Now they don't know what they're killing for.'

Ganci was made a man of honour in 1980, when he was only 20. Growing up within the walls of a mafia dynasty, he had very little choice in the matter. 'His father's sons were destined to join the organisation. Part of his decision to collaborate was to free his own sons from the family tradition. "Even if my wife doesn't go along with my decision and disowns me," he told me, "my boys will always be marked as the sons of a *pentito*, so they will be barred from the organisation." '

When Ganci told his wife that he had killed her father, he said, 'You can leave me. I would understand.'

Isabella, who for three years had followed her husband from one maximum security jail to the next, turning up once a month on Italy's most inaccessible and inhospitable islands, broke down and cried, 'What have they done to our lives?'

The daughter and granddaughter of mafiosi, Isabella must have known what her husband was. She probably guessed he had something to do with her father's murder. 'Maybe she did know,' his lawyer agrees. 'But to hear him confess to it was something else entirely. Mafia women are accomplices. They don't ask questions, most of the time they just keep quiet and give their support. It's better not to talk about it, that way you never know for sure. But once her husband gets arrested, she has to confront who he is, and what he has done. After Ganci's confession, his wife said one thing. "I support my husband's decision." She was incredibly strong. She really loves him.'

By a transformation partly the result of a Catholic inheritance, a mafia killer who decides to repent and confess, in the eyes of law-abiding society becomes a hero. But for the woman who has stuck by him through all his years of stalking and killing, the process is reversed. When he confesses, she sees clearly for the first time how bad he really is.

Cosa Nostra has its own hermetically sealed 'logic', within which the murder of a best friend or even a child can be justified. When faced with death, betrayal or confession, mafia men and women seem to wake up from a deep trance. Women who knew their husbands were killers are profoundly shocked to hear it. Men who thought they were doing the right thing break down when confronted with the reality that they were not.

For Ganci, a man who, in his professional capacity, must

have got a lot of satisfaction from watching people's heads explode, the turning point was the kidnap and murder of the 13-year-old boy Giuseppe Di Matteo. After he heard about this pointless and cruel crime, the view from his top security prison was strangely altered. 'I know how you strangle someone, because I've done it with my own hands,' he told his lawyer. 'How could I ever look my son in the eyes again, if I had strangled a child?'

Ironically, Ganci's son took his change of heart very badly. Collaborators' children are often stigmatised, picked on and bullied at school. Before their father defected, both of Ganci's children, a boy of 11 and a girl of 14, enjoyed the kudos of having a mafia boss as a father. The boy could not accept that the father he adored and looked up to as a hero, was now an *infame*, a traitor, a scab.

The first Italian mafia defector was the wretched Leonardo Vitale, who decided to confess everything after his arrest in 1974 (see Chapter 2). He was disbelieved, diagnosed insane and committed to an asylum before being definitively silenced by his former associates.

But a major breakthrough by Italian organised crime investigators came when Judge Giovanni Falcone brought home the Sicilian Tommaso Buscetta from Brazil in 1984, with the announcement that the once powerful Cosa Nostra boss had decided to collaborate.

Buscetta had been on the run from the mafia and US law enforcement when he was arrested in Brazil. Since he was out of their reach, Buscetta's mafia rivals had begun systematically murdering his family. The Brazilian police had pulled out his fingernails to try to make him confess to being the mastermind of an international heroin trafficking operation, without eliciting a word. But when Giovanni Falcone flew out to hear Buscetta cross-examined, he finally showed some willingness to talk. Those who know him are convinced that it took one key person to persuade Tommaso Buscetta to collaborate – his wife.

As an aspiring mafioso in Palermo, Buscetta had already shown a compulsive interest in women, which later got him into trouble with the Commission. At 16, ambitious and restless, he had pursued a beautiful girl from his neighbourhood, Melchiorra Cavallaro; they started meeting in secret, she got pregnant and they married in 1946. But after four months of married life, Buscetta got bored and moved to Turin. He returned to Palermo in December just in time for the birth of his daughter.[2]

But he couldn't settle down. At 18 he was already initiated, a made member of Cosa Nostra, and doing pretty much his own thing. By the mid-1950s, Buscetta was travelling between Italy and the US, using several aliases, making contacts in the heroin trade, and with other women. He settled in Mexico under an alias, where he was joined by his Sicilian mistress, Vera Girotti. The couple moved to New York, and were living in Queens when Buscetta had unexpected visitors: his wife Melchiorra and their children. Unfazed, he settled his wife in an apartment in New York, and continued to live with his mistress.

Such behaviour is viewed in a dim light by the Commission, who regard a long-term mistress as a security risk. Casual relationships with beautiful dumb women are fine, almost obligatory to enhance the mobster's social status, but longer relationships can get nasty when they break up, and a mistress scorned might reveal information about her ex-lover's associates. The other, frequently quoted rule, that a wife must never be publicly humiliated by her husband, again has much less to do with respect, than the fear of what the wife might say in anger.

It was later said that Buscetta was dropped by the Commission because of his disorderly love life, but there is no evidence for this. According to his lawyer, Luigi LiGotti, Buscetta never cared for rules. 'Buscetta is an extraordinary person. He has always done what he wants. He has never sought permission: he knew he wouldn't get it, so he just went ahead, and got away with it. He has had lovers, jealous scenes, women fighting over him – and he has always been part of Cosa Nostra.'³

Wanted by Italian and American police, Buscetta went to Mexico for plastic surgery to create a new face. Studying 'before' and 'after' pictures, it is very hard to spot the difference. Not even his children noticed any change. But the episode created a myth around him: the invisible man; master of a thousand disguises. This reputation gathered momentum: during the Palermo mafia wars, when members of his family were being eliminated with mechanical regularity, people whispered about the dangerous avenger who would return to Palermo unrecognised to exterminate his enemies, and who might already be in their midst.

In 1971 Buscetta was expelled from the US but continued to expand his drug operation; he travelled frequently to Paraguay and moved to Brazil. Cristina Guimaraes was sunbathing on the beach at Copacabana, when she became aware of a man staring at her. She was 19, pretty and blonde; he was 45, thickset, with a square face and protruding eyes. She was a law student, who spoke five languages, the daughter of a successful Brazilian lawyer. She found him charming and her family took to him immediately. They moved in together, and he went to work for her brother, an insurance broker. Later, she discovered that he was already married. Not to one woman, but two. And that he had several children.

For a short time they lived together in luxurious surroundings. But Buscetta was arrested by the Brazilian police the following year and extradited to Italy on a murder charge. He spent five years in the Ucciardone prison in Palermo, where his reputation preceded him: as a high-ranking mafioso he enjoyed conditions of comfort and ease; his meals were brought in to him from the city's top restaurants, and the other prisoners waited on him. During this time he married Cristina.

On his release, Buscetta skipped probation and escaped to Brazil on a false passport before his enemies could reach him. Cristina and the children joined him, and they set up home on a ranch in the Amazon basin.

A bloody mafia war had ended with the Corleonesi taking over the Palermo clans, including Buscetta's family of Porta Nuova. While Buscetta lived high in South America, his enemies started exterminating his family in Sicily. In September 1982 his two sons Benedetto and Antonio disappeared. Next his son-in-law, his favourite brother and his nephew were shot dead in Palermo. As news of the systematic murder of his family reached them, Buscetta and his new family went underground. But while dodging Cosa Nostra's assassins, they were arrested by the Brazilian narcotics department.

While the US and Italy competed to extradite him, and the Brazilians tortured him, Cristina went to the US Embassy again and again, begging them not to send her husband back to Palermo, where the mafia was sure to eliminate him, and would probably target her and the children as well.

Cristina is always portrayed as a smart woman. She must have known what she was getting into when she married Tommaso Buscetta in Palermo's top security prison. According to some sources, her background was not very different from his: her father was a lawyer who carried a gun, and had earned himself 'powerful friends and a shady reputation'.[4]

Caught between the police and the mafia, Buscetta finally began to think about protecting his family. But when he came home to Sicily to begin his collaboration, he claimed the moral high ground, saying he no longer recognised the honoured society he had joined as a young man. Why should he defend an organisation that had forgotten the notion of honour, with his silence?[5] The mafia, he said, was 'not fuelled by principles of honesty and moral rectitude as I had once believed, but was in fact a conspiracy whose sole end was to protect its members from being caught committing crimes'.[6]

Antonio Manganelli, then a police investigator working with Falcone, later became head of the special department for the protection of *pentiti*. (He has since been appointed chief of police in Palermo.) The phenomenon of mafia defectors has grown so big that one has to obtain permission to see Manganelli from the Ministry of the Interior – a pilgrimage of paperwork along endless bureaucratic corridors. His office, in a concrete desert beyond the southernmost stop of the Rome metro, is guarded by police with submachine guns.

Manganelli is softly spoken, tanned, perfectly manicured, and perfectly mannered. He has no doubt that Cristina was responsible for Buscetta's change of heart. 'Behind Buscetta, this charismatic personality, is a truly remarkable woman. She understood that collaboration was the only way, she begged him to do it. She is an extraordinary woman, undoubtedly much more cultured than most mafia wives . . . The way her mind works is clear, concrete and efficient – she goes straight for the solution to a problem.

'She has done a lot for him. She adopted his children from another marriage, she took them to Brazil, gave them a new life, and brought up their own two children – very well, in my opinion . . . All the time he was in Brazil, and in Italy, she struggled on alone . . . When I met her she was holding together this extended family, and living exactly like any other American woman. She spoke perfect English, and was studying and working as an interpreter.'

The American witness protection plan is designed to make people disappear: it works perfectly well, unless you have a famous face. Buscetta's notoriety has made it very difficult for his wife to start again.

'She was recently living in an American town where nobody has even heard of the mafia, where there shouldn't have been any question of anyone finding out who he was. She had settled down well there. One evening, they showed a TV programme on the American mafia. At the start and finish of the commercial break, the programme had a logo, a single image: Buscetta's face. That same evening, the coloured lady who lived opposite phoned to say, "Hey, we saw your husband on TV! He's famous!" So the next day the family had to move out.'

Buscetta became the most celebrated supergrass of all time. But his glory is fading as other, newer defectors take the stage. 'Buscetta loved the limelight,' says his lawyer Luigi LiGotti.

'He always says: "The worst day will be when they turn off the spotlight." Other *pentiti* have overtaken him in importance. He has said everything he has to say.'

A great self-publicist, Buscetta has tried to hang on to the mystique. Recently his picture was published in a popular Italian magazine after 'ten agonising hours' under the plastic surgeon's knife – an operation which was clearly more for the purposes of youth enhancement than disguise. He now looks like one of the *Thunderbirds* puppets.

After holding the family together for years, Cristina is suffering from nervous exhaustion. In 1995, she was ill and had trouble walking; her husband decided to take her and their son on a cruise to perk her up. A reporter from the weekly magazine *Oggi* – the Italian equivalent of *Hello!* – was also on board, and elicited an interview, with pictures, from the supposedly anonymous supergrass. The news caused a national scandal. When they came into dock, a police helicopter winched three passengers off the ship and whisked them away to safety.

The mafia's God is strictly Old Testament. Cosa Nostra has always exercised dominion over the blood family, and from time to time a mafioso is forced to prove his loyalty by sacrificing a loved one. But when the clan loses credibility, the mafioso tends to return to his wife and children. A man who has understood that he has been a slave all his life, could not wish to see his children enslaved in their turn. Unfortunately, most mafia members only reach this conclusion when their criminal career is over.

Nino Calderone was a powerful mafioso. His brother Pippo was head of the Commission, and guaranteed him a position of authority in Catania. Nino owned two service stations, a motor parts trade and a portfolio of illegal imports that financed the clan's drug trafficking and laundered the profits. He and his wife Margherita Gangemi used to spend Sundays and holidays with their friends, Catania *capo* Nitto Santapaola and his wife, Carmela Minniti. The two couples were godparents to each other's children, which practically made them relations.

When his brother Pippo was murdered in a leadership struggle in 1978, Nino Calderone hung on, hoping his friendship with Santapaola would protect him. One evening soon after Pippo's death, the Calderone family called in at the Santapaola house, unannounced as usual. Carmela was at home, but she was strangely tense and guarded. She told them her husband was out, and that she was sorry, she couldn't invite them for supper because there were workmen in, and there wasn't a thing in the house.

This strangely cold reception confirmed Calderone's worst fears: that his friend had killed his brother. It struck him that Santapaola was going to kill him too. 'And not just me. I realised that Nitto, my friend, whose wife was a friend of my wife's, knew me so well that if he was going to do the job properly, he'd have to kill my wife as well, since it was obvious I always told her everything.'[7]

He decided to run. In February 1983 Nino Calderone headed for the south of France. His wife stayed on in Catania, sorting out their financial affairs, getting the children organised, packing the minimum necessary without drawing anyone's attention to the fact that the family was leaving town.

They settled in Nice; the former mafia boss rented a shop and set himself up in the laundry business, this time cleaning clothes. In spite of their financial difficulties and their new humble lifestyle, he was improbably happy. Perhaps momentarily forgetting that his career in Cosa Nostra was washed up, he prided himself on the fact that he had liberated his family from a future in the mafia. When his daughter asked if they were ever going home, he said: 'You're a big girl now, you know who I was in Catania. If we had stayed there and someone like me, a mafioso, had asked for your hand, I would have had to say yes . . . now you can marry whoever you want. You don't have to marry a mafioso and live on the run, or in hiding, or constantly tortured by fear.'[8]

The new life had its alarming moments. One day a notorious killer from Palermo, Pino Greco, who was living in Nice at the time, brought in a pair of trousers. Calderone ducked behind a washing machine. He couldn't tell whether Greco was coming for him, or whether he just wanted his trousers cleaned. The gangster was supposed to pick up his cleaning on Thursday, and Calderone spent the whole day hiding in the back. When Greco turned up, Margherita slammed the trousers down on the counter, and charged him a ridiculously high price. 'What?' Greco protested, 'that much for one pair of trousers? I'm not coming back here.'

'Doesn't bother me,' she retorted. 'That's what it costs, and if you don't like it, don't come back.' He didn't go back.[9]

While Calderone and his wife were eking out an honest living in Nice during 1984, Tommaso Buscetta was unravelling the mysteries of Cosa Nostra's recent history. Soon afterwards, a warrant went out for Calderone's arrest. Police tracking the couple put taps on the telephone lines to their families in Sicily. During one conversation with her mother, Margherita let slip a couple of details which gave away their whereabouts. Calderone was arrested in 1986, and imprisoned in Marseilles, awaiting extradition to Italy.

The mafia tracked down Calderone in Marseilles. After a series of threats on his life, including an attempt to burn him alive in his cell, he was thoroughly rattled. It was clear that he wouldn't survive the trip from his cell to the courthouse if he returned to Italy. Meanwhile Margherita and the children had fled their home in Nice when she found out there were mafia killers on their trail. In December 1986, Giovanni Falcone received a phone call from France. A woman's voice said: 'My name is Margherita Gangemi. My husband Antonino Calderone would like to talk to you.'

A couple of days later, Manganelli and Judge Falcone arrived in France to debrief the latest defector. Knowing it was vital to gain the confidence of the collaborator's wife, Manganelli arranged a meeting with her the evening before. She was clearly in desperate straits. The wife of a once powerful

mafioso, she was only just managing to feed the children by
scrubbing the stairs of apartment blocks.

When Manganelli and Falcone went to see Nino Calderone
the next day, he refused to speak without first talking to his
wife. Since no one knew where Margherita was, they waited
the whole day, hour after hour in awkward silence, before she
was eventually found. Husband and wife spent a long time in
earnest conversation, after which Calderone announced that his
collaboration could officially begin.

This was long before the law guaranteed mafia defectors a
basic income and somewhere to live, and Manganelli and his
colleagues were forced to improvise. 'We used to interrogate
Calderone for a week every month. One day, as we were
leaving France, not due to return for three weeks, we realised
that we were leaving Signora Calderone with three children
and a dog and absolutely no way of feeding them. She is a very
dignified person, and was going to let us leave without saying a
word. I said, "Here is the advance payment for the next stage of
your husband's collaboration." But it wasn't the advance
payment, it was our own money.'[10]

Calderone was moved to Italy to testify, and serve the
remainder of his sentence. He was depressed, bitter and
tortured by self-loathing. Every time he was taken out of prison
and moved to a safe house for interrogation, his wife was there,
with their youngest child, to meet him. 'Every time,. this
woman's presence was a sign of faith – it was a great boost for
him,' Manganelli remembers.

Money was still a problem, and Margherita kept the family
going by sheer force of will. 'She worked as a nurse during the
day, and in an old people's home at night. After work, she
would go home, make supper for the children, then she'd be
on her feet all night, looking after old people, who need
attention every ten minutes. At the weekends, she would do
the cooking in a scout camp, for 200 or 300 people. Then on
Monday, she'd start again. She never got a moment's rest. She
never slept.'

After Calderone's release, the couple planned to move to the US. The arrangements were in place, with documents and plane tickets supplied, when officious police detectives told them they would have to leave their dog behind. They refused. It was only by Manganelli's intervention that the family finally left on schedule, to begin a new life, with their dog. 'You can never underestimate the wrench that people suffer, leaving everything for an unknown future in a foreign place. Of course they couldn't leave their dog, after everything that family had been through.'

Since settling in the States, Margherita has put all the children through college. 'Thanks to her efforts, it's working out for them,' says Manganelli. 'It's the best example I've seen of a mafia family making themselves a normal life.'

It's a long way from the heady social life of the Catania mafia, the holidays on the Ionian coast, wedding parties, and christening parties. Instead of sitting down for dinner with 500 glamorous guests, Margherita Gangemi cooks for 300, paid by the hour. Her husband's collaboration has meant some difficult personal choices for her too. Recently her mother died but she did not go back to Catania for the funeral: she knew that her presence would only make things difficult for her relatives.

Margherita Gangemi seems humble and hard-working by nature. What did it mean to her, being married to a powerful mafia boss? 'If you think about it,' says Manganelli, 'it's not as if he was a hit man who left the house after dark and went off to shoot somebody. He had his petrol stations and his bar – it wasn't as if she was married to some sort of bandit – she was a businessman's wife. He financed the clan's drug trade. It's clean work – that is, it seemed to be clean, he didn't have to go about strangling people.

'Yes, she understood that the mafia was behind all this, she understood that he was someone important, but it's different from being married to a thief who goes out at night and robs houses. It's easier to pretend you don't understand the evil behind it all.'

★

The Italian version of a witness protection programme, as Manganelli admits, is years behind the US Marshal Service. In the late 1980s it was still in its infancy, while frightened or disillusioned mafia members defected in increasing numbers. But the issue of 'penitent' mafiosi giving evidence has become controversial. Voices warn that the system is open to abuse by lazy investigators too willing to prosecute on the word of a turncoat with an axe to grind. In a couple of instances, investigators have been accused of taking risks in their single-minded pursuit of the testimony they need.

Francesco Marino Mannoia, a tough and ambitious mafioso from Palermo, married Rosa, the daughter of mafia boss Giuseppe Vernengo, in September 1978. It was quite usual for an up-and-coming young mafioso to improve his prospects by attaching himself to one of the major dynasties. Rather more unusual was that Marino Mannoia's long-standing girlfriend, Rita Simoncini, had just told him she was pregnant. Marino Mannoia had no intention of breaking off his love affair, and began a parallel life. His girlfriend lived near him and his wife in Palermo, and when her daughter Cristina was born, they saw more of each other than ever. Rita inhabited the edge of her lover's life: his mother adored her, and his younger sister Enza was her best friend and confidante through what must have been emotionally testing years.

Marino Mannoia was a skilled heroin refiner for the Palermo *cosca* or clan – headed by the triumvirate of Rosario Spatola, Stefano Bontade and Salvatore Inzerillo – which was all but exterminated in Totò Riina's takeover in 1982. He managed to escape the slaughter and placed himself with implacable professionalism at Riina's disposal. Riina found him an excellent soldier: hard, serious, inscrutable – a mafioso of the old school. And an excellent chemist.

Having survived the putsch, Marino Mannoia was arrested in January 1985. While he was in prison in the spring of 1989 he learned that his brother Agostino – his closest ally and informant in the organisation – had disappeared. Police found his car abandoned, with blood spattered all over the interior.

When they went to inform the family, his mother, a tough woman with an instinctive mistrust of the police, didn't flinch. After a long silence she said: 'If he comes back, fine. If not, patience.'[11]

Francesco Marino Mannoia's sister and his aunt were both involved in mafia activity: during the preparation for a murder, guns were often hidden among their household rags or in their knicker drawer. After his arrest, Marino Mannoia's sister went to visit him in prison every week, and kept him up to date with what was going on in the neighbourhood. She knew everyone and could give him information on the alliances and plots going on in his absence.

During his imprisonment, according to his lawyer, Marino Mannoia's girlfriend kept up a continual, subtle pressure to draw him away from the mafia family he had married into, to distance himself from the carnage that lay putrefying around Cosa Nostra. The Corleonesi meanwhile were watchful of any sign that he might intend to collaborate. When he made the decision – a terrible wrench for a mafioso with his scruples, his discipline, his hard attitude – he let Falcone know through the only person he could trust.

It was late one September afternoon in 1989, when Rita Simoncini arrived at the offices of police chiefs Gianni De Gennaro and Antonio Manganelli. 'This woman turned up, and asked to talk to us. She was with her daughter, and we understood that the situation was pretty serious, so we asked a young woman from the office to take the little girl out for a pizza. We talked to her till late. When we had assured her she could count on the utmost secrecy, and that Judge Falcone would go and interrogate her husband as soon as possible, she said goodbye. As she was leaving, we asked her where she was going, if she was on her way back to Sicily, and she said, "Oh no, I checked into a hotel near the station, I'm going there."

'We thought it probably wasn't wise for her to go, because she might have told someone where she was going. We took her and her daughter to a house we use for undercover operations, where there's a bed, and got sheets from my house.

The next morning, two of our men accompanied Rita
Simoncini back to this hotel to get her luggage, and the
receptionist said, "Oh signora, you didn't come home last
night. There were two men looking for you. They waited all
night." '

Marino Mannoia's collaboration with Giovanni Falcone
started slowly, and continued for months as gradually he
revealed the inside workings of Riina's war machine. Part of his
motivation for becoming a collaborator was to leave his wife
and marry Rita Simoncini. His wife, who was a Vernengo first
and Marino Mannoia's wife second, agreed, with her father's
blessing, to a divorce.

As soon as Marino Mannoia agreed to talk, his family was
offered protection. According to Manganelli, they refused.
'The motive was simple: love. His sister, Enza, had just got
engaged, and wouldn't leave Palermo. The older women didn't
want to leave her behind.' The women's decision is perplexing.
They did not disapprove of Marino Mannoia's decision, but
they wanted to remain in Palermo and carry on as usual. They
put it about that they disowned him, and stayed. Either they
thought they could keep the news of his collaboration secret, or
they were convinced Cosa Nostra would not harm women.

'We tried to convince them,' says Manganelli. 'A woman
from our Anti-mafia Department went to meet Marino
Mannoia's sister a couple of times in a supermarket. They
walked around with their trolleys, looking at packets of food
and talking, without looking at each other. But she wouldn't
hear of leaving. In some respects, they were mafia women to
the bone.'

On 23 November 1989, just over a month after Francesco
Marino Mannoia began to collaborate, as his mother, aunt and
sister left their house in Bagheria and got into their car, gunmen
ambushed them and sprayed them with bullets. They died in
the street in a mess of blood and shattered glass.

The reason for the women's violent death, according to
Palermo deputy chief prosecutor Guido Lo Forte, was their
active involvement in mafia business: 'The women had

officially dissociated themselves from Francesco Marino Mannoia once he started to collaborate. But in reality, they were
helping him, taking messages, looking after his financial
interests, managing his income, and hiding weapons for him.
Giuseppe Lucchese, capo of a rival family, found out the
women were working for the collaborator. He said, "Women
give the orders in that house," and put them under surveillance.
As soon as he had proof that the women were working on
behalf of the defector, he had them killed.'[12]

The criminal sub-groups that hunt in the waters around the
Santapaola family in Catania include the Savasta clan, a group
continually tearing itself apart and re-forming with new allies
and enemies, and the casualty rate is high. Riccardo Messina, a
hit man for the group, was arrested in May 1994 and found
himself facing a series of heavy charges. As a member of a small,
volatile criminal group, he felt no great moral obligation to
protect his associates and, encouraged by his wife, Liliana
Caruso, decided to collaborate.

People knew the couple were close, and that Messina
listened to his wife's advice. So that when news leaked out of
the prison that Messina's daily routine had changed, his wife
began to receive solicitous visits. Liliana Caruso later described
the visits to magistrates in Catania.

The first sign of trouble was when Liliana's friend Domenica
Micci came to call, bringing her best friend Santa Vasta, smiling
and kissing her on both cheeks, and patting the children. Once
the two women — wives of the Savasta clan leader and his
deputy — were seated at the kitchen table, they asked Liliana
Caruso for news of her husband. Was it true he was planning to
talk? If she needed money, they could help — after all, they had
always been good friends. If Liliana wanted to leave him, they'd
understand, they could help her out. Who would want to be
married to an *infame*?

The women offered their support with smiles: it was their

duty to support the families of imprisoned members of the group. They were here to help. Off they trotted, with much smiling and patting, leaving her to give their offer some thought.

Not long after, the ladies paid another visit. Liliana sent the children out to play, and told her friends they were wrong: her husband had no intention of betraying the family, it was just talk, there was nothing to worry about, and she didn't need money. The smiles faded off her friends' faces.

The following day they were back. They told her their husbands, the boss Nino Puglisi and his second-in-command Orazio Nicolosi, would like to talk to her. Both men were in hiding; she would be taken to a secret location. She could bring the children.

Liliana mentioned this invitation to her husband the next time she saw him. Realising his former allies would try to kidnap her, and probably the children as well, to stop him talking, he warned her sternly not to go.

Instead of going to meet the bosses in their remote country hideout, Messina's wife reported the threats she had received. Every time her unfriendly neighbours paid a call, she relayed their threats to magistrates investigating the Savasta clan. But although news of her husband's collaboration was circulating in Catania's ancient backstreets, Liliana Caruso and her children were not protected.

'She was offered protection,' says magistrate Francesco Puleio, 'but it would have meant moving to a secret location in the north, and her husband didn't want her and the children to leave without him. He needed his wife near him.'[13]

On the afternoon of 13 July 1994, less than a month after Messina first hinted that he would collaborate, his wife and her mother, Agata Zuchero, set out to report yet another threat from the Savasta women. On her way out, Liliana remembered she had to buy the children's tea. She told her older daughter, aged 11, to let the basket down from the balcony on its long string, so she could put the shopping in it and her daughter could pull it up. The girl stood on the balcony, basket at the ready, staring absently across at the neighbours' balconies, their dusty geraniums, their shutters closed against the afternoon sun. Suddenly she heard an explosion in the street. She looked down. Her grandmother was lying on the ground. She recognised her father's friend Nino Puglisi standing over the old lady, pointing a gun. She looked at the grocer's across the road, expecting her mother to come running out. Instead of her mother, Orazio Nicolosi, another friend of her father's, burst out of the shop with a gun in his hand, and the two men ran away.

More than a warning to silence Messina, the double murder was a message to other *pentiti*. Liliana Caruso's mother came from the slums of Catania but had no involvement in organised crime (her father had passionately disapproved of her getting mixed up with a mafioso). By murdering a woman entirely unconnected, the Savasta clan showed that they would create scorched earth around anyone who dared to talk. Solidarity with traitors had to be discouraged.

But the tide had turned against them. In November 1996, the boss Nino Puglisi and his lieutenant Orazio Nicolosi were given life sentences for the murder of Agata Zuchero and Liliana Caruso. Their wives Domenica Micci and Santa Vasta were given four years each. Riccardo Messina, who had brought a civil case against his wife's murderers, was awarded damages.

Riccardo Messina has subscribed to a judicial system foreign to his upbringing – a sign that he has crossed the line between the criminal underworld and 'civil' society. But his lawyer suggests that such a crossing is never definitive. If that system had let him down, she implies, he would have resorted to violence. 'He would have obtained justice by himself.'[14]

13. Marriage Most Foul

April Woltemate's connection with the South Philadelphia mafia began with the end of her first marriage. She was an unconventional girl from a decent middle-class Catholic family, flirting with the wild side of South Philadelphia. He was a gangster looking for a girlfriend.

'A new casino had opened up and me and four other girls went out to this place in South Street. It was June fifteenth 1982. This guy kept sending drinks over all night. I was just separated from my husband, I was having fun with the girls. We didn't want to bother with the guys. At the end of the night I went over and thanked him for the drinks.

'He got my phone number – I wouldn't give it to him, but he found it – and he kept on calling my parents' house until I had to talk to him. So we went out . . . We went down the shore to the casino, for dinner. I was just separated, I had babies, I wasn't looking for a boyfriend.'

But Ron 'Cuddles' DiCaprio was not to be dissuaded, and April couldn't resist the attention. She looks battered by her experience, and her cheeks are flushed with thread veins, but she is tall and slim in a dark red fitted jacket and black ski pants, and her blue eyes and high cheekbones are faithful relics of her good looks. Her words slur a little and her voice swings from low to high in mockery of her former innocence.

She had been through college and done an accounting course, was home with her parents and putting her life together again, when her admirer swept her into the mob haunts of the South Philadelphia waterfront. 'We started going out, down to the shore, with a bunch of his friends. One time we were asked to leave the casino – I was so embarrassed. We were undesirables. I came from such a proper background, it was so different . . . I think Ron was attracted to me because I was

everything he wasn't. None of them had made it through grade
school. I came from a good family, had a good education, raised
as a proper Italian Catholic girl, you know . . .

'I thought he was a bookie, a bartender, no big deal. He
taught me how to do the numbers game [an illegal lottery], so I
became a bookie. I thoroughly enjoyed it. Those accounting
skills, I put them to good use! I kept great books! It was fun.'

We are sitting in the corner of a cosy, noisy bar in rural
Pennsylvania in winter, drinking red wine in the middle of the
afternoon. April has given up smoking, but she gets up and
buys me a packet of cigarettes. A man at the bar recounting an
interminable story in a braying voice is on his third listener.

April, whose hands have aged more than her face and her
short, strawberry blonde hair, doesn't seem to have put the past
very far behind her. She talks enthusiastically about her early
love affair with the mafia.

Social life revolved around the mob: every occasion was an
excuse for the men to get together. 'There were two sets of
friends: the husbands with the girlfriends, and the husbands
with the wives. I saw both. The wives knew their husbands all
had girlfriends, but I don't think they cared. They got money
and their one night out a week. They didn't care what the guys
did the rest of the time. Weddings were a wife thing. They
were always like, a Sunday after the football game, or a Friday
night before the football game started.'

As April discovered, weddings are often used for mob
business. 'At one wedding, I happened to walk into the back
room, and I walked into the middle of their initiation
ceremony. They were making a man a member. They burn a
piece of paper, a tissue, in his hand, and they draw blood, they
do the whole spiel. There they were in a circle and I could see
like a fire in the middle. And I was like "Oops, sorry guys", and
made a real fast exit.'

Being a gangster's girlfriend was hard work. She had to
shine. 'We were always dressed up. Every day. It was like a job.
It was fun at the start, but you kind of get tired of it. He would
take me to the store and I would try everything on and he

would buy it for me.' At weddings the competition was fierce. The wives would jostle, each one a blazing Christmas tree, to outshine the rest, and trash each other's outfits. April was having a good time. 'At that level, I knew them as people, not as murderers and killers and things like that, they were nice guys, y'know, and the girls were fun.'

The fun did not last. Seven months later, everything changed. Cuddles DiCaprio and his running mate, Joe Rico, were ambitious to 'make their bones': to commit a murder so they could be made members of the mafia. DiCaprio needed April, who was still living at her parents' house, for logistical support, probably because she had a better brain than the two men, and because nothing seemed to rattle her, but mainly because she had a clean record and an unsuspectable address. April admits that part of her was excited by the gangsters' plotting, part of her too frightened to raise any objection.

'Joe Rico had given me a shoe box and a map and told me to hide them. The box was done up with tape. Of course, being a female, I'm shaking it, weighing it . . . and then I realised: Holy shit, this is a gun in this box. I looked at the map, and it didn't mean anything to me. So I put it away.

'One night, it was the third week of January, Ron took a phone call at my house, then him and Joe went out. When they came back, they asked me for the box and the map. Now I knew what was in the box. They asked me for a pair of gloves. And they had changed their clothes: they had old clothes on, which I had never seen – they were always dressed up. So they took the box, and said they were going to take care of a problem. I thought they meant they were going to go out and scare the guy . . . surprise!'

Over an hour later Ron exploded back into the house, hyped up and ranting: 'He was really ticked off because Joe had let him down. He was yelling: "It was the first time Joe had shot anybody. He lied," he said, "he told me he'd whacked somebody before. I had to yell at him to shoot him. He almost shot *me*." '

'OK,' April imitates her own voice, tiny and breathless.

'He gave me this bag of money and said, "Count the money and make sure there's no blood on it," so I counted the money and there was like 7,000 dollars, and he said, "OK, go hide it in the back of the basement." Then he told me to wash the clothes.'

DiCaprio was still talking. 'He said "Can you believe this guy? He shoots the guy three times. Still alive. I go to his pocket to take out a penknife, and I stab him in his neck. I go take a piece of rope, this guy's still alive. Joe goes and gets the man's car, backs it up. There was Christmas presents in the trunk, there was a baseball bat. So we used a baseball bat to hold the trunk open, and throw him in, and he's still alive and saying Help me, help me." Joe slammed the trunk down and they went and parked the car. Then they came right to my house.

'We were up till five o'clock in the morning. Joe Rico and Ron and I. Ron fell asleep on the couch snoring. Joe was sitting, all psyched up – and he never touched his hair. He has it slicked back, right? He's just killed a man, right? and he's sitting like this, with his arm up, kind of like half lounging, not messing his hair up. I'm on the floor, thinking, He's not messing his hair! he's just killed a guy and he's worried about his hair.

'They were glad because the weather was so cold that the body would freeze and it wouldn't smell. Then they were worried that somebody might hear him because he was still alive when they parked the car, saying "help me". Every time they heard sirens, they were convinced they'd found the body.

'Joe couldn't wait for morning to come because he wanted to go around the corner and tell the guys what they did . . .'

Greater surprises were to come. The morning after the murder, Ron turned up on April's doorstep and presented her with a small velvet box. Inside was an engagement ring. 'He said "When are we going to get married?" And I said "But I'm still married. I gotta get a divorce first." The guy was in a real hurry to get married.'

April was not so keen. Since she had started seeing Ron,

things had not been easy, and she had discovered that getting away from a gangster wasn't easy either. She had tried to leave him, and he had followed her and threatened to harm her parents if she didn't go back to him. He had beaten her up and threatened to kill her children. He had told her friends to stay away from her. She was isolated and trapped, with an engagement ring winking at her from its little box. April's voice is flat. 'The reason he was so keen for the wedding to happen as soon as possible was because a wife at that time could not testify against her husband.'

Waiting for her divorce, April was able to stall for time, but she was aware that she could not turn down DiCaprio's marriage offer. She knew too much about his crimes, not because she had spied, or asked, or even wanted to know, but because he had told her. Now he was going to make her pay for it. Like many women who allow themselves to slide into relationships with mafiosi, April had blinded herself to the consequences of her boyfriend's criminal activity. By the time she was forced to open her eyes, it was too late to extricate herself. Worse was to come, when Ron 'Cuddles' DiCaprio received instructions to kill his best friend, Pat 'the cat' Spirito.

'Pat? Oh yeah, he was a nice guy,' says April in a low voice. 'They killed him because he was supposed to go to a hit and he never showed up. And then he wasn't splitting the money right with his crew. When Ron got the order that this was going to happen, we were told to be closer with him, so he wouldn't suspect anything. That's the way they do it. It's always your best friends.

'And so we had to start hanging out with him. I was real quiet – I was trying hard to figure a way out. The whole time I was looking at this guy and thinking, You're gonna be dead.'

Ron drove the car the night Pat 'the cat' was shot. This time, the gangster's girlfriend was in on the plot from the first. After the murder, April went with Ron to a bar in New Jersey where they exchanged greetings with enough people to give them an alibi. Then they went out for dinner, just the two of them. Ron was in high spirits but still anxious, waiting for the sign that the hit had gone without a hitch. He talked about nothing else from the prawn cocktail to the coffee.

Ron DiCaprio did not disguise his haste to march April to the altar. It was November 1983. 'We were out Friday night, and I was out with Salvy Testa and a couple of guys. Sal and I were about the same age, and we were pretty good friends. But then again I didn't know he'd killed six people. We would just kind of hang out together. I was out till about six in the morning, playing poker machines.'

April had no way of getting out of this wedding. Not even going out all night with another man could put off her bridegroom. The reception, the following day, was the kind of lavish affair that lights up the mafia wives' weekend. The guests were all invited by Ron. All April had to do was show up in a white gown chosen and bought by her husband.

'There were 350 guests. The only pictures we had were the ones the FBI took outside,' she laughs. 'No cameras allowed. It was like a scene out of a movie. A couple of guys would come in and whole tables would stand up. I was standing there with my next-door neighbour. And he was saying to me "Jesus Christ, April, do you know who they are?" ' She laughs, almost a sob. 'He had his hand on my shoulder and he said: "What have you done?"'

'My parents didn't know what was going on. I never let them know. He had this hold on me, he knew I would never let anything happen to them. That's how he controlled me. You've got to understand, at that time the wiseguys ruled the city. They ruled.'

On their wedding night, the happy couple went out for dinner down to the shore. That night, April got food poisoning so badly that she ended up in hospital having her stomach pumped. She believes that her husband, having made sure she could not testify against him, was trying to poison her.

Seriously frightened, she went back to her parents' house, to convalesce. Ron was in and out of prison for the whole of the next year. The following winter, he was released from jail late

one night, and she went to pick him up with her father. She
dropped him off at their house and got back in the car.

'I said, "Look. Just leave me alone. I'm not going to say
anything to anybody, just let me go." But he wouldn't give me
a divorce. He kept coming around threatening me. He was
doing really nasty things. He came to where I was working,
tore the office apart. He followed me. So I went to the police,
tried to get a bond so he couldn't follow me.' The FBI, always
on the lookout for weak points in the mafia's armour, quick as
a flash offered April their support. 'They sent an agent round,
who said, "Is there anything I can do?" They wanted me to
testify against DiCaprio. I said "No, thank you." ' She laughs,
for a long time.

Her words go a bit blurry here. She talks fast, skipping
between one sequence of events and another. 'They told me
that he was going to . . . trying to . . . yeah he did. He went to
the boss to get permission to kill me.

'He was pretty violent, he grabbed me on the street, used to
beat me real bad, grab me when I was with the kids. I'm telling
you, it was like a movie. Joe Rico came into the restaurant
where I was working one night with a leather coat over his
shoulders, and two guys behind him. He said, "Everybody out,
now." Joe told me that I had to go back to Cuddles. I don't
remember what I said. It probably wasn't real nice.' She laughs
her jerky, wheezy laugh.

DiCaprio realised the FBI were encouraging his wife to
become a state witness, and made another attempt to kill her.
This time he hired a hit man. The FBI found out about the
plan, and sent one of their men to pose as the hired killer.
Then, naturally, an FBI agent told April what had happened
and asked whether she would like to reconsider becoming a
witness. 'They bullied me a little bit . . .' she admits, without
rancour. 'I was the easiest target to get what they wanted . . .'
Although she was cleverer than these mobsters – she had always
looked down on her husband and his friend – she realised that
they weren't just playing at being bad guys, and that she
probably couldn't protect herself from them for much longer.

The gangland adventure had turned sour. April finally agreed to testify against DiCaprio. 'It wasn't something I wanted to do. It was something I had to do. The wiseguys had done twenty-two murders by this time between them. It was ridiculous: twenty-two guys were dead. And it just wasn't stopping.'

She agreed to testify but refused to enter the witness protection programme. Instead, she played the mob at their own game. 'I never went home the same way twice. I knew all the tricks, because Ron had told me. I learned their way of doing things, so I knew what they were looking out for. I was trained,' she laughs. But the mob's intimidation intensified, and April ended up in the programme, kicking her heels in Texas. She did a degree in Houston, where her college friends thought she was from a biker gang.

April went to testify before the grand jury, and fell for one of her FBI bodyguards. On the first day she took the stand, agent Jerry Waltomate spent time trying to calm her down. He took her for lunch in the break, and she was too nervous to eat. When the hearing was over, they stopped for supper on the way back to her accommodation. She was highly strung and in serious need of care and attention. 'I really couldn't eat anything. Drank a couple of Margaritas though. Jerry took me upstairs, put me to bed, alone . . . I had nightmares, I was in a pretty bad way, and he took care of me.'

Ron DiCaprio was convicted on murder and racketeering charges, and sentenced to twenty years. April's marriage to FBI agent Jerry Waltomate released her from the witness protection programme, and she came home to freezing, suburban Pennsylvania. They now live in a neat little close in a tidy little house with dove grey carpets you can't walk on in your shoes, fitted furniture and a hysterically affectionate fluffy white dog that April calls 'The Rat'. Jerry has a firm handshake, he is precise and polite. Her teenage kids clump in and out with loud hellos.

'It's so different being with Jerry,' she admits as she swings her Range Rover down the suburban roads, each with its grandiose name and neatly trimmed verge. 'Jerry's so straight-laced . . . oh my God . . . you can't get any straighter. Ron was

really jealous, but Jerry's very protective. He's very very very
protective. We go for dinners with the other FBI couples, and
. . . you know, I just don't fit in. I mean, you should see their
shoes.'

Meeting the wives and lovers of mafia members, there is one
question that almost never arises: 'What is *she* doing with *him*?'

Most of these women were, or still are, powerfully attracted
to the mafia underworld – to the status they enjoyed as wives,
the money, and the excitement of living on the edge. April let
herself be drawn into the criminal underworld, without
questioning it, until circumstances forced her to confront the
fact that her lover was a murderer. What seems in retrospect
like a sudden revelation is usually the point at which there's so
much unsavoury evidence shoved under the carpet that the
door won't close.

The mafia marriage is usually a trade-off: the wife benefits
from her mafioso husband's status and respect, she gets money,
and reflected glamour; in return, she has to put up with having
weapons, or drugs, concealed about the house; mixing only
with close family, and accepting her husband's long absences, as
well as having total strangers, on the run from the police,
staying in her home.

In the USA a wife cannot testify against her husband; in Italy
a woman cannot be prosecuted for aiding and abetting a
member of her family. But a mafioso needs more than the
protection already afforded him by the law. He needs someone
he can trust. Relations between mafia 'brothers' are fickle;
when things turn sour a mafioso's wife is often the only person
he can rely on.

Marriage is a strategic business: an ambitious young man may
yoke himself to a distinguished mafia family by marrying the
daughter. Sam Giancana, boss of the Chicago crime family in
the 1950s and 1960s, was determined to catch a useful fellow
with a future in politics, and hitch him to one of his daughters.

Sam's daughter Antoinette recalls that the only time she gained her father's approval was when she was dating a smart young lawyer called Tony Tisci. 'Tony was a protégé of my father's, a man for whom he had big political plans . . . my failure to marry Tony was never forgotten.'[1] Sam persisted in his ambition and Tony Tisci married his second daughter, Bonnie.

Giancana's control of his daughters' emotional affairs was absolute: Antoinette discovered that her father sent his boys round to scare off any unsuitable suitors. Like many first-generation Italian-Americans, Sam Giancana set great store by appearances. When Antoinette got divorced, he never forgave her, and never spoke to her again.

A good mafia wife knows everything and says nothing, but her husband must keep his side of the bargain and treat her with proper respect, at least in public. The Sicilian mafia defector Gaspare Mutolo once observed that a good marriage is a safeguard against information leaking out. 'The man of honour who respects his family and doesn't betray his wife creates a tranquil home. If he betrays his wife, he will fuel gossip and spite, and risks having "family" business discussed in public.'[2]

Mutolo's self-righteous view of a good marriage is typical mafia hypocrisy: a mistress is essential to the mafioso's reputation and self-esteem. What he must not do is publicly humiliate his wife. He may commit adultery, by all means, but a minimum of tact is required.

Judge Giovanni Falcone described Cosa Nostra as 'decidedly conservative' and 'conformist', both in its lip service to traditional Christian values, and in its outward disapproval of extra-marital relations. 'A man who has had more than one wife, or who has had public affairs, who is not capable of self-control in sexual or emotional matters, is not considered trustworthy in business. The only important woman for a mafioso is, and has to be, the mother of his children. The others "are all whores" . . . He must conform to the key values of the family, and see to it that mother and children are respected and provided for. For the rest, he can do what he likes, as long as he is discreet about it.'[3]

What emerges from Falcone's analysis is a clear division between rules and reality: Cosa Nostra's 'code of honour' is invoked, for the purposes of public relations, to show that the mafia defends traditional family values. When Totò Riina (known as 'The Beast', serving eight life sentences for murder) faced his principal accuser, mafioso turned supergrass Tommaso Buscetta (a man who has had three wives) in court, Riina refused to speak, saying he could not talk to someone with such low moral standards.

For many men, belonging to the organisation is proof of manliness; being a mobster legitimises the use of violence. The one thread that binds the experience of mafia women, from southern Italy to the USA, is the constant battering they endure at the hands of their husbands. Men whose daily routine demands bullying and threatening behaviour seem to feel that their manhood is constantly being tested.

Cristina Culicchia, girlfriend of Sicilian hit man Antonino Titone, describes how he used to come home drunk, rip his clothes off and grab her, holding his gun to her head. As he fucked her at gunpoint, he made her say, over and over again, 'Ninu is the best, Ninu is the best, Ninu is the best . . .'[4]

Behaving like feudal lords, 'men of honour' still exercise droit de seigneur. Bernardo Brusca, the son of an old and respected *capo* from the Sicilian town of San Giuseppe Iato, abducted the flame-haired Antonina, had sex with her and then married her, in a ritual known as 'reparational marriage'. Her family thought it a good match, and once she was married, her dented honour was perfectly repaired.

Although Cosa Nostra's 'code' states that mafiosi may not divorce, or marry divorced women, this rule applies only when it is useful. It may be applied, for example, as an excuse for murdering or expelling a mafioso who has fallen from grace. Many mafiosi get away with it, with no loss of face. Brusca's son Giovanni followed his father's impetuous lead. He saw a woman with long dark hair who lived in San Giuseppe Iato, and decided he wanted her. Rosaria Cristiano, the woman in question, was married to a local builder, with a child, but this did not deter the young boss (his nickname, *'u verru*, 'the swine', refers to his behaviour with women). He knocked on her door one day and told her to pack her things and go with him. We do not know whether she was happy to go, or what she told her husband, but she packed, and went.

Since then, Giovanni Brusca and Rosaria have had a child, Davide. After Brusca's arrest, in May 1996, Rosaria attacked a journalist with her handbag in a Palermo courtroom, for printing unflattering accounts of his life.

Even women who have turned state's evidence and shopped their mobster husbands sometimes remain ambivalent about the organisation. There is a lingering fascination that leaks from even the most watertight account of escaping from a life of hell with a mafia boss.

Margherita Petralìa's husband, Sicilian mafioso Gaspare Sugamiele, walked out after fourteen years of marriage. She describes life married to the mob as lonely and miserable. He often stayed away for days at a time; if she asked him where he had been, he beat her. And yet, years after they split up, after she betrayed him and testified against his family, she still returns to her home town several times a year, and something inside her seems to cry out against her exclusion from the clan.

I met Margherita in Sicily at the peak of the holiday season, the first week of August, when the whole of Italy takes off for the beach. A sirocco was blowing hot sandy wind under a cloudy sky. Margherita had flown down from Milan to visit her children, now in their early twenties, and was driving her mother's tiny old Fiat 500, a white bubble car with red plastic seats. Evidently she was used to much more powerful vehicles. We sat on a park bench in the middle of Trapani, an ancient port in the west of Sicily, smoked cigarettes and stared back at the old men and children who circled us.

Margherita was only 13 when she met Gaspare Sugamiele. She was tagging along with her sister and her boyfriend, after her mother had sent her out to be her sister's chaperone. When her mother discovered that Margherita had been seen holding hands with one of the boys, she was gated. Gaspare was unsuitable, her parents said, from the wrong kind of family. But in spite of her mother's vigilance, Margherita and Gaspare carried on meeting in secret, until they decided to take matters in hand, and slept together. From that moment, she knew everything would change: she would have to marry him or her family would be disgraced.

If her family was unhappy at the match, his parents weren't exactly cock-a-hoop, either. An important mafia family from Paceco, a small town near Trapani, they had hoped to form a useful alliance through their son's marriage, and already had a suitable girl in mind. 'His uncles used to make a real fuss of him at dinners and parties,' Margherita remembers. 'They used to say to me: "You've hooked yourself a good catch, you know. If it wasn't for you, he might have done very well for himself . . ." It was said in quite a threatening way.'

She was only 19, but already had a strong character, and didn't like being pushed around. From the very first, she clashed with her father-in-law. 'They never accepted me, they considered me inferior. They used to say "You're nothing to do with this, you're not a Sugamiele." I used to say "And I'm proud of it." '

Her big dark brown eyes flash defiance under long thick lashes. In spite of her defiant manner, she looks fidgety and tense. Now 44, and a mother of three, she has good skin and prominent cheekbones emphasised by her short haircut. She wears lots of gold, a white T-shirt with little bows at the neck, a very short miniskirt which she keeps pulling down over her thighs, and white trainers.

Her husband's family did their best to isolate her. He was very much in awe of his father, and allowed his family to tease and bully his new wife. When she defended herself, he would round on her, telling her she should have more respect. Margherita's sister-in-law, Antonia, had made a good match, with an important mafioso. Her pedigree and her marriage placed her above Margherita, who felt increasingly aggrieved. Antonia was included in discussions about family business, but when Margherita entered the room they would all fall silent, or change the subject. In later years, when Gaspare went into hiding, Antonia would always know where he was; Margherita, to her humiliation, would not.

'My sister-in-law was sweet to my face, but I didn't trust her. I never knew what she was saying behind my back. They didn't trust me either. Now and then, my husband did talk to me about things that were bothering him, but mostly they left me out of it. They never thought of me as one of the family.'

An open, confident, assertive woman, Margherita began to shrink into the role of mafia wife. She saw no one apart from her husband's family and her parents. Like other mafia wives, she was not permitted to have friends of her own. She attended weddings and baptisms, big family events, and she was made a godmother. The mafia families in the area were linked by rituals which soldered their friendship: they were best men at each other's weddings, they were godparents to each other's children. The circle grew tighter.

Margherita became increasingly bitter at her exclusion from her husband's life. 'I was supposed to bring up the children and keep quiet, and if he slapped me around, I had to take it and keep my mouth shut. He didn't want the girls to go to school, and he stopped me going into higher education. He didn't believe women should be educated.'

This attitude is widespread in mafia families. Southern Italian women are feisty and powerful personalities, and men seem to struggle for much of their lives to hang on to some power of their own. The mayor of a small Sicilian mafia stronghold describes problems faced by women who are forbidden to work. 'There are bright young women leaving school with qualifications, hopes and ambitions, and then most of them marry men who won't let them get a job. Most of the men here consider a wife who works to be a poor reflection on her husband's ability to provide. These women get terribly depressed and disillusioned.'[5]

Even in sixties America, Rosalie Bonanno, wife of the New York mobster Bill Bonanno, required a good deal of courage to test this prejudice, when she signed up for adult education classes. 'For a first-generation Sicilian-American (especially one in my husband's world) to allow his wife to go to school and leave his children was a very progressive act, bordering on heresy.'[6]

Margherita Petralìa's mother-in-law was the only member of her husband's family she got on with: 'She confided in me – she used to say she'd been putting up with bullying and violence all her married life. She didn't dare open her mouth to complain, she was completely enslaved by her overbearing husband. What brought us together was that we suffered the same treatment – only I fought it, and she didn't. Her daughter Antonia was terribly rude to her. She behaved like one of the men, and treated her mother just like the men did.'

After two years of marriage, Margherita made a discovery that shocked her profoundly. Her husband came in at seven o'clock one morning. His shoes were covered in mud and vine leaves, and his clothes were dirty. He seemed very agitated, and asked her if the carabinieri had been looking for him. He gave her the dirty shoes and clothes, and told her to clean them. If anyone came to look for him, he told her, as he got ready to go out again, she was to say that he had come in before ten o'clock the night before.

As she scrubbed her husband's shoes, she turned on the radio news, and heard that there had been a murder in a vineyard, near where they lived. The pieces fell crashing into place. Although she was aware that her husband was a member of the mafia – the couple had spent their honeymoon visiting his exalted mafia connections in their places of exile all over Italy – she had never thought of him as a murderer.

She later described her reaction: 'When he came back, I made lunch, and we sat down to eat. But I couldn't eat a thing. I just stared at his hands, wondering how he could have killed a man. He felt me staring at him, and was obviously uncomfortable. That evening he didn't go out, for once, and we went to bed early. After a few moments, he reached out his hand to touch me, but I couldn't stand to have his hands on my skin.'[7]

At that point, she wanted to know everything her husband

was doing. She hung around behind closed doors, listening to conversations, and eavesdropping on meetings when she took food or drink to the men discussing business.

It is difficult to believe that Margherita didn't know about her husband's crimes before the night of the vineyard murder. It was certainly no secret that he carried a gun. 'He was like a kid with a toy,' she says. 'He wanted me to see the guns, but I didn't want them anywhere near the children. I made him take them away.'

One summer, feeling isolated and frightened when her husband was spending long periods away from home, she sat down and wrote an account of her life. Scrawling over the pages of an exercise book, she unleashed her loathing for her husband and his family, and railed against the mafia. She detailed crimes they had committed, named members of the clan, and their contacts among local dignitaries, teachers and judges.

'I am the wife of Gaspare Sugamiele,' she began. 'I am his wife in the sense that a long time ago I married him, but in reality I am his servant, his whore, for him to have his way with when the urge takes him, I'm also his punchbag whenever he feels like lashing out. If I dare to open my mouth, I get a good kicking. Unfortunately I wished all this on myself, and now I've got three children to look after, so there's nothing I can do.'

This dismal text was written over two nights in June 1983, when she thought her husband was going kill her in one of his violent rages: it would be her testimony from beyond the grave. But having written this potentially lethal document, she didn't do anything with it. She kept it hidden in the house. Perhaps she wanted him to find it, so he would realise how miserable she was, and that, with all the information she held about the family's mafia activities, she had some power over him. But for the moment, she let it lie.

In the early years Margherita was madly in love with her husband, but gradually she had been hardened by his cruelties. 'I was tired, fed up with him. I never knew where he was. It

turned into a love-hate thing. I wanted to get away but I knew
he'd come after me and probably kill me. We didn't sleep
together any more, I couldn't stand to touch him. I used to
bring the children into bed with me, or sleep on the sofa.'

Not long after she had written the diary, Gaspare came home
and started packing a suitcase. 'He had a smile on his face. He
just said: "I'm leaving. I'm not going to live with a whore any
longer." '

When Margherita demanded an explanation, Gaspare's father
called a family conference, and announced, in front of her
parents, that she had had an affair. 'He said, "You've been
unfaithful to my son. Take this money and go away." I said, "It
sounds like the perfect opportunity." ' She sounds feisty
enough now, but something sticks in her throat.

Had she had an affair?

'Yes. He was an old friend and I needed someone to talk to.
But he fell in love with me and wanted to leave his wife – I
mean, honestly. So I had to end it. Then he confessed the
whole thing to his wife, and I think she must have told
someone.'

After her husband left, Margherita continued to live defiantly
in Paceco, with her two daughters, aged 11 and 9, and her 7-
year-old son. It wasn't easy. Her in-laws cut her dead or
exchanged insults whenever they met, which was fairly
frequently, as they still lived 50 yards away. Margherita is a
tough woman, and it became a point of pride to carry on living
in her home town, but her situation was impossible. She would
have to make a dignified retreat, or find some way of getting
back at the family. She still had the diary. One day in June
1985, two years after writing it, she handed the little exercise
book over to the police.

Margherita Petralia testified against her ex-husband's family,
and her diary became a vital piece of evidence in a wider
investigation into the Paceco mafia. But even her master-stroke
against the family was not as lethal as she had hoped. Under
cross-examination, Margherita had to admit that many of the
allegations in her diary were hearsay. Nonetheless, investigators

had sufficient evidence to convict her husband and his sister Antonia on charges of mafia association.

Margherita finally left Paceco and moved to Milan in 1989. One of her daughters came with her, but she didn't like the big city and went back to Sicily. Her older daughter stayed at home. She has since got married and had a baby. Margherita's son did his military service and then he went to live with his father, who by this time had been released from prison. 'He lives rent-free, he's got his car, his mobile phone, he loves it. It's about time he got something out of his father.'

Isn't she afraid her son will turn into a mafioso?

Half an hour into our conversation, Margherita had begun fidgeting with her car keys. Now she stands up, and stamps out a cigarette. 'I don't think he's interested in that stuff. His father is fixated with all the rituals and traditions; my son just wants to have an easy life and lots of money, without getting a job.'

She talks clearly and spontaneously, but there is something about Margherita Petralìa's version of her life that won't quite fall into place. She tells it like a triumph against the mafia, her courageous escape. But she has lost everything. Ignominiously thrown out by her husband, publicly reviled as an adulteress in full view of the whole town, betrayed by her children, she has had to flee to the north and start all over again. She is broke, her grandchildren are growing up without her, she works night and day in an old people's home. And she hates the cold.

14. All for Love

In public, the wife of a mafioso enjoys the prestige of being married to the mob; in private, she is forced to endure the humiliation of his infidelities. The mafioso may claim to be the soul of honour, but a mistress is essential to his entourage: she is the symbol of his power and wealth. 'The girlfriends get the best deal. They get presents, they get cars, clothes and jewellery, they get taken out to the best restaurants, and they don't have to clean up after him!' says Brenda Colletti, wife of a Philadelphia hit man (see Chapter 2). Mafia mistresses are walking showcases of what the mafioso's money can buy. And most of them are not the marrying kind.

Lucia★ is a high-class prostitute whose 60-year-old mother runs a brothel in downtown Naples. I was introduced to her by a carabiniere. On our way to her place, she leans out of the taxi window and buys 60 Marlboro from a street vendor. We take the lift to her apartment in a high-rise block near the law courts. Her bouncy hair is hennaed bright orange and she wears high-heeled boots. 'This is my bedroom – isn't it gorgeous? It's so feminine.' The double bed is a sea of pink satin. There are pictures of her all over the walls.

Lucia has been arrested three or four times, mostly for prostitution. She was briefly famous when her lover, a Camorra boss, was arrested for cocaine trafficking and extortion in the mid-1980s. He had been using her apartment as a cover, and making her pay him protection money on her prostitution business.

She admits that mobsters can be very attractive. 'Some women love the life. They just can't resist it. The men bring you flowers, buy you presents, book you a restaurant table.

*Not her real name

They are fascinating guys, you know, they lavish all this attention on you. All the girls in the neighbourhood just swoon all over them. When you're out with them you can see that people are afraid of them. It's very exciting. Around here they are big shots, walking all over the trash beneath their feet. But if they ever leave Naples and go somewhere else, with all their money, they are nobody. So they never leave.

'Some of the men have a mask: they have two different realities going on. I was with a man like that. I met him when I was going out with another boy, who was really good-looking and had loads of money, we were really happy. Then he got shot. I don't know who shot him – oh, you know, it was something to do with the mafia but I don't know who did it. When it happened I just cracked up. This guy was really sweet to me, he looked after me and talked me round, when I recovered he was still here . . . he'd bring me presents, flowers, jewellery . . . I really fell for him.

'He was involved in drugs, arms, extortion, the whole lot. Yeah, I knew all about it. People used to tell me things about what he was up to, but I didn't care. The person I knew was sweet and kind and loved me – that's all I cared about.

'When he was arrested I found out that my phone had been tapped, and he'd been using my name in a lot of his business transactions – and my mother's name. I was arrested and charged with possession of firearms, drugs, mafia association . . . it was unbelievable. They said I had been paying him protection money, but it's not true, it was money I owed him, I was paying him back.'

Lucia got four years, reduced to two suspended on appeal, and did four days in prison for living off immoral earnings. Even in prison she enjoyed the afterglow of being a mobster's girl.

'When I went to jail I was so terrified, these women just talked about heroin all the time. Then the TV news came on, and there was my picture, and this great splash "The Boss's Woman". They all looked at me and everything changed.

They made my bed, brought me a carton of Marlboro, made me coffee. It was great. I wasn't going to say any different.'

It's not just girls from the poorer neighbourhoods who dream of going out with a gangster. Francesca Bourelly was 25 when she met Naples Camorra boss Ciro Mariano, notorious and charismatic capo of the Spanish Quarter. He was in his forties, a gangster with a criminal record, married to a woman with the same background as him, with teenage children. Francesca was from a respectable middle-class family; she lived with her parents, a teacher and a lawyer, in the Vomero, a leafy district high above the city.

When they met, he was living underground in Naples, she was working in a tourist office. She was pretty, tall and thin, with long brown hair; in her T-shirts, designer jeans and flat leather shoes, she looked the antithesis of the mafia woman. He wasn't much to look at, but she knew his reputation.

A friend of theirs (who prefers to be nameless) says it was not the danger that attracted Francesca to the mafia boss. On the contrary – she was worried about being arrested and a couple of times said she was afraid someone was following her. But there was a sense of adventure in this life: while Ciro Mariano was in hiding, he travelled all over Europe; when he could, he would send an ambassador to bring her to him, on a first-class flight. He wasn't holed up in some rural hideout, he was lying beside swiming pools in Spain.

'As far as I could tell, he was much more in love with her than she was with him, but she let herself be wooed. She knew he was married, she knew he was Ciro Mariano and what that meant. She did once ask me if I thought she was going to get into trouble.'

The couple had been seeing each other for about six months when he was arrested on his way to meet her for dinner. She waited for him at the restaurant for a while, then realised something must have happened, and slipped away. There was a warrant out for her arrest, but she disappeared, went to stay with a relative in Rome.

The warrant was revoked after a month, and she returned to

Naples. The papers got hold of the story and ran banner headlines: WOULD YOU LET YOUR DAUGHTER DATE A MAFIA BOSS?

No more was heard of Francesca Bourelly in Camorra circles. 'As soon as he was arrested, Ciro went straight back to his wife. Of course, everybody does.'

Once they are in prison, mafia bosses rely entirely on their wives. Not many mistresses would be trusted to do what a wife has to do: everything from laundry to legal representation, and spying on his associates. While he is hiding, a mafioso's mistress is likely to be escorted by one or more of her lover's men – partly for her own safety, but mainly so he can be sure of her fidelity. But as soon as he is sent to prison, she is free to go.

A woman in that environment has to look after herself, and history has recorded spectacular betrayals by women who, needing protection, allow themselves to be charmed. Luciano Leggio, the creepy and cold-blooded Corleone boss, was strangely attractive to women, who shielded him from arrest on several occasions. In 1948 Leggio murdered a young trade-unionist in Corleone, Placido Rizzotto, who had resisted the mafia's manipulation of the labour market. After his violent death, he was hailed as a hero of the Left.

Years later, when Leggio escaped from prison, he was found living in pampered ease at the house of two unmarried sisters in Corleone. Although usually parsimonious, the old ladies had been seen staggering home with shopping bags full of exotic and delicate foodstuffs. When police searched the house, they found guns hidden in the basement. One of the sisters, Leoluchina Sorisi, now white-haired, had once been engaged to Placido Rizzotto.

Some women cannot resist the seduction of power, which lures them from the victim to the victor. One Calabrian woman, still red-eyed from mourning her husband, sought comfort in the arms of the man who had killed him. This move seemed such a clamorous betrayal that magistrates suspected her of murder.

Concetta Managò married her teenage sweetheart when she was just 17. They were both from ordinary working-class

families in Palmi, on the northern Calabrian coast. Francesco
Condello, her young husband, had no connection to the
'Ndrangheta, until he and his brothers got into a stand-off with
local gangsters, the Gallico brothers. The problem seems to
have started when Francesco wanted to open a bar and disco
near the beach. It was impossible to open a place like that
without the local clan's permission, but Francesco was going to
go ahead anyway, and made no secret of his plans.

The Gallico brothers couldn't let this provocation pass. In
1977, Francesco Condello's younger brother was shot dead. He
was just 16. Condello did not go to the police. He sought the
protection of the ruling mafia family and, as the traditional
Calabrian blood feud dictates, went into hiding, to prepare to
avenge his brother's murder.

Salvatore Boemi, grizzled prosecutor in Reggio Calabria,
reconstructs the couple's transition across the line from law-
abiding society to organised crime. 'They entered another
world. Condello wouldn't give evidence against his brother's
killers, but as soon as they got out of prison, he murdered them
systematically, one by one. Concetta Managò, just 18, who had
married a normal lad with no previous convictions, suddenly
found herself hitched to a dangerous killer on the run. Their
honeymoon period, their first flush of love, was spent in hiding,
dodging his enemies.'[1]

But Concetta, who had married the boy next door, fell for
the outlaw. 'He became notorious, a local hero. People
believed he was right to avenge the brutal murder of his young
brother. Her husband was in the papers, he was on the TV
news, he'd earned a lot of respect; she was young, and she was
impressed. She was proud to be his woman.'

While Francesco Condello was in hiding in the hills above
Palmi – 'Ndrangheta members involved in a feud never go far
from home – his wife became his life support. She hid guns or
moved them for him; drove him around; helped him set up
meetings with other clan members. Condello was in hiding for
twelve years as the feud raged and the two families tried to
drive each other out. Because of his personal prestige, his clan

benefited from a high profile, and collected protection money all over Palmi. Businessmen delivered kickbacks to his wife.

'She was free to come and go because no one ever thought to follow her,' says Boemi ruefully. 'Pretty stupid really, because women are the lifeline for any man in hiding. This woman had only been married a year – frankly, it was obvious she would be in close contact with her man. If only we had followed the women a little more often, we would have caught a lot more mafiosi.'

As the war between the Condello and Gallico clans continued, more than fifty people died in tit-for-tat killings. There was only one way the feud could end. In 1989 Francesco Condello was killed by a bomb which exploded as he got into his car. His wife, who had been dreading the news of his violent death every day for years, heard that something was wrong and went straight out to look for him. He had been betrayed by one of his own guards, who knew exactly where he would be and when. They were supposed to watch the car and check for explosives; instead, they had allowed his enemies to execute him.

'At this point, the boss's wife, respected, feared, at the hub of the organisation, found the whole group falling to pieces around her. She felt terribly exposed. Soon after her husband's death, she was invited to a meeting with Domenico Gallico, the *capo* of the enemy clan. She agreed to go and meet him, she said later, because she was afraid her children would become targets. It does sometimes happen that the children of a warring family are killed to prevent the feud being rekindled years down the line.

'And in the strange way things sometimes turn out, Concetta Managò ended up having a relationship with her husband's sworn enemy.'

Boemi, an avuncular, private man, admits he finds the whole thing baffling. 'She has always been drawn to powerful men, perhaps that was the attraction. Gallico was a big boss. She says he was kind to her. She had known him when they were growing up, and she felt protected. From his point of view there was a certain triumph in having a relationship with the widow of his lifelong enemy.'

Gallico had another motive for pursuing a love affair with Concetta Managò. The feud was still going on, and he needed information on the rival clan's movements. Perhaps this was Concetta's chance to punish her husband's men for betraying him. Perhaps she was just looking after her own interests. Safely ensconced in the enemy camp, she told Gallico where three of her husband's men were in hiding. Gallico hunted them down and killed them.

A few months after Concetta Managò crept to her enemy's bed, he was arrested. Not long afterwards, she was charged with mafia association and murder. Magistrates interrogated her about her affair with Gallico, suspecting her of plotting her husband's death. She denied the charge. To this day, she swears she always loved her husband, and only slept with his enemy to save her children.

While awaiting trial, Managò was placed under maximum security provisions designed for dangerous mafiosi. She was bewildered and frightened. Her children were staying with their grandmother, who was letting them run wild. 'When I spoke to her,' says Boemi, 'she was going out of her mind. She was worried about the children, and solitary confinement was driving her crazy. She had said she would collaborate, but no one had taken her seriously.'

Salvatore Boemi summoned Concetta Managò as a witness for the prosecution. Calabrian magistrates have had very little help with their inquiries from 'Ndrangheta defectors, because the clans are tightly knit and family based. With Managò's help, Judge Boemi was able to reconstruct in detail twelve years of mafia war. 'In Calabria, young people sometimes decide to collaborate because they want to start a new life – sometimes even unmarried people need to get out, start again. It is much more difficult for older people to talk about crimes committed by their relations. Someone like Concetta Managò, who has watched the mafia destroy her life, wakes up one day and realises that the legal system offers a way out of a desperate situation.'

She was convicted of murder for her part in the killing of her three former allies, but after giving evidence against the 'Ndrangheta clans, Concetta Managò got out of prison in 1994 after serving a short sentence, at the age of 33. Her three children went to live with her in a secret location, under assumed names. She has a new man in her life.

The criminal underworld seems to encourage driving ambition and infidelity, which sometimes fatally combine. A Neapolitan widow, Alessandra Maninetti, who became a collaborator, shone a bright light on the underside of life in a Camorra family infested with treachery, adultery and greed. Crawling from the wreckage, she was determined to avenge the man she loved, even though he had betrayed her.

When she turned up at the police station in January 1988 and said she wanted to talk, Maninetti was in serious trouble. Raffaele Nuzzo, the husband she adored, had been murdered, betrayed by his closest friends. Her husband's brother Nicola Nuzzo had been murdered by his wife. There was no one left she could trust. Maninetti's fear and paranoia was given a sharp edge by the quantities of cocaine she was consuming. She wanted to send the killers to prison and get her revenge.

Nicola Nuzzo had been an important ally of Raffaele Cutolo, the megalomaniac who ruled Naples from inside prison (see Chapter 1), but he had found Cutolo's dictatorship oppressive, and had gone over to the other side. He got rich from a protection racket which skimmed money from building sites in Acerra, in the Naples hinterland. He had also been a protagonist in the scandal of the decade: negotiations for the release of the Christian Democrat MP Ciro Cirillo, taken hostage by the Red Brigades in 1981.

According to Alessandra Maninetti's testimony, in the early 1980s Nicola Nuzzo's wife, Carmela Frezza De Rosa, began an

affair with a shady creature of the Naples underworld, Franco
Vicino – a doctor, a former terrorist, now a mafia associate.
'Everybody knew she was Doctor Vicino's lover,' Maninetti
later told investigators. 'The whole town was talking about it.'[2]

At the mention of Carmela Frezza De Rosa, Judge Paolo
Mancuso, who brought the prosecution against the Acerra
clans, just smiles. 'She's an extremely hard, extremely determined woman.'[3]

In 1986, the boss, Nicola Nuzzo, was under house arrest, but
was moved to hospital, suffering from kidney trouble. His
brother Raffaele kept him informed of what was going on in
the neighbourhood. He also informed him about his wife's
affair. Nicola went crazy and attacked his wife in front of
another of her former lovers; when he tried to intervene,
Nuzzo laid into him. He tore up her picture and slashed her
clothes with a razor.

The family was riven with backstabbing and scheming,
fuelled by cocaine. While her husband was in hospital, Carmela
handed bundles of cash – the profits from his extortion racket –
to her lover; they planned to cut her husband out of the
business altogether. Then they decided to murder him.
Carmela told one of her faithful soldiers that her husband had
turned state's evidence, and was going to land them all in jail –
when she promised him a share in the protection racket, he
pretended to believe it. He agreed to find hit men to do the
job.

On 6 September 1986, Nicola Nuzzo was found dead in his
hospital bed. His skull had been smashed with a hammer.
Alessandra Maninetti went straight to the hospital when she
heard the news, and found Carmela and her lover Franco
Vicino already there. 'Vicino, who had hardly ever spoken to
me before, pulled me to one side and told me it must have been
the secret services who killed him, since Nicola had recently
been interviewed about the Ciro Cirillo affair. I asked him why
they hadn't just shot him. He said they must have wanted to
bash his brains in and make him lose his memory, without
actually killing him.'

When Raffaele heard about his brother's violent end, he summoned Carmela to his home, and accused her of murder. When she denied it, he beat her up. Alessandra came home to find her sister-in-law running out of the house, battered and bruised, screaming that Raffaele had lost his mind. Alessandra was furious: 'I told my husband he should never have let Carmela in the house – I was afraid of her. I thought she was dangerous.'

By this stage, Alessandra Maninetti, who was hoovering up cocaine at an alarming rate, was becoming increasingly paranoid and frightened, and begged her husband to tell her everything that happened. She knew Raffaele would be next on the hit list, and wanted to know what was in his mind. He told her he was planning to murder Carmela's lover. 'He said he wanted to punish Carmela, but not to kill her. He said that whatever she had done, she was still the mother of his brother's children.'

Raffaele sent a hit squad – including Carmela's son Pasquale – to shoot Vicino, but they only managed to wound him. Raffaele rang him to warn him to stay away from his brother's business, and his wife.

The circle drew tighter. Everybody was plotting behind each other's back, lying to each other, convinced – with the help of cocaine, the untruth drug – that they were cleverly deceiving everyone else.

Ignoring the danger, and believing he had right on his side, Raffaele Nuzzo summoned members of Carmela's faction, and persuaded them to join in his conspiracy against her. He formulated a plan to kill Vicino that looked like a rehearsal for his own murder. He told his wife: 'They're going to invite Vicino to a meeting to discuss how to kill me. Only it won't be my death they're planning.' While he was being driven to the meeting by a couple of friends, Vicino was dispatched with a bullet in the back of the head.

Since his brother's brutal murder, Raffaele had lost control. He was trying to muscle in on a racket run by a group of mafiosi. He had been irascible and violent with his men, and had even cracked one of them over the head with a pistol butt.

He had been playing around with the wives of his own soldiers. 'There were women queuing up to sleep with him – they wanted money and jewels off him. Some of them succeeded,' admitted his wife, Alessandra. 'There were plenty of people with a motive for killing him.'

The showdown was not long in coming. Raffaele was summoned to a meeting at a bar in the main piazza in Acerra. The night before, Alessandra heard him telephone one of his men and ask him to go with him to the bar, armed with a gun. In the early hours, one of his associates rang up and asked him for a kiss over the phone. Later his wife realised the significance of this Judas kiss.

He set out alone on the morning of 4 June 1987. He arrived at the meeting place and bought coffee for a friend at the bar. They put down their cups, and stepped outside. A man turned from the bar and shot Raffaele in the back several times. As he fell to his knees, two masked men outside the bar shot him from either side. At that moment, a car screeched to a halt, and a masked man got out carrying a machine gun. He fired at Raffaele, who was sprawled on the pavement, and hit a passer-by who was carrying a baby.

Isolated and afraid, Alessandra Maninetti panicked. She got a friend to take her to a shooting range, so she could learn to fire a gun. She tried to talk to Carmela, who slammed the door in her face. 'I don't know if my sister-in-law had a role in my husband's death,' she told investigators much later. 'I remember that when Franco Vicino was killed, Carmela said that whoever had killed him would pay for it. But that's all I know.'

Maninetti decided to collaborate and turn in the whole family. Her husband's second brother, Giovanni, her last ally in the world, would shortly be released from prison. She was convinced that if she didn't do something, he would be murdered as soon as he got out.

Once she had cleaned up her cocaine habit, Judge Paolo Mancuso found Alessandra Maninetti an exemplary witness. 'She was very good-natured, very much in love with her husband, completely devoted to him. And determined to send

the killers to jail. At one point, she had to go into prison to
identify the killers – it must have been a very frightening
experience, but she was quite firm. She stood in front of their
cells and identified the murderers. She looked them right in the
eye. They had to look away. They couldn't meet her gaze.'

The trial ended with thirty-five convictions. Carmela Frezza
De Rosa was found guilty of mafia association and murder.
Alessandra Maninetti started a new life with her two children,
satisfied that she had done her duty by her husband: 'I had
sworn to get my revenge for the death of my brother-in-law
and my husband, through the only means available to me,
which was the law.'

The day her lover was shot dead with several rounds from a
Kalashnikov, Giacomina Filippello walked into a police station
in Campobello di Mazara and said she wanted to talk. 'She
didn't have any noble ideals about collaborating,' says magistrate Alessandra Camassa. 'This was in 1991, before the law
offered protection to mafia defectors. She did it for love. It was
a vendetta for love.'[4]

For over twenty-four years, Giacomina Filippello was the
mistress of Natale L'Ala, a mafia boss on the run – first from his
wife, then the police, and then his own men, who betrayed and
finally murdered him. Her collaboration proved for the first
time that women – even in western Sicily, where Cosa Nostra
is considered to be at its most inflexible and chauvinistic –
know a great deal about mafia business, and are sometimes
better adapted to the life than their men when the going gets
rough.

Filippello, now 47, lives under state protection in an
apartment on the outskirts of a big city. She opens the door
cautiously, and looks at me sideways through thick blue
eyeliner. She is a large woman compressed into a little black
lace top, with a short black skirt clamped over her bottom, a
pink artificial flower in her black hair, and pink lipstick applied

with generous abandon. She shows me into an apartment like a
bachelor pad, anonymous and unloved.

She first met Natale L'Ala at the age of 17. Her father kept a
brothel, which was frequented by men of honour and their
friends. L'Ala was dodging arrest, and Giacomina's father was
ordered to take him in. When the precocious, rebellious
teenager came home from boarding school, she found a strange
man living in her house.

'He was good-looking, but he was 43 – to me that was like
an old man. He had this air of authority, which I couldn't
stand. All my life I'd had people telling me what to do.
Everyone treated him with enormous deference, but I just
answered back.'

He found her teenage petulance exciting, and they began a
combative courtship. If she wore something too revealing, he
would make her change her clothes. She would make
extravagant demands, and he would send one of his men to find
whatever she wanted. One day her mother found them kissing.
He turned round and announced: 'I love your daughter. I am
going to leave my wife to be with her. If she won't have me, I
will kill her.'

It was the most romantic thing Giacomina had ever heard.
She was deeply impressed by Natale and his friends, by their
aura of power. 'They stood up and kissed my hand whenever I
walked in the room. Even though I was still a girl, they treated
me with respect. I began to believe that I could be someone.'

L'Ala was eager to get away from her parents, who were
appalled that a mafioso had seduced their daughter – worse still,
a mafioso married with children older than his teenage lover.
He had skipped probation, so all he had to do was get himself
sent home: he turned himself in to the police, who immediately ordered him back to Campobello, exactly as he had
planned. Giacomina waited for him on the station platform,
suitcases in hand, till he arrived under police escort. She still
remembers the presents he brought her that day: a green dress,
a pair of green high-heeled shoes, fishnet stockings with little
flowers down the seam, a pair of black lace panties.

Giacomina loves to talk dirty. She talks about her passion for Natale, the way he made love to her so sweetly. She talks about how he touched her when they danced, how she once clawed a hole in his shirt on the dance floor in a moment of passion. She talks about visiting him in prison: how the guards used to leave them alone together and she brought the place down with her squealing. She reads me erotic love poems written in red felt pen which she keeps in a shoe box.

L'Ala's nephews headed the Campobello mafia, and their alliance with the Palermo clans gave them a share of the heroin trade. She knew he dealt in smuggled cigarettes and gold, but she refuses to accept that he dealt in drugs. She knew – through her own intuition, things she overheard, things he told her – he had driven the car on a number of shootings.[5] She knew where he got hold of guns, and where he hid them, that he ran a protection racket. When he was sent into internal exile, L'Ala carried on business as usual: 'He never seemed to work, but we were never short of money. People would send him cheques. This was the most secure time of his life. He had friends, respect, power. He didn't even carry a gun.

'We were very happy. We still argued continually. I was wound like a spring.' She flicks through a pile of snapshots, cigarette clamped between fat fingers. 'See this woman?' A distant group shot from the early seventies shows two couples in an uncomfortable pose. 'She was murdered by her husband when he discovered she had been sleeping with another man. When I found her picture in Natale's breast pocket, I slashed my wrists. Look.' She shows me a jagged scar.

It was not a peaceful coexistence. When L'Ala was in his mid-fifties he was arrested for kidnapping and raping a woman.[6] To punish him for another infidelity, Giacomina reported him to the police for possessing firearms. Once he threatened to kill her for talking to a man from her balcony. 'He accused me of flirting and beat me, so I went to sleep in the other room. In the middle of the night he came in and said, "Get up, I'm going to kill you."

'He dragged me downstairs. I was screaming, "What have I

done?" There was a storm raging outside. He said he was going to take me out to the woods where no one would hear me. I thought I was going to die. When we got to the front door, he said, "Go back upstairs." Oh my God, the kisses, the tears – that night we made mad, passionate love.'

A small, grey-haired old man comes in and sits down, waiting for Giacomina to make lunch. He is her new beau, rumoured to be retired from the secret services. The sun pours in across the concrete tenement block. She cooks spaghetti and talks about how she misses home – the smells, the familiar landscape of her childhood. 'I will never go back to Sicily.'

In 1982, Natale L'Ala's nephews, leaders of the Campobello clan, were murdered. The same day, he and his men fled to England to wait for things to calm down, and plan their next move. Giacomina stayed behind in Campobello to watch the fallout. She noticed that one of L'Ala's men, who had initially gone into hiding, started going out unguarded during the daytime. She realised he must have made a deal with the rival clan, the Versa family, led by Nunzio Spezia and backed by the Corleonesi. Others started creeping out of hiding. 'I was aware that they'd stopped coming to ask me how Natale was, if he was all right, if he needed anything. I was able to see how things were panning out.'[7] She went to join L'Ala in England just before Christmas, with the painful news that his men were deserting. He refused to contemplate going on his knees to beg Nunzio Spezia for mercy. They stayed in a series of hotels across southern England; she remembers driving through the endless rain with his hand resting on her leg. 'Whenever we stopped at a hotel or a pub, people would turn their heads to look at us. My husband was always well dressed in velvet suits and boots, with a leather jacket. We always caused a stir.'

Eventually they returned to Campobello, on 1 April 1984, after two years smuggling and laundering money for his mafia contacts across Europe. On 1 August he was driving his car when two gunmen on motorcycles bore down on him. They shot him in the shoulder and shattered the windscreen. Bleeding heavily, he managed to swing the car from side to side so they couldn't get abreast of him. He could see them clearly in his rearview mirror. One of them ran out of ammunition, the other one handed him his gun. Using techniques he learned at the wheel of a getaway car, L'Ala spun the car and lost them.

'He called his friends from outside Sicily, and got himself a bodyguard. He bought a nice big bulletproof car. From that day on I never knew from one moment to the next if I was ever going to see him again. He was jittery, and afraid to sleep. One of us always had to be awake. I would stay up till three or four in the morning, then when I got up, he would go to bed. If I went out, I was followed everywhere. We were nervous wrecks. I don't know how we got through those years.'

As Natale began to lose his power, Giacomina found her strength. She demanded to be informed of everything that happened, and was present at all meetings with his few remaining men, where the main topic of discussion was how they were going to kill the rival boss, Nunzio Spezia. 'I had become *mafiosetta*, cunning. I didn't miss a thing. He wasn't careful enough.'

In 1986 L'Ala was imprisoned on a drug trafficking charge and Giacomina chained herself to the lamp-post outside the prison to protest his innocence. While he was inside, he made friends with a couple of low-lifers, and after his release they turned up at the house, saying they needed somewhere to stay and offering their services. Giacomina was not convinced. 'I didn't trust them. Quite honestly I didn't like the look of them ... the way they behaved wasn't ... right. Natale wasn't looking out for himself.'[8]

She suspected they had a spy in their midst. 'Every time we planned a strike on the Versa clan, they would attack us. We were going to hit them on 31 December. On 28 December Natale and one of his men were having a drink in a bar, when someone shot at them.'

L'Ala was badly hurt. He was hit in one eye and a bullet had smashed his jaw. Giacomina drove him to hospital and stayed at his bedside. A few days after the shooting, Judge Paolo Borsellino went to visit him. Not long before, another mafioso from the rival Versa clan in Campobello had turned state's evidence. 'They both knew the mafia was going to kill Natale. Judge Borsellino said that if Natale collaborated, he could save his life. But Natale told him, "I was born a man of honour, and I will be a man of honour till I die." '

L'Ala came home from hospital in a pitiful state. His jaw was wired and he couldn't eat. He had lost one eye, but Giacomina couldn't bear to tell him. She kept it covered and dressed it every six hours, pretending it was getting better. Misery made her furious. One day she noticed she was being followed and turned on her stalker. 'I went right up to him and said, "If you touch a hair of my man's head I will come after that bastard your leader and rip his heart out with my teeth." '

On 7 May 1990, Natale L'Ala was ambushed in a grocer's shop in Campobello di Mazara. 'They shot him twenty-eight times in the back of the head. The police called me and I went straight down there. The shopkeeper was hurt. Bottles of olive oil and milk had smashed all over the floor, there was blood and wine everywhere. I slipped and nearly fell. I tried to take him in my arms, I thought he might still be alive.

'The street was filling up with people who wanted to see what I would do. I stood up. I was soaking wet, covered in blood. I took the gun out of his belt and walked away.'

It was Paolo Borsellino who persuaded Giacomina to talk. 'He was a lovely person, so understanding. I felt very close to him. When he talked to you you never felt he was the big man behind the desk. He was a real friend to me. I suppose he made me believe in the legal system.'

As soon as she decided to collaborate, she was moved to a convent, where the nuns did their best to ignore her black lace knickers and her stockings hanging from the crucifix.

She was questioned repeatedly by magistrates investigating the Campobello mafia, and testified in the trials of ninety mafiosi. During one examination, she admitted that being with her had damaged Natale L'Ala's career. Despite this humiliation, the mafioso's mistress got her revenge on the gossips and the traitors. 'I was the lover of a boss – I was no one: I should never have talked. Where I come from, they call someone like me *infame*: a traitor. Collaborating with the law was my vendetta. It's as if I'd shot those men myself. I wanted to show how much you can love someone, even if you haven't got the certificate to prove it.'

Giacomina Filippello sits in the gloom of her temporary flat, surrounded by memories. We have smoked ourselves to a standstill. There are pages of poetry and photos scattered all over the table. It's getting dark, but she doesn't get up to turn the light on. She holds fast to an image of her lover as a mafioso of the old school, a man of honour. 'He did a lot of good. If he could help someone, he would, even if it meant taking money from his own pocket. He never betrayed a friend. The mafia, the beautiful mafia I used to believe in, the mafia Natale brought me into, made me what I am. For him, the mafia meant helping people at any cost; helping the weak, even if they had to commit a crime to do it. Even if it meant committing murder, they had to do it. In the old days they always killed people for a good reason.'

15. Vendetta by Law

In June 1991 Morena Plazzi, a young magistrate from Romagna recently arrived in Sicily, was investigating a murder near Partanna in the west of the island. The victim was a 24-year-old man, Nicola Atria, who had been shot by unidentified assailants in his restaurant. Among the women at the autopsy, Plazzi saw the victim's widow, who struck her as dignified and thoughtful – not the usual mafia type at all. 'There was a strange contrast between the man's family, who were all in black, all weeping noisily, and this girl, who looked utterly alone, keeping her feelings to herself. She didn't look like she belonged with the rest of them.'[1]

Judge Plazzi called the woman in for questioning. Piera Aiello was 23, with a young child. She said she had witnessed her husband's death: he had been shot by three masked men whom she thought she recognised. This was already more than most mafia widows would divulge. After a couple of conversations, Judge Plazzi thought Piera Aiello might agree to collaborate. She contacted Paolo Borsellino, and sent her to Marsala to see him.

One of Borsellino's deputies in Marsala was Alessandra Camassa. In a hot Sicilian July, she is on holiday at her house by the sea, with soldiers patrolling the garden. Her daughter is clomping around in clogs, while her baby son Paolo, named after Borsellino, is asleep upstairs. Camassa worked closely with Borsellino until his assassination in 1992, and it was while working with him that she came into contact with a series of female collaborators.

'Piera Aiello's relationship with Borsellino was fundamental,' says Camassa, 'because for someone who comes from such a different environment, to meet a person like him was very gratifying. He was nothing like her preconception of a magistrate. She used to call him "uncle". The way he conducted the interviews was very funny. When the little girl got fidgety, Borsellino would sit her in his chair at the desk, where she could draw pictures and play with the ornaments. He would find somewhere else to sit.'

A soldier goes by in the sunny garden. The feather in his hat and the muzzle of his rifle are just visible over the hedge. 'Piera Aiello was unusual for a mafia wife, because she wanted to find out, she wanted to know everything. She gave us a lot of detailed information on the Partanna mafia. It wasn't vendetta she was after – she isn't the type. She didn't have a particularly high opinion of her husband, actually she thought he was a *cretino*. She wanted to get away, to start a new life.'

I was able to speak to Piera Aiello on the telephone only after an elaborate arrangement through an intermediary. She is not in the least nostalgic about her husband's family. 'I come from a normal family, nothing to do with the mafia – I didn't understand what it meant until it was too late.' She was 14 when she first tried to leave Nicola, who was then her boyfriend. 'His father came to see me and told me that if I left his son, he'd kill me. They forced me to marry him.'

Partanna, which stands on a hill in the rich farmland of the val del Belice, had been badly hit by an earthquake in 1968, which opened the way for speculation by local politicians and mafia clans. In 1983 the deputy mayor was murdered, but there were no convictions. A war between clans erupted in 1989, and in two years there had been thirty murders in a population of only 9,000. People had been blown up by car bombs, or disappeared – almost every family had suffered a death. But there were no witnesses. It was the biggest secret war Sicily had seen in years.

Nicola Atria's father was a shepherd and a mafioso, who built his power base by extorting protection money from farmers. But when he came into conflict with the Partanna mafia over a drug deal, he was dropped by his own clan. In November 1985, Don Vito Atria was shot dead out in the fields.

Nicola solemnly swore to avenge his father's death. He tried to get in with one of the mafia clans – he needed allies and armed back-up – but since his father had been disgraced and summarily executed, he could never be a man of honour. He started hanging out with *piciotti*, low life and mafia footsoldiers, trying to get closer to the killers and discover the details of his father's murder. At the same time, he started dealing heroin, doing business with the very people who had killed his father.

His wife and younger sister Rita both tried to warn him he was taking stupid risks. 'Even his sister later admitted that Nicola would deal drugs with anybody,' says Camassa. 'He wasn't very bright. He told his wife everything he did, even though he knew she didn't approve. He felt this duty to avenge his father like a great weight on his shoulders. He was tense and frightened, he had to talk to somebody. Sometimes he would burst into tears and tell his wife he was afraid.

'Piera Aiello tried to change him, dissuade him from this insane revenge mission. But he didn't even try to hide anything from her. Once he left the house carrying a submachine gun. Another time she caught him putting one of her stockings in his pockets – when she asked him what he was doing, he told her he was going out to shoot somebody. She tried to stand in his way, and he beat her. She would turn the place over, and find packets of heroin and handguns. She used to tell him he had to get rid of the stuff, and threaten to leave him, but he still seemed to need to confide in her. Mafia life is very strange that way.'

Piera's father tried to distract Nicola from his vendetta fixation by setting up the couple with a pizzeria in Montevago, a hilltop town 15 kilometres from Partanna. For a while, it seemed to work, but soon he was back to his old ways, sitting round a table with his *piciotti*, shooting his mouth off about revenge. On the day the pizzeria opened, they invited a few friends to celebrate. After the last guest had gone, they were clearing up, and their three-year-old daughter was playing on the floor, when three men in stocking masks burst in carrying guns. They shot Nicola and left. Piera held him in her arms as he died.

Not long after, the magistrate Morena Plazzi was offering Piera Aiello an escape from the ruins of her life. 'She was only 25. She didn't want to spend the rest of her life in a small town, shut indoors, the widow of a mafia murder victim. She had been living under terrible strain, expecting them to come for him any time. She felt the mafia like a great oppressive force hanging over her home.'

Everyone who dealt with Piera Aiello in the early days of her collaboration says the same thing: that she was very sure of herself, very confident, and never wavered in her resolve. She was proud, and would turn up for interviews wearing a fur coat, just to prove that she wasn't doing it for the money.

'With my background, I didn't have a very positive idea of lawyers and magistrates,' she admits. 'I had very little idea of justice as the world outside sees it. My husband would rather have died like he did than talk, but that's the kind of man he was. The first time I went to the courthouse I was quite scared. I was very worried about my daughter. But they understood what I needed, they made me feel safe, they explained all the pros and cons of becoming a collaborator, and what protection they could offer me. That was before I said a word.'

Piera and her little girl disappeared into the protection programme, and were ushered off to an unknown destination under assumed names. Soon afterwards her husband's sister Rita took the same path. 'I didn't tell anyone before I started collaborating, not even my parents. Rita called me herself, after she had talked to the police. She asked me what my life was like, and I told her, then I just left it to her to decide. You can't tell someone to do a thing like this, everyone has to find their own path, to do whatever they have to do in life.'

A month later, Paolo Borsellino got a telephone call saying a young girl from Partanna wanted to talk to him. Rita, just 17, went to see the judge and his colleagues for the first time in November 1991. A passport photo shows her with heavy features, untidy brown hair and intense hazel eyes. 'She was a strong character, very self-possessed,' says Plazzi. 'She was proud, and quite undaunted by her surroundings. She was quite clear that she wanted to send the people who killed her father and brother to prison.'

Rita's collaboration began under conditions of the utmost secrecy. Not even her mother could be told. Every day she took the school bus as usual, but got off near the courthouse in Sciacca. As her friends were coming out of school, the carabinieri dropped her off at the bus stop. One night, she and her mother heard a knock at the door, and a man's voice said he was looking for Rita. They didn't let him in. The next day, Rita was taken into protective custody.

The carabinieri called her mother and explained the situation. A woman born and bred in a mafia household, Rita's mother, Giovanna Cannova, sensed a terrible betrayal. She blamed her daughter-in-law Piera Aiello – she had fallen out with her son after he married Piera, and they had not spoken for five years. The carabinieri put Rita on the phone, but her mother was inconsolable.

Giovanna Cannova stormed up to the courthouse, demanding to see her daughter. One of the magistrates met her at the entrance: 'She wanted to give Rita a good thrashing, said she had brought shame on the family: "She's mad, she doesn't know what she's talking about, she has accused a lot of innocent people. Mafia! What does she know about mafia? It's Piera Aiello's fault: she's put these ideas in her head. Give me back my Rita." '[2] She even reported Paolo Borsellino to the police for kidnapping. A few days later, Rita rang her mother again, to tell her she was safe, and was with Piera. 'The happy couple,' her mother sneered. Rita put the phone down.[3] Over the following months, Rita, who had always had a difficult relationship with her mother, tried to persuade her to leave Partanna, and go to live with her. But she refused.

'Rita Atria's mother is a monster,' says Alessandra Camassa. 'Rita begged her to go with her. Why wouldn't she go? She had lost her husband, and her son, there was nothing for her to stay for. But after her daughter collaborated, she didn't want to know. Rita was always trying to protect her mother, she often asked us to try and persuade her to go with her. She used to tell us what a hard life she'd had. Well, she obviously didn't love her children very much.'

Her mother's violent reaction made Rita's decision even more painful. For a time, she lived with Piera Aiello in Rome, a strange, disconnected existence. Piera, who admits she is quite happy lounging about all day in her pyjamas, was never interested in going out, and they spent a lot of time hanging round the flat. Her family shut her out completely. Rita was planning to visit her older sister Anna Maria in Milan, but at the last minute her sister refused to see her. Rita was devastated. Under police escort, she travelled down to Sicily to spend New Year's Eve with her mother. Once they were alone, her mother threatened her. 'She said that if I were to collaborate with the magistrates, she would see to it that I met the same end as my brother Nicola,' Rita told the carabinieri the next day.[4] Things began to look up when Rita met a boy and started dating, filling her diary with longings.

Rita had seen her father killed when she was 11, and her brother had been murdered when she was 16. She worshipped her father, and was proud of his mafia connection. 'She used to say "I am an Atria. That name carries a guarantee" – meaning in the mafia sense of the word,' Camassa remembers. 'She was self-assured and proud. She always used to say no one would suspect her of collaborating because she was an Atria, and an Atria would never talk.

'Rita was a mafiosa – a boss in a skirt. She used to hide guns for them. She had grown up with the mafia mentality, and had created this completely false version of reality, which she even tried to get me to believe. From her earliest childhood, she had invented a father who was good, who found lost sheep and restored them to their owners, when in fact her father had stolen the sheep and the farmers had to pay him to get them back.

'She had grown up identifying completely with the values of her family. When she started talking to us, she would tell us things which obviously shocked us, and seeing our reaction, she would suddenly see them in a different light. She was a deep

person, sensitive and intelligent. She was aware that her father
had been in prison, but she had decided to believe that this was
not because he had committed any crimes, but because some
stupid judge had put him there. When we gave her the facts to
read about what he had actually done, she began to realise what
kind of a man he really was. It was a devastating process for
her.'

Hours of interviews with the two young women illustrated
what is meant by 'mafia logic'. Piera Aiello was not from a
mafia family; when she and Rita Atria described the same
event, they described it in completely different ways. 'With
Piera Aiello you never had to explain what she meant, or why
she described it in that way. You could just write down what
she said. But with Rita Atria, you had to explain the
significance of what she said, which emerged bit by bit. For
example, she would say "My father couldn't have committed
that murder." What she meant was: He would not have killed
that person, because that person was insignificant. He would
have killed his father, who was more important. We had to
untangle the logic to get to the facts.'

But the facts were there, and the two women provided
detailed answers to twenty years of mysteries, including the
unsolved murder of Partanna's deputy mayor. Another woman,
Rosalba Triolo, also from Partanna, began to collaborate at
around the same time. She had left her husband and had been
having an affair with a mafia hit man who got his thrills from
coming home at night and telling her who he had murdered
and how. Before long Triolo, who was none too bright,
incriminated herself by talking about a planned murder on a
tapped telephone line.

Police gave Triolo the option of collaborating or going to
prison. 'She was a very stupid woman, she didn't seem to have
any powers of analysis at all,' says Camassa. 'She just reeled off
the facts that she knew, in exactly the same order, in exactly the
same words, every time we tried to interrogate her. She was
like a record, just went round and round. In the end she said

she had told us everything, and when we let her go, she went straight back to her husband.'

Rita and Piera continued living in Rome, moving to a new secret address every few weeks. Rita's boyfriend left to work abroad. Meanwhile, Rita's relationship with her mother did not improve. She felt isolated and homesick. Her mainstay during this time was Paolo Borsellino, who worried about his young collaborator and often expressed concern to his colleagues about how she would cope away from home, without her family.[5] He talked to her on the telephone every few days. But perhaps more than loneliness, Rita Atria's slow awakening, her realisation that her brother was just a cheap smack dealer and that the father she idolised was a villain, broke her heart.

On 19 July 1992, Paolo Borsellino was assassinated by a car bomb as he pressed his mother's doorbell in the via d'Amelio in Palermo. For the young collaborators spurned by their families, he had become like a father. A week after Borsellino's death, alone in her apartment in Rome, Rita Atria wrote in her diary: 'Now there's no one to protect me. I can't go on.' She closed the notebook and left it on her bedside table in the seventh-floor flat. Then she threw herself out of the window.

The old town of Partanna perches on a hill in the rolling countryside of western Sicily. A smart new road approaches the town through sprawling cement developments, rusted cranes and half-built houses and sweeps up towards the town on concrete stilts. But when I got to the top of its elegant curves, there was no exit: I was swept all the way down again, and rattled into town on the old road.

On either side were ruined houses and crumbling walls. Over twenty years after the earthquake destroyed parts of the town, it was still badly in need of repair. The church roof had collapsed, leaving a gaping hole which had lost tiles like teeth. Houses had bulged and toppled in the quake and lay by the roadside where they fell. Ten years after the disaster, any money made available went straight into the bank accounts of local mafiosi, who signed contracts with their own construction companies, and built themselves new villas with the profits. Instead of repairing the old church, they built a new one beside it. Hundreds of local people whose houses had been destroyed were temporarily rehoused in huts and prefabs on the edge of town – where they remain.

On the day of Rita Atria's funeral, nobody in Partanna's quiet centre had any comment about her short life and lonely death. Hardly anyone seemed to remember her at all. She was a national heroine, but her fame had yet to reach her home town.

If it was difficult to think of Rita's last hours, alone in a rented flat in a strange city, it was harder to think of her mother. Six months before she died, Rita had written in her diary that her mother was on no account to go to her funeral.[6] A waitress in a bar – who couldn't recall Rita Atria but thought it was a shame – said she'd heard that her mother had gone out of her mind, and was being cared for by nuns in a hospice on the edge of town.

By four o'clock, several cars had arrived at the cemetery gates, bringing anti-mafia protesters from Palermo. That week, a group of women had begun a hunger strike in Palermo's central square, to protest against the government's corruption and inactivity. A few of them had made the journey to Partanna, carrying copies of poems and bunches of flowers. A group of local people, mostly women, stood among the gleaming tombstones, holding on to each other's arms and watching the strangers.

The coffin was hoisted on to the shoulders of a small group of women. At the front was photographer and Green politician Letizia Battaglia, who had spent three years taking pictures of bullet-riddled corpses. At the back was Michela Buscemi, who had testified against her brothers' killers and been ostracised by her family. Behind the coffin, openly weeping, came a young blonde woman, Rita's sister Anna Maria, heavily pregnant and leaning on her husband.

The accusing presence of a group of anti-mafia campaigners made the local people uneasy. Eyes searched the unfamiliar faces during Mass. The coffin was draped with an Italian flag, and a couple of local dignitaries showed up at the last minute, looking uncomfortable. Rita Atria was a difficult local heroine.

The mayor stepped forward, wrapped in a tricolour sash like a cake decoration, to give his address. He spoke about courage, youth and dedication to ideals. He did not once mention the mafia. The priest intoned: 'Lord: Forgive your servant for her sins . . .'

'*Rita non ha peccato, ha parlato*' – Rita did not sin, she talked – 'And what she said was the truth,' a voice called out. After a shocked silence, a ripple of applause passed through the crowd, and echoed for long minutes around the cypress trees as, one by one, everybody joined in.

A few weeks after the funeral, Rita's mother crept down to the cemetery and found her picture, glazed and framed on the new marble tomb. She took out a hammer and smashed it.

The prosecution case against the Partanna mafia was based largely on the testimony of Piera Aiello, Rita Atria and Rosalba Triolo. After the first convictions, a number of mafiosi followed their example and agreed to collaborate.

Lately, there has been much criticism of the use of mafia defectors as witnesses, but Judge Camassa is adamant. '*Pentitismo* changed the way we were able to work. People have no idea how difficult it was to conduct an investigation before we had collaborators. There were no letters, almost nothing written down. I monitored a phone tap for a year and got *nothing*. As soon as the law offered the *pentiti* protection, 350 people came forward immediately. The testimony of women who had no previous convictions was even more valuable. Without the collaboration of these women, our case against the Partanna mafia would have been dropped.'

Piera Aiello still moves house several times a year. Last

winter she was burgled, and lost the few precious possessions she had accumulated. She returns home from time to time to visit her family. 'It isn't easy,' she says. 'Things are a bit strained between us. They accept me for what I am, but they can't understand the choice I made. I'm just trying to live a normal life, I've got a degree now, and my little girl's in school.

'I'm a simple person. I just like slopping around the house. I've never asked for money for collaborating: I get the state subsidy, and I never even asked for that. This life is pretty hard, but I can't complain. I did what I had to do. I don't go out much because I've got a young child, but I have made friends – people can see what I am, even if they don't know who I am.

'The first few months were the hardest, I couldn't stop thinking about my husband getting shot right there in front of me. I had times of real darkness. But pride carried me through. I had made a decision and taken control of my life.'

A year after Rita's death, Piera Aiello challenged mafia women to come forward and tell police what they know.[7] 'The wives of mafiosi always know everything. If they were to talk, it would be the end of Cosa Nostra. If they don't talk, they could still do a lot to persuade their men to change. A woman can make her husband do anything she wants. As long as the women remain silent, the mafia will never be beaten.'

Biographies

Piera Aiello

Married Nicola Atria, the son of a mafioso from Partanna, western Sicily. During their stormy relationship, she tried to stop him dealing drugs and committing murders for the mafia. When Nicola's father was killed, he tried to get revenge, but in 1991 he was shot dead in front of Piera and their little girl. At the age of 23, Piera Aiello turned state's evidence as a way of getting away from the mafia environment and starting a new life. She and her daughter live under protection, and she has recently got a degree.

Rita Atria

Sister of Nicola Atria, Rita was just 11 when her adored father, a mafia boss, was murdered. When her brother Nicola was shot dead in 1991, she was just 16. Although raised in a mafia family, she decided to turn state's evidence. She was taken to Rome under protection, where she lived with her sister-in-law, another state witness, Piera Aiello. Depressed and frightened after the assassination of Paolo Borsellino in July 1992, Rita Atria killed herself.

Antonietta Bagarella

Schoolmistress and sister of Corleone boss Leoluca Bagarella, she married Salvatore Riina in 1974 while he was in hiding from the police. Antonietta ('Ninetta') was charged with acting as go-between for the Corleonesi, and became the first woman proposed, though not sent, for internal exile on mafia-related charges. She lived with Riina in hiding for twenty-five years, and had four children, whom she educated at home. When her husband was arrested in 1993, she took the children home to Corleone. After her oldest son Gianni was arrested in 1996, she wrote a letter to *La Repubblica* newspaper, claiming her family was unjustly persecuted. In 1997 he was sentenced to four and a half years for mafia association.

Serafina Battaglia

Wife of a mafioso who was murdered in a long-running feud between Palermo clans in 1960. She urged her son, Salvatore Lupo Leale, to avenge the dead man; she even found him a bodyguard, and a gun. Before Salvatore could arrange the revenge killing, he was shot dead. Serafina Battaglia went to court to testify against her son's killers, but after nine years of hearings all over Italy, the defendants were acquitted.

Antonina Brusca

Married to Bernardo Brusca, boss of San Giuseppe Iato, mafia stronghold in western Sicily, allied to the Corleone clan. Antonina is descended from a mafia dynasty, as is her husband, and they raised three sons in the tradition. One of them, Giovanni Brusca, was arrested in 1996 for the murder of Giovanni Falcone. His mother made several feisty speeches in his defence to the press. To her disgust, two of her sons have become collaborators. Her husband and three sons are now all in jail, and Antonina lives with her daughters-in-law and their children.

Michela Buscemi

Grew up in the slums of Palermo, the eldest of eight brothers and sisters. Her brother Salvatore was murdered in 1979 by the mafia after selling contraband cigarettes without the boss's permission. A younger brother, Rodolfo, was also killed, to prevent him avenging his brother. Michela testified against their killers in the maxi-trial of 1985–86 in Palermo, but had to withdraw after she received a message threatening her six-year-old daughter. After she testified, her mother ostracised her and her husband lost his job. She remains an active anti-mafia campaigner.

Liliana Caruso

Married to Catania hit man and member of the Savasta clan Riccardo Messina, with two children. After he was arrested in 1994 and decided to collaborate, she refused to go into protection. Domenica Micci and Santa Vasta, the wives of the Savasta clan bosses, tried to threaten him by intimidating her. When she reported them to magistrates, Liliana Caruso was shot dead with her mother, Agata Zuchero, in front of her daughter. Messina continued his collaboration, and successfully sued the killers.

Brenda Colletti

A former go-go dancer, she married Philip Colletti, small-time hit man for the South Philadelphia mafia. Pleaded guilty to a series of gun charges committed by her husband, in order to gain status within the mob. They stored a bomb in their house, and had a shooting range in the basement. She planned to commit a murder, but was prevented from carrying it out by her husband. She and Philip both became collaborators in 1994, when she was 28. He is still in prison and she has left the witness protection programme. Their four-year-old son lives with Philip's parents.

Giuseppa Condello

Wife of 'Ndrangheta boss Nino Imerti, who controlled the town of Villa San Giovanni in Calabria. When Imerti went into hiding after the shooting of the rival boss Paolo De Stefano, Giuseppa and her sister Caterina, known as 'Junior', ran the extortion racket in his place. Giuseppa maintained contact between family members; 'Junior' was expert at extracting protection money. The clan members communicated by radio, but police located their wavelength. In 1990 the police descended, and in 1992 a judge in Reggio Calabria handed down sentences to the whole clan, including both women.

Rosetta Cutolo

Older sister of Raffaele Cutolo, 'il professore', founder and Messianic leader of the Nuova Camorra Organizzata. Rosetta lived with her mother in Ottaviano, near Naples, and never married. She is said to have held the reins of the NCO from 1979 until Cutolo's empire fell apart in 1982–83. She evaded arrest when police broke into her house while she was holding a meeting in 1981, and went into hiding until she gave herself up to police in February 1993, aged 55. While serving a five-year sentence for mafia association, she has been acquitted on nine murder charges.

Teresa Deviato

Widowed at 43 when her husband was murdered in 1991, she took over her husband's neighbourhood, the via dei Tribunali in central Naples. With her son from her first marriage, Vincenzo Saetta, she built up a lucrative extortion racket. Saetta was head of a gang of armed robbers, which carried out regular raids on banks and post offices. One of her sons died of a heroin overdose in 1996. Shortly afterwards, Deviato was arrested and charged with extortion and mafia association, after a listening device placed in her house recorded her counting money and guns. She is currently in prison awaiting trial.

Santa Margherita Di Giovine

Known as Rita, she was born in Calabria; her mother was related to the powerful Serraino clan. Rita moved to Milan with her mother and many brothers and sisters in 1963. Her mother started a heroin business, which she ran with her eldest son Emilio. The whole family was engaged in the traffic, which also involved many of their neighbours. When Rita married, her son became a dealer too. At its peak, the family was importing up to 150 kilos of heroin a week, as well as guns and anti-tank missiles to support their Calabrian cousins in their war for domination. In 1993 Rita Di Giovine was arrested in possession of 1,000 Ecstasy tablets and decided to testify against her whole family, starting with her mother.

Patrizia Ferriero

Married to Camorra boss Raffaele Stolder, she took over his

cocaine dealing when he went to prison. Stolder managed to serve a prison sentence in a hospital bed thanks to his wife, who rigged his diagnosis. She kept records of cocaine dealing and bribed police. Her driver and bodyguard was a former carabiniere. She was arrested in 1991 after police discovered an underground safe beneath her apartment containing drugs and guns, which provided access to banks in Naples, via the sewers.

Giacomina Filippello

Lover of mafia boss Natale L'Ala for twenty-four years. When she was 17 and he was 43, they went to live in his territory, Campobello di Mazara, in western Sicily. When his powerful nephews were murdered in 1982 in a takeover bid, he fled to England and Giacomina followed. Two years later he returned, and was wounded in an attack. After another attack, she began to take control, plotting to kill his enemies and keeping guard. But in 1990 he was shot dead, and she turned state's evidence to get her revenge. Her testimony contributed to the conviction of the Campobello clan. She now lives in hiding, under protection.

Margherita Gangemi

Married mafioso Antonino Calderone in Catania. His brother Pippo, head of Cosa Nostra's Commission, was murdered in 1978. They eventually fled to Nice in the south of France with their three children. Calderone was arrested in 1986, and imprisoned in Marseilles. With Margherita's encouragement, he decided to collaborate. He was eventually extradited to Italy, and after testifying in a series of trials, moved with his family to the United States, where they live under protection. While he was in prison, Margherita worked to put all the children through school.

Cristina Guimaraes

Daughter of a wealthy Brazilian lawyer, she met Sicilian mafioso Tommaso Buscetta in Rio when she was 19. He was on the run from two wives, and police on two continents. They moved in together, and got married while he was in prison in Palermo. After his release they moved back to Brazil, where he was arrested, accused of running an international heroin ring. In 1984, under Cristina's persuasion, he agreed to collaborate with Judge Giovanni Falcone, and gave evidence in the maxi-trial. They now live in the USA under the witness protection programme, with their two children and his various children from other marriages.

Immacolata Iacone

Daughter of a Camorra member, met Raffaele Cutolo, self-appointed leader of the Nuova Camorra Organizzata, while visiting her brother in prison, and married him in 1983. She is not known to have been involved in any of his criminal activities, but has made statements to the press on his behalf. He is serving life for murder, and spent years of his sentence in solitary confinement. For the last five years, Immacolata Iacone has petitioned to have her husband's child, and plans to bring her case before the European Court.

Maria Imbraguglia

Wife of Giuseppe Mandalari, who is known as the mafia's accountant. She worked for him at his office in Palermo. They were arrested together in 1994, and are both on trial for money-laundering for Cosa Nostra. The prosecution alleges that when he was out of town, his clients – including Corleone boss Salvatore Riina – would deal with her. He is also accused of rigging trials and elections through his Masonic connections. He is 63 and in very poor health; she is 58.

Tatiana Imparato

Daughter of the Camorra boss of Castellammare di Stabia, Umberto Mario Imparato. She was a law student, her mother a teacher from the Veneto. Her father was shot in a battle with the police; her brother was killed soon afterwards. She was arrested in May 1993 for accepting a kickback from a contractor but released shortly afterwards. Now resident in northern Italy.

Felicia Impastato

Married a mafioso from Cinisi, west of Palermo, called Luigi Impastato, who worked for the boss Gaetano Badalamenti. They had two sons; the eldest, Giuseppe (Peppino for short), became a Communist and campaigned against the mafia, with his own radio transmissions, leaflets and demonstrations. His father threw him out of the house. In 1978 Peppino was killed, in a bomb explosion made to look like a bungled terrorist attack. The assassination was established as a mafia crime, but no individuals were indicted. Felicia lives alone, assisted by her surviving son Giovanni, fighting to reopen the investigation and clear her son's name.

Pietra Lo Verso

Married to a prosperous horse butcher, Cosimo Quattrocchi, they lived in Palermo with their children. He started doing business with a meat cartel in Catania, who nearly ruined him. When he went elsewhere to buy meat, he was murdered with eight of his employees in what became known as the piazza Scaffa massacre, in 1984. She tried to sue the presumed killer, horse dealer Antonino Fisichella, but he was acquitted. Since then, two of her sons have gone to prison for possessing guns and drugs.

Concetta Managò

Married Francesco Gallico from Palmi in Calabria as a teenager. Soon afterwards, his brother was shot dead by the 'Ndrangheta, and Francesco got involved in a blood feud which was to last the next twelve years. He was killed by the rival Gallico clan in 1989. Almost immediately, Concetta Managò went to live with the leader of the enemy family, Domenico Gallico. She says it was to protect her three children from revenge attacks, but she also helped Gallico inflict further damage on her husband's clan. A few months later, Gallico and Managò were arrested. She was tried and convicted of murder, and agreed to turn state's evidence. In 1994 she was released from prison, and now lives under protection with her children.

Alessandra Maninetti

Married to Raffaele Nuzzo, from a Camorra clan in Acerra, near Naples. Her brother-in-law, Nicola Nuzzo, was a powerful Camorra boss. Nicola's wife, Carmela Frezza De Rosa, conspired with her lover, terrorist turned camorrista Franco Vicino, to murder him, and Nicola Nuzzo was battered to death in his hospital bed. Vicino was then murdered by Raffaele Nuzzo. In 1987, Raffaele was gunned down outside a bar by several of his former allies. Alessandra decided to turn state's evidence, in revenge for the murder of her husband and his brother. Carmela Frezza De Rosa was arrested with the rest of the clan in 1990.

Vincenzina Marchese

Sister of mafioso Pino Marchese, she married the Corleone clan number two, Leoluca Bagarella, in 1991. Shortly after the wedding, the couple vanished. Her brother Pino was arrested and became a collaborator in 1992, after being betrayed by Corleone chief Salvatore Riina. Bagarella was arrested in 1995, but there was no sign of his wife. Collaborators later revealed she had killed herself. Her body has never been found.

Pupetta Maresca

Born Assunta Maresca, she married Camorra boss Pasquale Simonetti, known as Pascalone 'e Nola, in 1955, aged 17. He was murdered by mafia rival Antonio Esposito eighty days after the wedding; she shot Esposito in revenge. She gave birth to a son, Pasqualino, in prison. On her release after fourteen years, she became the lover of drug baron and Camorra boss Umberto Ammaturo, and gave birth to twins. Pasqualino disappeared when he was 18. She called a press conference and publicly defied the ruthless Camorra supremo Raffaele Cutolo in 1982. Subsequently served four years for murder and extortion, crimes she still denies. Now lives alone in Sorrento.

Carmela Marzano

'Donna Carmela' married the Camorra boss Luigi Giuliano when she was 13. They have had six children, but one died of heart trouble. Luigi was once leader of the Giuliano clan which runs the Forcella district in the heart of Naples, and has spent long periods in prison for smuggling cigarettes and drug trafficking. Carmela and her male children are frequently arrested; she claims the family is unjustly persecuted.

Anna Mazza 'the Black Widow'

Her husband, Gennaro Moccia, boss of Afragola near Naples, was murdered in 1976. Her 13-year-old son Antonio then shot his father's killer. After her husband's death, the Moccia family routed two other clans. She was banned from Naples a number of times, and has spent a total of five years in prison, but has never been convicted of mafia crimes. In the 1980s the family accumulated a fortune through extortion and building contracts. Her sons, Angelo, Luigi and Antonio, are all detained; her favourite, Vincenzo, was murdered in 1987.

Maria Filippa Messina

Wife of the Catania boss Antonino Cintorino, she took over his clan at the age of 24 when he was given a life sentence in 1993. She collected protection money, and imported arms from Yugoslavia. She was planning a massacre of the rival group when police bugged her home. She was arrested in February 1995 and is currently being held in isolation in a maximum security unit reserved for mafia members.

Carmela Minniti

Wife of Nitto Santapaola, supreme boss of Catania Cosa Nostra, said to be the second most powerful man in Sicily after Salvatore Riina. While he was in hiding for over ten years, Carmela spent a lot of time with him, but also held meetings with their lawyer and brought him information. He was arrested in 1992, and she continued to have meetings with the lawyer. When her two sons were arrested in 1994, she broke down in public outside the courtroom, and appealed for their release. She was rumoured to be on the point of collaborating when she was shot dead in 1995 by an enemy of her husband's.

Carmela Palazzo, 'Cerasella'

Married with a child by the age of 12, she dealt heroin for her family, the 'Palazzetti', in the Mercato district of Naples. Had another three children by different men. She and her brother Vincenzo Palazzo dealt in speedballs (heroin and cocaine cocktails). Favourite brother Francesco was shot dead in front of her. She tried to become leader of the clan, but was accused by relatives of embezzling funds, and was forced to step down. Out of spite, and to avenge her murdered brother, she became a collaborator in 1991. She was subsequently dumped from the protection programme for unruly behaviour.

Saveria Palazzolo

Married to Bernardo Provenzano, who was Salvatore Riina's running-mate in the 1950s (they were known as 'the Beasts'). Provenzano has been in hiding from the police since 1969. She was doing business for him, investing money, buying property and setting up companies, in consultation with the man known as the 'mafia's accountant', Giuseppe Mandalari, until a warrant was issued for her arrest in 1983, and she went into hiding. Years later, when she was granted an amnesty, she brought her two sons home to Corleone. They spoke fluent German and English, and had been very well educated, but were not registered as Italian citizens. Provenzano, rumoured to be Riina's substitute, is still in hiding.

Margherita Petralìa

Married mafioso Gaspare Sugamiele from Paceco, near Trapani in western Sicily; they had three children. His family controlled Paceco, and had links with the Catania Cosa Nostra. Angered by her husband's prolonged absences, and frequent beatings, Margherita wrote a diary, detailing his mafia connections and crimes. After they had separated, she delivered the diary to the police. Sugamiele and his sister Antonia both went to prison on mafia charges. Since 1989, she has lived alone in Milan. Her son still lives with his father.

Amalia Pizza

A young mother of two, separated from her husband, she lived in Nola, near Naples, an area run by Camorra boss Carmine Alfieri. Two of her brothers were ambitious to join the mafia, but were murdered by Alfieri's men. Amalia at first collaborated with the police, then, together with her father, in 1992 shot the man who killed her brothers. When she got out of prison, aged 33, she moved in with a man who beat her to death. Her children are living with her mother. Her father is still in prison for murder.

Grazia Ribisi

Sister of the 'terrible brothers', gunmen for the Agrigento mafia. In 1984, the 'terrible brothers' made a bid for control of Palma de Montechiaro in southern Sicily. In the ensuing war, three of them were killed. The rest of the clan went into hiding, and Grazia Ribisi, who remained at large, became the focus of police inquiries. During this time, police placed a listening device in her bedroom. When the Allegro family tried to pull out of the conflict, Grazia Ribisi was heard cursing their treachery. She was arrested at the age of 50, and charged with mafia association, but she was acquitted, and received compensation for wrongful arrest. Her husband died in prison, and she lives with her two daughters in Palma de Montechiaro.

Angela Russo, 'Grandma Heroin'

Daughter of a Palermo mafioso, she grew up to be his surrogate son. When she got married, she started dealing in drugs, and by the time she was in her seventies 'Grandma Heroin' was dealing out of her own home, using three generations of her own family, with the smallest children selling on the street. She used to carry kilos of heroin to the mainland in a battered suitcase. The whole family was arrested in 1981, including her daughters and one granddaughter. During the trial, her son Salvino threatened to testify but his mother managed to destroy his nerve. She went to prison for five years, and died in 1990.

Rita Simoncini

Pregnant when her boyfriend, mafioso Francesco Marino Mannoia, married a mafia boss's daughter, Rosa Vernengo, in 1978, she had the child, called Cristina, and continued living near the couple in Bagheria, near Palermo. Mannoia was arrested in 1985, and was in prison when his brother was murdered. In 1989, Rita Simoncini finally persuaded him to collaborate. It was she who travelled to Rome, to discuss his decision with the chief of police, and was immediately offered protection. Shortly after he began to talk, Marino Mannoia's mother, aunt and sister were all killed by Cosa Nostra. He obtained a divorce and now lives with Rita and their daughter under protection.

Giuseppina Spadaro

Daughter of heroin refiner Tommaso Spadaro, who is serving thirty years for drugs offences, Giuseppina (Giusy) grew up in La Kalsa, a mafia-run bomb site in the heart of Palermo. She married Pasquale Di Filippo, one of Corleone boss Leoluca Bagarella's top aides. When her husband was arrested and subsequently became a collaborator, in 1995, she and her sister-in-law Angela Marino, who is married to Emanuele Di Filippo, called a press conference to announce they had disowned their husbands.

April Waltomate

Separated with two children, she started dating mobster Ron 'Cuddles' DiCaprio in South Philadelphia in 1982, and became a bookkeeper with the mafia. DiCaprio made her help him destroy evidence after a murder, and involved her in plans for another killing. He then forced her to marry him, to keep her from testifying against him. They married in 1983, but afterwards he tried to murder her. She agreed to collaborate with the FBI, and testified before the grand jury. DiCaprio went to jail, and April subsequently married her FBI guard, Jerry Waltomate. She lives with her husband and children in Pennsylvania.

Notes

Introduction

1. *La Repubblica*, 23 June 1996.
2. Corrado Stajano, *Mafia: L'atto d'accusa dei giudici di Palermo*, Riuniti, Rome, 1992 (first edn 1986), p. 14.
3. Pino Arlacchi, *Gli uomini del disonore*, Mondadori, Milan, 1992, p. 163.
4. La donna nella criminalità organizzata. Report to parliament by the Osservatorio permanente sulla criminalità, Ministry of the Interior, May 1996, p. 297.
5. *Panorama*, 1 August 1993.
6. Figures from Antonio Manganelli at the Department for Protection of Collaborators, January 1997.

1: Camorra Godmothers

1. Isaiah Sales, *La camorra, le camorre*, Riuniti, Rome, 1993, p. 136.
2. Ibid., p. 137.
3. *La Repubblica*, 28 August 1990.
4. Interview with assistant chief prosecutor Italo Ormanni, Rome, 28 May 1996.
5. Interview with Italo Ormanni.
6. *L'Ora*, 23 February 1982.
7. Ibid.
8. Sergio De Gregorio, *I nemici di Cutolo*, Pironti Ed, Naples, 1983, p. 44.
9. Procedimento penale a carico di Alfano Nicolò + 15, examination of the witness Giacomina Filippello, 22 July 1991.
10. *La Repubblica*, 31 May 1996. The speaker was the Sicilian mafioso Gaspare Mutolo.
11. Corrado Stajano, *Mafia: L'atto d'accusa dei giudici di Palermo*, Riuniti, Rome, 1992 (first edn 1986), p. 71.
12. Gigi Di Fiore, *Potere Camorrista*, Alfredo Guida, Naples, 1993, p. 159.
13. *Il Giornale di Napoli*, 9 February 1993.
14. *Unità*, 11 September 1981.
15. *Il Giornale di Sicilia*, 9 February 1993.
16. *Il Mattino*, 17 March 1987.
17. From Cutolo's *Poetry and Philosophy*, quoted in *Oggi* 1981.
18. Sergio De Gregorio, *Camorra*, Società Editrice Napoletana, Naples, 1981, p. 106.
19. *Giornale di Sicilia*, 9 February 1993.
20. Interview with Antonio Laudati, Naples, 11 September 1995.
21. Misura di prevenzione contro Ciro Mazzarella + 19, Tribunale di Napoli, 27 July 1992, p. 33.
22. Umberto Vecchione, deputy chief of Criminalpol, described the scene to the *Giornale di Sicilia*, 9 February 1993.

23. Applicazione di misure di prevenzione, Anna Mazza + 9, Tribunale di Napoli, 10 April 1990, p. 48.
24. Ibid., p. 26.
25. Ibid., p. 39.
26. Alfonso Lamberti, judge in the court of appeal, was arrested on corruption charges in 1990.
27. Misura di prevenzione . . ., p. 19.

2: The Women who Want to be Boss

1. Diego Gambetta, *La mafia siciliana*, Einaudi, Turin, 1992, p. 216.
2. Giovanni Falcone, *Cose di Cosa Nostra*, Rizzoli, Milan, 1992, pp. 98ff.
3. Interview with deputy chief prosecutor Guido Lo Forte, Palermo, 6 May 1996.
4. Norman Lewis, *The Honoured Society*, Eland Books, London, 1991 (first edn 1964), p. 77.
5. Lucio Galluzzo et al., *Objettivo Falcone: magistrati e mafia nel Palazzo dei veleni*, Pironti, Naples, 1989, p. 107.
6. Diego Gambetta, *La mafia siciliana*, Einaudi, Turin, 1992, p. 35.
7. Henner Hess, *Mafia: le origine e la struttura*, Laterza, Bari 1993 (first edn 1970), p. 146.
8. Ibid., p. 51.
9. Giuseppe Pitré, *Usi e costumi, credenze e pregiudizi del popolo siciliano*, Palermo, 1898, vol. II, a classic treatise on mafia daily life and behaviour, quoted in Franco Ferrarotti, *Rapporto sulla mafia: da costume locale a problema dello sviluppo nazionale*, Liguori, Naples, 1978, p. 77.
10. Salvatore Lupo, *Storia della mafia*, Donizelli, Rome, 1993, p. 183.
11. Interview with Teresa Principato, Palermo, 6 May 1996.
12. 'Ci sono donne nella mafia?', essay by Giovanna Fiume in history and social science magazine *Meridiana*, 7–8, 1990, p. 293.
13. Interview with Antonio Laudati, Naples, 11 September 1995.
14. *Giornale di Sicilia*, 28 February 1994.
15. Ibid.
16. Interview with Luigi Gay, 24 May 1996.
17. Interview with Giuseppe Narducci, 12 September 1996.

3: Naples Loan Sharks

1. Isaiah Sales, *La camorra, le camorre*, Riuniti, Rome, 1993, p. 41.
2. Interview with Antonio Laudati, Naples, 11 September 1995.
3. Jimmy Burns, *Hand of God, the Story of Diego Maradona*, Bloomsbury, London, 1996, p. 135.
4. Giovanni Falcone, *Cose di Cosa Nostra*, Rizzoli, Milan, 1992, p. 126.
5. Interview with Don Massimo Rastrelli by Luigi d'Alise in *La Voce della Campania*, October 1995, p. 28.
6. Marco Monnier, *La Camorra*, Argo, Lecce, 1994, p. 151.
7. Recorded on 26 March 1995.
8. Procedimento penale contro Teresa Deviato + 16, Tribunale di Napoli, July 1996.
9. Interview with Gabriella Gribaudi, Naples, 23 May 1996.
10. Trial in progress at time of writing.

4: Extortion: The Deadly Protectors

1. Enzo Ciconte, *'Ndrangheta dall'unità a oggi*, Laterza, Bari, 1992, p. 362.
2. The name 'Ndrangheta is said to derive from the Greek *andragathos*, meaning a man of courage and valour. It has only recently come into general usage to describe the Calabrian mafia.
3. Ciconte, *'Ndrangheta*, pp. 205–6.
4. Interview with assistant chief prosecutor Salvatore Boemi, Reggio Calabria, 20 July 1996.
5. Corte d'assise di Reggio Calabria, sentenza contro Antonio Imerti + 40, 14 November 1992. The story of Giuseppa Condello is based on transcriptions of radio conversations contained in this document, and on interviews with Salvatore Boemi, who led the investigation.
6. Interview with historian Salvatore Lupo, Catania, 19 June 1996.
7. Richiesta per l'applicazione di misure cautelare contro Antonino Cintorino + 40, Procura Distrettuale della Repubblica, Catania, 22 December 1995. The story of Maria Felippa Messina is based on transcripts of conversations reprinted in the prosecutor's report.
8. Interview with Salvatore Lupo.
9. *La Repubblica*, 9 February 1995.
10. Tribunale di Catania, Misure di custodia cautelare nei confronti di Vasta Maria Rosa + 4, 7 November 1994, p. 3.
11. Tribunale di Catania, richiesta di convalida del fermo nei confronti di Niciforo Lucia + 10, 25 June 1994.

5: Vendetta

1. This account of Amalia Pizza's life and death is compiled from conversations with carabinieri intimately involved with the case, who prefer not to be named.
2. Interview with Luigi Gay, deputy chief prosecutor, Naples, 24 May 1996.
3. Norman Lewis, *The Honoured Society*, Eland Books, London, 1991, p. 26.
4. Ibid., p. 28.
5. Jerry Capeci and Gene Mustain, *Gotti: Rise and Fall*, Onyx/Penguin, New York, 1996, p. 67.
6. Ibid., p. 66.
7. Tim Shawcross, *The War against the Mafia*, Mainstream, Edinburgh, 1994, p. 164.
8. Leonardo Sciascia, *La Sicilia come metafora*, Mondadori, Milan, 1984 (first edn 1979), p. 14.
9. Procedimento penale a carico di Alfano Nicolò + 15, examination of the witness Giacomina Filippello, 22 July 1991.
10. Giorgio Chinnici and Umberto Santino, *La violenza programmata*, Franco Angeli, Milan, 1989.
11. Nino Calderone with Pino Arlacchi, *Gli uomini del disonore*, Mondadori, Milan, 1992, p. 171.
12. *L'Ora*, 16 July 1981.
13. *Giornale di Sicilia*, 16 July 1981, cited in *Con e contro: le donne nell'organizzazione mafiosa e nella lotta antimafia*, ed. Anna Puglisi and Antonia Cascio, Centro siciliano di documentazione Giuseppe Impastato, Palermo, 1986.

14. Lewis, *Honoured Society*, p. 28.

15. Enzo Ciconte, *'Ndrangheta dall'unità a oggi*, Laterza, Bari, 1992, p. 57.

16. Luigi Lombardi Satriani debating the role of women in the mafia, in *Le ragioni della mafia: studiie ricerche di quaderni calabresi*, ed. F. Faeta et al., Jaca Books, Milan, 1983, p. 175.

17. Ciconte, *'Ndrangheta*, p. 64.

18. Interview with assistant chief prosecutor Salvatore Boemi, Reggio Calabria, 20 July 1996.

19. Interview with deputy chief prosecutor Nicola Gratteri, Reggio Calabria, 10 June 1996.

20. Tribunale di Milano, examination of the witness Santa Margherita Di Giovine, in the trial of Gianfranco Agnifili + 149, 5 June 1996.

21. Ciconte, *'Ndrangheta*, p. 223.

22. Interview with Salvatore Lupo, Catania, 19 June 1996.

23. This account was largely supplied by Agrigento journalist Franco Castaldo.

24. Interview with Teresa Principato, Palermo, 6 May 1996.

25. Interview with Grazia Ribisi's lawyer, Salvatore Russello, Palma de Montechiaro, 12 September 1996.

26. *Giornale di Sicilia*, 18 April 1992.

27. Ibid.

6: The Sins of the Mother

1. *La Repubblica*, 24 May 1996.

2. Interview with Antonio Laudati, Rome, 26 September 1996.

3. Interview with Salvatore Lupo, Catania, 19 June 1996.

4. Interview with Liliana Ferraro, Rome, 28 May 1996.

5. *L'Ora*, 13 July 1971.

6. *La Repubblica*, 12 June 1996.

7. *Il Messaggero*, 26 June 1996.

8. The letter ran over a full page in *La Repubblica* on 23 June 1996, and was followed by commentaries and debates which ran for days.

9. *Panorama* magazine, 7 December 1995.

10. *La Repubblica*, 12 June 1996.

11. Marco Nese, *Nel segno della mafia: storia di Luciano Leggio*, Rizzoli, Milan, 1975, p. 42.

12. *Uno sguardo dal bunker: cronache del maxiprocesso di Palermo*, ed. Aurelio Angelini et al., Ediprint Diapason, Syracuse, 1987, p. 122.

13. Claire Sterling, *The Mafia*, Hamish Hamilton, London, 1990, p. 60.

7: The Breeding Ground

1. Tim Shawcross, *The War against the Mafia*, Mainstream, Edinburgh, 1994, p. 162.

2. Ibid., p. 247.

3. George Anastasia, *Blood and Honor*, Zebra Books, New York, 1991, p. 418.

4. Walter Rizzo et al., *Il governo della mafia*, Arbor, Palermo, 1994, p. 37.

5. Claire Sterling, *Crime without Frontiers*, Warner/Little, Brown, London, 1995, p. 108.

6. Alexander Stille, *Excellent Cadavers*, Pantheon, New York, 1995, p. 383.

7. *Giornale di Sicilia*, 16 May 1993, quoting her interview on the Costanzo show.

8. Interview with Amato Lamberti, Naples, 12 September 1995.
9. *Il Mattino*, 31 May 1991.

8: Battle for the Children's Souls

1. *La Repubblica*, 10 March 1996, reported the scene in the words of the collaborator Giuseppe Monticciolo.
2. Interview with Luigi LiGotti, Rome, 1 July 1996.
3. ANSA, 20 July 1996.
4. Ordinanza di custodia cautelare in carcere against Enzo and Giovanni Brusca + 19 others, Tribunale di Palermo, 7 June 1996.
5. Interview with Santino Di Matteo's lawyer, Lucia Falzone, Caltanissetta, 14 July 1996.
6. Anna Puglisi and Umberto Santino, 'Le donne e il pentitismo', essay published in *Narcomafie*, 9, October 1995.
7. Interview with Pupetta Maresca, Sorrento, 17 May 1996.
8. Interview with deputy chief prosecutor Guido Lo Forte, Palermo, 6 May 1996.
9. Interview with Frank Friel, Bensalem, Philadelphia, 7 November, 1995.
10. *Giornale di Sicilia*, 9 May 1993.
11. This account comes from an interview with deputy chief prosecutor Nicolò Marino, Catania, 21 June 1996.
12. Interview with Guido Lo Forte, as above.
13. Enzo Ciconte, *'Ndrangheta dall'unità a oggi*, Laterza, Bari, 1992, p. 46.
14. *La Repubblica* and *Il Corriere della Sera*, 28 June 1995.
15. *Giornale di Sicilia*, 28 June 1995.
16. Ibid.
17. *L'Unità*, 28 June 1995.
18. Interview with Nino Scarpulla, Palermo, 9 July 1996.
19. Paper delivered by Giancarlo Dionisi of the Servizio Centrale di Protezione to the Convegno su Minori Oltre il Processo, Palermo, 25 April 1996.
20. Interview with deputy chief prosecutor Nicolò Marino, as above.

9: The Drug Trade: Women's Work

1. Tribunale di Napoli, processo contro Raffaele Stolder + 45, udienza 26 April 1994. Ferriero was convicted and sentenced to seven and a half years.
2. This was confirmed by a calligraphy test in court.
3. Umberto Santino and Giovanni La Fiura, *Dietro la droga*, Gruppo Abele, Turin, 1993, p. 178.
4. Titti Beneduce, 'Donne di Camorra', essay in *Cosa Nostra Napoletana: rapporto sulla Camorra 1992*, ed. Vita Faenza, Publiprint, Naples, 1993, p. 113.
5. Trial in progress at time of writing.
6. *Giornale di Sicilia*, 26 March 1983.
7. Interview with Piera Mattiolo, Palermo, September 1992.
8. Marina Pino, *Le signore della droga*, La Luna, Palermo, 1988, p. 27.
9. Interview with Amato Lamberti, Naples, 14 September 1995.
10. Interview with Salvatore Esposito, Naples, 27 May 1996.
11. Anna Puglisi of the Centro siciliano di documentazione Giuseppe Impastato, 'Le donne dentro l'organizzazione mafiosa', lecture delivered in Messina, 27 May 1993.

12. Pino, *Le signore*, p. 79.
13. Ibid., p. 97.
14. Ibid., p. 86.
15. Interview with Maurizio Romanelli, Milan, 27 September 1996.
16. Tribunale Ordinario di Milano: processo contro Gianfranco Agnifili + 149, udienza 9 May 1996, Milan: examination of the witness Santa Margherita Di Giovine. This account of life in the Di Giovine family is taken from a transcript of the case, 9 May–6 June 1996.

10: No Such Thing as a Businesswoman

1. *L'Ora*, 28 February 1983.
2. *Giornale di Sicilia*, 14 December 1994.
3. Salvatore Lupo, *Storia della mafia*, Donizelli, Rome, 1993.
4. Umberto Santino and Giovanni La Fiura have carried out a painstaking reconstruction of companies which reveal the mafia businessmen's entire family tree, in *L'impresa mafiosa*, Franco Angeli, Milan, 1990.
5. Pino Arlacchi, *Mafia Business*, trans. Martin Ryle, Oxford University Press, Oxford, 1988, p. 208.
6. Interview with Antonio Laudati, Rome, 26 September 1996.
7. Antoinette Giancana and Thomas C. Renner, *Mafia Princess*, Corgi, New York, 1985, p. 106.
8. Interview with Umberto Santino, Palermo, 30 April 1996.
9. Interview with Giacomo Travaglino, Naples, 21 May 1996.
10. *Giornale di Sicilia*, 14 December 1994.
11. Interview with Maurizio Delucia, Palermo, 9 July 1996.
12. Decreto di non luogo a procedere contro Francesca Citarda, Tribunale di Palermo, 11 February 1983, reprinted in Anna Puglisi and Antonia Cascio (eds), *Con e contro: le donne nell'organizzazione mafiosa e nella lotta antimafia*, Centro siciliano di documentazione Giuseppe Impastato, Palermo, 1986, pp. 38–42.
13. Renate Siebert, *Le donne, la mafia*, Il Saggiatore, Milan, 1994, p. 188.
14. Corrado Stajano, *Mafia: L'atto di accusa dei giudici di Palermo*, Riuniti, Rome, 1992, p. 41.
15. Ibid., p. 21.
16. *Il Giornale*, 16 January 1993.
17. Liliana Madeo, *Donne di mafia*, Mondadori, Milan, 1994, p. 71.
18. Arlacchi, *Mafia Business*, p. 201.
19. Ordinanza di sentenza contro Abbate Giovanni + 706, Palermo, 8 November 1985, vol. 22.
20. Ibid., vol. 7.
21. Luigi Barzini, *The Italians*, Hamish Hamilton, London, 1987, p. 194.

11: Women Take the Stand

1. Interview with Giovanna Terranova, Palermo, 26 September 1996.
2. This moment in history is thoroughly documented in *Con e contro: le donne nell'organizzazione mafiosa e nella lotta antimafia*, ed. Anna Puglisi and Antonia Cascio, Giuseppe Impastato research centre, 1986.
3. Interview with Rita Costa, Palermo, 1 May 1991.

4. *Sole contro la mafia*, interviews with Michela Buscemi and Pietra Lo Verso by Anna Puglisi, La Luna, Palermo, 1990, p. 16.
5. Named in memory of Peppino Impastato, murdered by the mafia in 1978, see below, p. 173.
6. Interview with Felicia Bartolotta Impastato, Cinisi, 3 May 1991.

12: Life with the Supergrass

1. *Corriere della Sera*, 20 June 1996.
2. Tim Shawcross and Martin Young, *Men of Honour: Confessions of Tommaso Buscetta*, Fontana, London, 1989, p. 37.
3. Interview with Luigi LiGotti, Rome, 1 July 1996.
4. Alexander Stille, *Excellent Cadavers*, Pantheon, New York, 1995, p. 94.
5. Corrado Stajano, *Mafia: L'atto d'accusa dei giudici di Palermo*, Riuniti, Rome, 1992, p. 50.
6. Shawcross and Young, *Men of Honour*, p. 42.
7. Pino Arlacchi, *Gli uomini del disonore*, the biography based on interviews with Nino Calderone, Mondadori, Milan, 1992, p. 289.
8. Ibid., p. 293.
9. Interview with Antonio Manganelli, Rome, 29 June 1996.
10. Interview with Antonio Manganelli, Rome, 13 April 1995.
11. Liliana Madeo, *Donne di mafia*, Mondadori, Milan, 1994, p. 114.
12. Interview with Guido Lo Forte, Palermo, 6 May 1996.
13. Interview with investigating magistrate Francesco Puleio, Catania, 12 July 1996.
14. Interview with Messina's lawyer in Catania, Enza Angelini, 16 September 1996.

13: Marriage Most Foul

1. Antoinette Giancana with Thomas C. Renner, *Mafia Princess*, Corgi, New York, 1985, p. 22.
2. Liliana Madeo, *Donne di mafia*, Mondadori, Milan, 1994, p. 12.
3. Giovanni Falcone, *Cose di Cosa Nostra*, Rizzoli, Milan, 1992, p. 76.
4. Madeo, *Donne di mafia*, p. 127.
5. Interview with Maria Maniscalco, mayor of San Giuseppe Iato, 9 May 1996.
6. Rosalie Bonanno, *Mafia Marriage*, Avon, New York, 1991, p. 138.
7. From Margherita Petralìa's unpublished diary.

14: All for Love

1. Interview with assistant chief prosecutor Salvatore Boemis, Reggio Calabria, 10 June 1996.
2. Examination of the witness Alessandra Maninetti, 20 December 1988, cited in the sentence against Mario Fabbrocino + 34, Tribunale di Napoli.
3. Interview with assistant chief prosecutor Paolo Mancuso, Naples, 6 June 1996.
4. Interview with deputy chief prosecutor Alessandra Camassa, Trapani, 24 July 1993. Some of her comments quoted here are taken from further interviews in October 1993 and May 1996.
5. Procedimento penale a carico di Alfano Nicolò + 15, examination of the witness Giacomina Filippello, 22 July 1991. By law, the driver and the shooter are both guilty of murder.

6. Interview with magistrate Alberto Di Pisa, Palermo, 10 May 1996.
7. Procedimento penale a carico di Alfano Nicolò + 15.
8. Ibid.

15: Vendetta by Law

1. Interview with deputy chief prosecutor Morena Plazzi, Sciacca, July 1993.
2. Umberto Lucentini, *Paolo Borsellino: Il valore di una vita*, Mondadori, Milan, 1994, p. 195.
3. Sandra Rizza, *Rita Atria: una ragazza contro la mafia*, La Luna, Palermo, 1993, p. 102.
4. Ibid., p. 113.
5. Lucentini, *Paolo Borsellino*, p. 194.
6. Rizza, *Rita Atria*, p. 127.
7. *Panorama*, 1 August 1993, p. 63.

Bibliography

Nonostante la paura, Michela Buscemi, la Meridiana, Molfetta, 1995

Essere donna in Sicilia, ed. Simona Mafai, Editori Riuniti, Rome, 1976

La mafia in casa mia, Felicia Bartolotta Impastato with Anna Puglisi. Interview with the mother of Giuseppe Impastato, assassinated by the mafia aged 30. La Luna, Palermo, 1986

Le signore della droga, Marina Pino. Interviews with housewives who worked as drug couriers between Palermo and New York. La Luna, Palermo, 1988

Sole contro la mafia, Anna Puglisi. Interviews with Michela Buscemi and Pietra Lo Verso, who testified against the mafia. La Luna, Palermo, 1990

Rita Atria: una ragazza contro la mafia, Sandra Rizza. Life and death of a young collaborator. La Luna, Palermo, 1993

Con e contro: le donne nell'organizzazione mafiosa e nella lotta antimafia, ed. Anna Puglisi and Antonia Cascio. Press cuttings on women and the mafia. Centro siciliano di documentazione Giuseppe Impastato, Palermo, 1986

Le donne, la mafia, Renate Siebert, il Saggiatore, Milan, 1994, translated as *Secrets of Life and Death: Women and the Mafia*, Verso, London, 1996

Donne di mafia: vittime, complici e protagoniste, Liliana Madeo, Mondadori, Milan, 1994

The Walking Dead: the Life of Liliana Ferraro, John Parker, Simon & Schuster, London, 1995

Mob Girl, Teresa Carpenter, Simon & Schuster, New York, 1992

Mafia Princess, Antoinette Giancana and Thomas C. Renner, Corgi, New York, 1985

Mafia Marriage, Rosalie Bonanno with Beverly Donofrio, Avon, New York, 1991

Mafia e quotidianità, Renate Siebert, il Saggiatore, Milan, 1996

Un lenzuolo contro la mafia, Roberto Alajmo, Gelka, Palermo, 1993

Vi perdono ma inginocchiatevi: lettera ai mafiosi, Rosaria Schifani with Felice Cavallaro. The story of Vito Schifani, one of Giovanni Falcone's bodyguards killed with him in May 1992, by his widow. Tullio Peronti, Naples, 1992

Storia della mafia, Salvatore Lupo, Donizelli, Rome, 1993

Cose di Cosa Nostra, Giovanni Falcone with Marcelle Padovani, Rizzoli, Milan, 1992

The Honoured Society, Norman Lewis. Classic history of the Sicilian mafia through the story of the bandit Salvatore Giuliano. Eland Books, London, 1991 (first edn 1964)

Naples '44, Norman Lewis. An English intelligence officer stationed in Naples after the liberation. Eland, London, 1983 (first edn 1978)

Gli uomini del disonore, Pino Arlacchi. The Sicilian mafia recounted by the supergrass Antonino Calderone. Mondadori, Milan, 1992

Mafia Business, Pino Arlacchi, trans. Martin Ryle, Oxford University Press, Oxford, 1988

Mafioso: a History of the Mafia from its Origins to the Present Day, Gaia Servadio, Stein & Day, New York, 1976

Excellent Cadavers: the Mafia and the Death of the First Italian Republic, Alexander Stille, Pantheon, New York, 1995

Dieci anni di mafia: La guerra che lo stato non ha saputo vincere, Saverio Lodato, Rizzoli, Milan, 1990

La mafia siciliana, Diego Gambetta. Study of the mafia as a private protection enterprise. Einaudi, Turin, 1992

Mafia: L'atto d'accusa dei giudici di Palermo: Ordinanza sentenza per la corte d'assise a Palermo contro Abbate Giovanni + 706, Distillation of the magistrates' report on the maxi-trial ed. Corrado Stajano, Riuniti, Rome, 1992 (first edn 1986)

Uno sguardo dal bunker: cronache del maxiprocesso di Palermo, ed. Aurelio Angelini et al., Ediprint/Diapason, Syracuse, 1987

Rapporto sulla mafia: da costume locale a problema dello sviluppo nazionale, Franco Ferrarotti, Liguori, Naples, 1978

Le parole sono pietre, Carlo Levi. Contains an interview with the mother of murdered trade unionist Salvatore Carnevale. Einaudi, Turin, 1955

Cosa Nostra Napoletana: rapporto sulla Camorra 1992, ed. Vita Faenza, Publiprint, Naples, 1993

La mafia dell'eroina. Interviews with and writings by former Antimafia Commission chief, now speaker of the house, Luciano Violante. Edited by Daria Lucca, Riuniti, Rome, 1987

Non è la piovra. Twelve essays on the Italian mafia by Luciano Violante. Einaudi, Turin, 1994

Mafie e antimafia: Rapporto 96, ed. Luciano Violante, Editori Laterza, Bari, 1996

Il delitto come impresa, Raimondo Catanzaro. Mafia and business. Rizzoli, Milan, 1991

Rapporto sulla mafia degli anni 80, Gli atti dell'Ufficio Istruzione del Tribunale di Palermo, SF Flaccovio, Palermo, 1986

Ragazzi della mafia, storie di criminalità, ed. Franco Occhigrosso, Franco Angeli, Milan, 1993

La mafia, le mafie. Essays on the changing face of Italian organised crime, ed. G. Fiandaca and S. Costantino, Laterza, Bari, 1994

Mafia, politica e affari, 1943–91, Nicola Tranfaglia. Intimate relationship between mafia, business and politics. Laterza, Bari, 1992

Obiettivo Falcone: magistrati e mafia nel Palazzo dei veleni, Lucio Galluzzo et al., Pironti, Naples, 1989

L'impresa mafiosa: dall'Italia agli Stati Uniti, Umberto Santino and Giovanni La Fiura. Report on financial links between mafia families and companies. Franco Angeli, Milan, 1990

L'antimafia difficile, ed. Umberto Santino. Centro siciliano di documentazione Giuseppe Impastato, Palermo, 1989

La mafia interpretata, Umberto Santino, Rubbettino, Messina, 1995

Dietro la droga, Umberto Santino and Giovanni La Fiura. Textbook on how the international trade operates. Gruppo Abele, Turin, 1993

La violenza programmata, Giorgio Chinnici and Umberto Santino, Franco Angeli, Milan, 1989

La vita quotidiana della mafia dal 1950 a oggi, Fabrizio Calvi, Rizzoli, Milan, 1986

The Italians, Luigi Barzini, Hamish Hamilton, London, 1987 (first edn 1964)

Totò Riina, la sua storia, Pino Buongiorno, Rizzoli, Milan, 1993

L'inferno: profondo sud, male oscuro, Giorgio Bocca, Mondadori, Milan, 1992

Mafia: le origine e la struttura, Henner Hess. Study of mafia cultural roots and folklore. Edizioni Laterza, Bari, 1993 (first edn 1970)

Il governo della mafia, Walter Rizzo et al. History of Catania mafia, political intrigues and corruption in business. Arbor, Palermo, 1994

Nel segno della mafia: storia di Luciano Leggio, Marco Nese, Rizzoli, Milan, 1975

La Sicilia come metafora, Leonardo Sciascia. Mafia character and mores interpreted. Mondadori, Milan, 1984 (first edn 1979)

Raccolto Rosso: la mafia, l'Italia, Enrico Deaglio. Lively tour of the mafia hot spots and protagonists. Feltrinelli, Milan, 1993

Paolo Borsellino: Il valore di una vita, Umberto Lucentini. Biography. Mondadori, Milan, 1994

Missili e mafia: la Sicilia dopo Comiso, Paolo Gentiloni, Alberto Spampinato and Agostino Spataro. Sicilian anti-nuclear movement. Riuniti, Rome, 1985

Mafia vecchia, mafia nuova, ed. Nando dalla Chiesa. Includes essay by Giuseppe Fava on the mafia's control of industry: 'I quattro cavalieri dell'apocalisse'. Franco Angeli, Milan, 1985

I Siciliani, Giuseppe Fava. Interviews with Sicilians. Cappelli, Bologna, 1980

La mafia comanda a Catania, 1960–1991, Claudio Fava. Son of assassinated journalist Giuseppe Fava documents the mafia's control over Catania business and politics. Laterza, Bari, 1991

Totò Riina: 30 anni di sangue da Corleone ai vertici di Cosa Nostra, Giuseppe Martorana and Sergio Nigrelli, Musumeci, Quart, valle d'Aosta, 1993

Camorra, Sergio De Gregorio, Società Editrice Napoletana, Naples, 1981

I nemici di Cutolo, Sergio De Gregorio, Pironti Ed, Naples, 1983

Camorra: un mese a Ottaviano, il paese in cui la vita d'un uomo non vale nulla, L. Rossi. Interviews in Camorra boss Raffaele Cutolo's home town. Mondadori, Milan, 1983

Potere Camorrista, Gigi Di Fiore. Four centuries of crime in Naples. Alfredo Guida, Naples, 1993

Il camorrista, Giuseppe Marrazzo. Novelised version of the life of Raffaele Cutolo (later turned into a film by Giuseppe Tornatore). Tullio Pironti, Naples, 1984

La camorra, le camorre, Isaiah Sales, Riuniti, Rome, 1993

La camorra, Marco Monnier, Argo, Lecce, 1994

Uomini e affari della camorra: cronache di quotidiana violenza in un viaggio tra le storie dei clan, Fabrizio Feo, Edizioni Sintesi, Naples, 1989

I miei giorni della camorra, Domenico Santacroce. A magistrate's story. Boccia, Salerno, 1988

'Ndrangheta dall'unità a oggi, Enzo Ciconte. Exhaustive and fascinating history of the Calabrian mafia. Laterza, Bari, 1992

Manager Calibro 9, 20 years of organised crime in Milan, as told in the colourful words of the defector Saverio Morabito. Piero Colaprico and Luca Fazzo, Garzanti, 1995

Le ragioni della mafia: studi e ricerche di quaderni calabresi, F. Faeta et al., Jaca Books, Milan, 1983

La Mafia in Calabria, S. Gambino, Edizioni Parallelo 38, Reggio Calabria, 1977

'Ndranghete: le filiali della mafia calabrese, Diego Minuti and Antonio Nicaso. A look at Calabrian immigrant communities. Monteleone, Vibo Valentia, 1994

Africo, Corrado Stajano. The story of a Calabrian village. Einaudi, Turin, 1979

Gente di Calabria, Antonio Delfino. Interviews with locals. Editoriale progetto 2000, Cosenza, 1987

The Mafia: the Long Reach of the International Sicilian Mafia, Claire Sterling, Hamish Hamilton, London, 1990

Crime without Frontiers: the Worldwide Expansion of Organised Crime and the Pax Mafiosa, Claire Sterling, Warner/Little, Brown, London, 1995

Blood and Honor, George Anastasia, Zebra Books, New York, 1991

Mobfather, George Anastasia, Pinnacle, New York, 1993

Men of Honour: the Confessions of Tommaso Buscetta, Tim Shawcross and Martin Young, Fontana, London, 1989

The War against the Mafia, Tim Shawcross, Mainstream, Edinburgh, 1994

Gotti: Rise and Fall, Jerry Capeci and Gene Mustain, Onyx/Penguin, New York, 1996

Breaking the Mob, Frank Friel, McGraw Hill, New York, 1990

Scritti sulla mafia, ed. Linda Pantano, Istituto Gramsci Siciliano, Palermo, 1995

Articles, magazines, pamphlets

Osservatorio sulla camorra. Quarterly publication of the Fondazione Colasanto in Naples, directed by Amato Lamberti

Narcomafie 7–8, July–August 1990, Turin

Sicilia 102: caduti nella lotta contro la mafia e per la democrazia dal 1893 al 1994, Umberto Santino. Documentation of mafia victims by the Centro siciliano di documentazione Giuseppe Impastato, Palermo, 1995

Cesare Terranova In Memoria, with preface by Leonardo Sciascia, Palermo, 1982

'Ci sono donne nella mafia?' Giovanna Fiume, in *Meridiana: rivista di storia e scienze sociali*, 7–8, September 1989–January 1990

'Oltre il processo', by Giancarlo Dionisi of the Servizio Centrale di Protezione. Paper delivered to the Convegno su Minori, Palermo, 25 April 1996

La donna nella criminalità organizzata. Report to parliament by the Osservatorio permanente sulla criminalità, Ministry of the Interior, May 1996

La Voce della Campania. Independent investigative magazine edited by Andrea Cinquegrani, Naples

Mezzocielo. Sicilian magazine written and edited by women, ed. Simona Mafai, Palermo

Dalle donne la forza delle donne. Essays. Nuova Stampa di Mondadori, Milan, 1986

Legal documents

US District Court Eastern District of Pennsylvania, United States of America v John Stanfa + 7. Testimony of Brenda Colletti, 23 October 1995

Ordinanza sentenza per la corte d'assise a Palermo contro Abbate Giovanni + 706, Palermo, 8 November 1985

Tribunale civile e penale di Marsala, processo contro Alfano Nicolò + 15. Esame teste Giacoma Filippello

Tribunale di Palermo: ordinanza di custodia cautelare in carcere nei confronti di Mandalari Giuseppe e Imbraguglia Maria Concetta

Procura della Repubblica presso il Tribunale di Palermo, Dda. Esposizione introduttiva del PM nel procedimento contro Mandalari Giuseppe e Imbraguglia Maria Concetta

Tribunale di Palermo, ordinanza di custodia cautelare in carcere nei confronti di Brusca Giovanni + 19, 7 June 1996

Tribunale di Napoli, Applicazione di misure di prevenzione contro Anna Mazza + 9, 10 April 1990

Procura Distrettuale della Repubblica, Catania, Richiesta per l'applicazione di misure cautelare contro Antonino Cintorino + 40

Tribunale di Catania, ufficio GIP, richiesta di convalida del fermo nei confronti di Niciforo Lucia + 10, 25 June 1994

Tribunale di Catania, ufficio GIP, Misure di custodia cautelare nei confronti di Vasta Maria Rosa + 4, 7 November 1994

Tribunale di Napoli, Misura di prevenzione contro Ciro Mazzarella + 19, 27 July 1992

Corte d'assisie di Reggio Calabria, sentenza contro Antonio Imerti + 40, 14 November 1992

Tribunale di Napoli, Procedimento penale contro Teresa Deviato + 16, July 1996

Tribunale di Napoli, processo contro Raffaele Stolder + 45, udienza 26 April 1994

Tribunale di Napoli, sentenza contro Mario Fabbrocino + 34